Janner's Complete Speechmaker
Fourth Edition

'An invaluable addition to the library
of anyone who must speak in public . . .
I have read it and enjoyed it . . .
It's worth reading and worth having . . .'
*The Rt Hon George Thomas MP,
then Speaker of the House of Commons,
now The Rt Hon Lord Tonypandy*

JANNER'S COMPLETE SPEECHMAKER

Fourth Edition
Includes expanded compendium
of retellable tales

Greville Janner

Business Books Limited

This fourth edition was first published in Great Britain in 1991 by
Business Books Limited
An imprint of Random Century Limited
20 Vauxhall Bridge Road, London SW1V 2SA

Random Century Australia (Pty) Limited
20 Alfred Street, Milsons Point, Sydney
New South Wales 2061, Australia

Random Century New Zealand Limited
18 Poland Road, Glenfield
Auckland 10, New Zealand

Random Century South Africa (Pty) Limited
PO Box 337, Bergvlei, South Africa

First published in 1968 under the title *The Businessman's Guide to
Speechmaking and to the Laws and Conduct of Meetings.*
First published under present title in 1981
Second edition 1984
Reprinted 1986
Third Edition 1989
Reprinted 1989

Phototypeset by Deltatype Ltd, Ellesmere Port
Printed and bound in Great Britain by
Mackays of Chatham Plc, Chatham, Kent

British Library Cataloguing in Publication Data
A catalogue record for this book is available from the British Library

ISBN (Hbk) 0712650180
ISBN(Pbk) 0712650199

In-company and public communication training courses and consultancy by
Greville Janner and his team of consultants include: pitching for business
training; effective business presentation and speechmaking; radio and
television skills; report and business writing skills; effective telephone
techniques; and rehearsals and 'refreshers'.

For details, contact:
Effective Presentational Skills Ltd, Somerset House
37 Fortess Road, London NW5 1AD
Tel: 071–267 7792 Fax: 071–267 6394

In proud memory of my Father
Barnett Janner
Lord Janner of the City of Leicester
and with love to my mother
Elsie Janner
The Lady Janner CBE JP

Contents

Contents

Contents

Contents

The Author

The Hon. Greville Janner, QC, MP for Leicester West since 1970, is Chairman of Effective Presentational Skills. He and his colleagues have taught the arts of speechmaking and presentation to thousands of Britain's top business and professional people.

A Non-Executive Director of Ladbroke Group plc; author of over 60 books; member of the National Union of Journalists, the National Union of Mineworkers and the Magic Circle, and himself an eminent speaker of international renown, the author transfers his varied expertise into lively, practical and enjoyable reading. He speaks eight languages and his books have been widely translated.

Greville Janner is married, with three children and two grandchildren.

Introduction

In business or in social life, competent speechmaking brings success. Disaster on your feet lands you on your back. This new, fourth edition, is redesigned to keep you upright, articulate and successful in speech by showing you how best to think on your feet – to provide the maximum of practical help with the minimum of misery. It is based on a lifetime of experience of hugely varied audiences and of oratorical and presentational occasions in many parts of the world.

The book divides conveniently into four sections.

Book One describes the basic arts of speechmaking: nerve control, style, preparation, construction and delivery, audiences and occasions, technical aids – in short, the complete range of basic knowledge and guidance which is the essential equipment of the skilled speechmaker. I have rewritten much of this book and added many new chapters. As a teacher of presentation and of speechmaking, I am always learning. So here are the latest techniques and tips, as my trainer colleagues and I have developed them.

Whether you are addressing a meeting of colleagues or of employees at work, of shareholders in the UK or of stockholders in the USA, of family or of voters; whether you are making a presentation to commercial prospects or presenting a guest to an audience or prizes at a school, or proposing or responding to a toast at a wedding or a dinner, the techniques are essentially the same. Their application varies and is vital. Book One deals with them all.

You may have to chair a meeting, whether as major as a mass gathering or as minor as a company or social or charity committee. In the same book, I cover the rules on good chairing.

Book Two contains models – a selection of draft speeches for varying occasions. They should help you to make the best of your speechmaking opportunities and to minimize your prospects of tongue-tied collapse.

Book Three consists of classic oratorial gems.

Finally, in Book Four, I offer a greatly expanded compendium of my own favourite Retellable Tales. Forced to listen to literally thousands of speeches, too many of them excruciatingly boring, I have carefully accumulated an array of some 750 gems. I have used them all – for laughter, effect or emotional impact. Here are my favourites: stories, jokes and epigrams which shine with wit or with vivid language; which delighted audiences; and above all, which made me or others laugh, rejoice or just contemplate.

Watch moonlight on the Taj Mahal, dawn breaking over the Palace of Westminster, or the play and change of light over any other great building: it never appears the same twice. Go back to your Bible and re-read your favourite tales and the words will achieve new form and meaning. Put my Retellable Tales before different people or varied audiences – or even the same people or audience in different mood – and they will change their reflection in the mirror or the mood of that moment.

So select and adapt those that suit you and your style as well as your audiences and their reactions. With a modicum of that good fortune that every speaker always needs, but which is granted only on unpredictable and joyful occasions, these tales should provide you with a treasure house of spice for the seasoning of your speeches.

So why the fourth edition? Styles change. There were chapters and sentences to add, sections and phrases to chase away and I again submitted the Retellable Tales to the critical eyes and ruthless pens of my daughters, Marion and Laura. We argued our way through hundreds of stories. Out went those which they believed were irretrievably offensive. In came hundreds of others, selected and approved.

Revised, reviewed and renewed, restored and reindexed, my expanded Retellable Tales are a tribute to the united efforts of father and daughters – and are all offered on the usual basis: responsibility for all errors is accepted by the older generation alone!

My thanks, then, to Marion and to Laura and to all others who have contributed to the success of this new edition, including those who have (as will appear) given their consent to the republication of quotations. I thank those countless others whose speeches have provided me with examples – good and bad, worthy and laughable, splendid or sad – from whom I have culled both advice and retellable tales.

I thank those delegates to whom my colleagues and I in Effective Presentational Skills have taught the allied arts of presentation and speechmaking for helping to develop so much of the material in this book – and its sister Business Books publications, *Janner on Presentation*, *Janner's Complete Letterwriter*, *Janner on Communication* and *Janner on Competitive Pitching*.

Finally, my thanks to my partners in the business of training and

Introduction

coaching in speechmaking and presentation, Paul Secher and Leslie Benson and to our colleague trainers: Graham De Banzie, Sherri Cam, Caroline Janner, Deborah Lindsey, Phil Parry, Sarah Sherborne, Amanda Sieff and Kate Spiro. Our Effective Presentational Skills company has grown, along with the arts that it presents.

To you, my readers, I wish an overflow of those marvellous occasions when you return home from speechmaking, elated — knowing that the job was well done, the message duly delivered and the audience captivated and content.

GREVILLE JANNER
London, 1991

BOOK ONE

Speechmaking

PART 1

Preparation

1 Thinking on your feet

To succeed in speechmaking, you must think on your feet. You must operate your mind and your tongue in tandem, with body upright.

As a start, this means: recognizing, harnessing and controlling your nerves. We call that 'the confidence trick' – how to show confidence when you don't feel it, and then how to acquire it. It's a technique which colleagues and I have developed over many years, and it works.

To feel confident, you must look good, so here are the arts of body language, of eye contact and of deliberate movement and gesture.

Good speeches must be properly heard. Which means – voice production and projection.

Once settled into the job, you must combine style and content, performing, thinking and reacting at the same time.

An American President once said of his successor that he was so stupid that he couldn't walk and chew gum at the same time. A US Senator told me that the original quotation was even ruder – 'he couldn't walk and pass wind simultaneously!'

Thinking on your feet means being totally alert and able to use all parts of your body and brain at the same time.

So you need techniques of preparation. You must ask 'the four questions':

- WHO? Who are your audience – how many and where and in what environment and who makes the decisions?
- WHAT? What do *they* want? And then,
- WHY? Why are you there? What is *your* message? What (eg) ideas, products or services do you really wish to sell them, knowing who they are and what they will buy?
- HOW? what special techniques should you use – including notes, documentation and visual aids?

Then comes the structure of the speech itself. That includes constructing the skeleton. Plus the art of the 'sound bite' – condensing your message into a few sentences.

Then the techniques of delivery. Curiously, most of these techniques are easier to acquire than you may think. We teach people to do their speaking the easy way. For instance:

5

- Be yourself. Most people who are lively, articulate and animated in private conversation freeze up when they go before an audience. They become someone else. It's easier to be yourself and not to change . . . once you know how.
- You may think it easier to look at the ceiling or the floor, while you think. Once you get into the habit of looking at your audience, you'll wonder why.
- It's easier to sit back, relaxed, or to stand with one foot in front of the other and your head up and shoulders back, than it is to slouch. It's also better for your back.
- It's easier to pause . . . to speak slowly . . . to give yourself time to think what you are going to say, and your audience time to absorb what you've said.
- It's easier to use short, Anglo-Saxon words . . . crisp sentences . . . speech, punctuated and paragraphed like writing . . . instead of pompous, ponderous, jargonized language, in mighty, never-ending sentences.

Thinking on your feet, then, needs techniques. To learn them may not be easy. But everyone can do it. In this part I'll explain the rules. Try them, practise them, use them and you'll be amazed how quickly you'll absorb them.

To think clearly, you must prepare well. Preparing to make a speech means answering those four questions. Let's look at them again, in more detail.

WHO? Who are your prospective audience? How many of them and in what sort of environment or atmosphere?

Step One to success in any speech must be to *target your audience*; to recognize who you are aiming at; to spot your quarry, and then to get and to hold them firmly in your sights.

To get at least a general idea of your audience, start with research. Find out everything you can about the people you will be speaking to. Your aim will be better and the fact that you have taken pains will indicate that you are painstaking!

Personalize your approach and that will help reduce your tension.

If your speech is designed to bring results and you will need a decision, find out who will actually make it.

The former foreign secretary, George Brown, once attended a Labour party lunch, where the waiter handed round a basketful of rolls, served with an elegant pair of tongs. He placed a roll and a wrapped piece of butter on each person's plate. Not unreasonably, the Minister asked the waiter for a second pat of butter.

'I'm very sorry, sir,' the waiter replied, 'It's one roll and one pat of butter for each guest.'

'I don't think you know who I am,' said the eminent guest. 'I'm George Brown. I'm Foreign Secretary. I am the author of the economic miracle. I sit at the right hand of the Prime Minister. Please can I have another pat of butter?'

'I don't think you know who I am, Mr Brown,' said the waiter.

'No, I don't,' said Mr Brown. 'Who are you?'

The waiter paused and drew himself up to his full height: 'I am the waiter in charge of the butter!'

When you make important speeches, what matters is to spot who is in charge of the butter.

Next: as part of WHO? – WHERE? Study and if possible prepare your venue (Chapter 24) and make the best of your physical situation.

Then, WHAT? What do *THEY* want? To win, you must be market-led. You must be careful to ask and to answer this question before you move on to the next. Listen before you speak. Only when you have targeted your audience and their requirements do you move to the next question.

Your task is to satisfy your audience. Try to find out *their* requirements. Ask them, in advance and at the time. Address their wishes, their needs and their preferences or you will lose.

Then and only then do you come to question three: WHY? Why are you making the speech at all? What is your message?

Work out your message in advance. Spell it out from your early words and leave it well sunk into your audience as you depart. Whatever the occasion, plan to use it for your purpose, to plant your ideas or your message or, as on many social occasions, simply to provide pleasure to your audience.

Finally: HOW? What techniques will you use, to make the best of your message, knowing who your audience will be and what they want?

2   The skeleton of a speech

The human spirit can live, flourish and be much admired even when the human body is frail, ugly or misshapen. Some brilliant minds can capture and hold an audience with a rambling, poorly formed oration. Meaning and sincerity shine through and all is forgiven.

But to the business executive who wishes to make a speech in a business-like way, to the average speaker who wishes to put on an above-average performance, or to the poor or timorous orator, forced into public speechmaking, the structure of the speech is of supreme importance.

Create the skeleton, cloth it with sensible thought, and all that remains is to deliver it. But without a healthy skeleton, the entire speech collapses. So here are the rules on forming a well-built talk.

Any speech may conveniently be divided into three parts – the opening, the body and the closing. Take them in turn.

The first and last sentences of a speech are crucial. The importance of a clear, resounding and striking first sentence and a well-rounded peroration cannot be over-emphasized. You must catch the interest of your audience from the start and send them away satisfied at the end. So, when building your skeleton, spend time on 'topping and tailing'. Many skilled speakers write out their opening and closing sentences, even if the rest is left entirely unfleshed.

Assume, now, that you have established a relationship with your audience. You have led in with your thanks for the invitation to speak, topical references, personal remarks, introductory witticisms and greetings to old friends. Now comes the substance of the speech – any speech. It must flow.

Like a first-class book, chapter or article, most fine speeches start their substance with a general introductory paragraph which sums up what is to come, catches the attention of the audience and indicates the run of the speaker's thought. Each idea should then be taken in sequence, and should lead on logically to the next.

Just as each bone of the human body is attached to its fellow, so the ideas in a speech should be jointed. The flow of ideas needs rhythm. Disjointed ideas, dislocated thoughts, fractured theories: these are the hallmarks of a poor speech.

So jot down the points you wish to make. Then set them out in

8

logical order, so that one flows to the next. Connect them up, if you like, with a general theme. Start with the theme – and then elaborate, point by point.

Suppose, for instance, that you are explaining the virtues of a new product to your own sales staff. You begin in the usual way by asking for silence, smiling, looking round your audience and saying: 'Ladies and Gentlemen, sales staff of the X Company . . . It is a pleasure to see you here today, in spite of our reluctance to deprive the company's customers of your services . . .' Refer to Mr Y and Mr Z by name, congratulating them on their successes. Put your audience at ease. Tell them a joke or a story. Then launch into your theme.

'I have called you together today to introduce our new product.' (There it is, in a sentence.) 'Our research department has produced it. Now you must sell it. If you understand and exploit its full potential, you will not only benefit the company, but you should also add considerably to your own earnings.'

Personalize your message. Give your audience true incentive to listen. Whet their appetites for the substance to come. And remember the most important word in the English language has only three letters – YOU! That's the hook onto the interests of each person in your audience.

Now for the speech proper. First, name and describe the product in broad terms. Next, preferably with the assistance of diagrams, transparencies or slides, describe the product in detail. Then take its selling features, one by one: 'The following features are entirely new . . .' Spell them out and explain them. 'But the following features are retained – they were too valuable to be lost . . .' (Once again, maintain logical sequence.)

'So there, Ladies and Gentlemen, we have our new product – and you are the first to see it. You will be supplied with full sales literature within the next week. It will be available for your customers by . . . The rest is up to you. I wish you the very best of good fortune.'

Precisely the same rules of construction can be applied to any other discourse. Whether you are pronouncing a funeral oration over a deceased colleague or congratulating an employee on completing 25 years' service; whether you are making an after-dinner speech or haranguing your workers at the factory gates; whatever the circumstances, wherever the speech is made, if its skeleton is sound and solid, then even if the body is not as strong as it might be, the audience may not notice. Ignore the skeleton and the speech will prove a rambling disaster.

To summarize: introduce yourself and warm the audience . . . 'Good Evening, Ladies and Gentlemen . . .' Then say what you are going to say; say it; then say what you have said – Keep Your End Up.

3   In the beginning . . .

'In the beginning, God created the heavens and the earth.' What a marvellous first sentence, in the world's best-selling book!

Now pick up any national newspaper. Read the first sentence in any news story and it should grab your attention, excite your interest and tell you to read on. It will also encapsulate the theme.

Authors and journalists will tell you that they may spend as long on preparing the first sentence of a chapter or of an article as on the rest of the piece. A good opening is crucial to any presentation, written or oral.

Unlike the writer, speechmakers have the starting benefit of a few formal words to get used to the acoustics and to settle into their audience. Do not rush them. 'Ladies' . . . pause . . . 'and' . . . pause 'Gentlemen', – not 'Ladies-and-Gentlemen'. Look around and allow your audience to fix their attention on you, their minds on your words.

Next create rapport. Latch onto some aspect of the introduction you have just received, or to a topical matter of particular interest to your listeners.

My late distinguished father (to whose memory this book is dedicated) was an MP for a total of some 30 years and then a life peer. I was (and often still am) introduced as his son – often by that well-intentioned cliché: 'The distinguished son of a distinguished father.'

I have a standard opening which never fails: 'On behalf of my late father and myself – thank you for your kind introduction. When he was alive and active, we often got invited to meetings in mistake for each other. I treasure a letter, framed in the smallest room in my house, which was actually addressed to "The Rt Hon Lord Greville Janner QC MP, House of Commons, London" It begins: "Dear Sir or Madam!" The man was taking no chances!'

Listen to experienced speakers and you will find that they have opening gambits of their own – and you will find a batch of some favourite standbys at the start of my Retellable Tales.

Once you have created contact with your audience and reassured them that they will be interested in your theme and will not be bored by your presentation, then – and only then – you launch into your

11

subject. Your first sentence should be like those in the book or the newspaper – aimed precisely at the issue. Here are some random examples from front pages:

- 'The Prime Minister will return from his overseas visit tonight to find his Government in visible and increasing disarray over its controversial decision to . . .'
- 'The American space shuttle returned to earth yesterday from an eight-day mission . . .'
- 'British Coal yesterday closed a pit where the National Union of Mineworkers had withdrawn essential safety cover . . .'
- 'British American Tobacco announced yesterday that it is withdrawing from direct sale distribution in Britain, with the loss of over 1,800 jobs, mostly in Liverpool . . .'

You could start any of those sentences with the words: 'Did you know that. . . ?', or 'We have come together because . . .', or 'It is essential for our industry/organization that we should recognize that . . .', or 'As our local/trade newspaper announced on its front page today . . .'

Sprinters who make a bad start can rarely win the race. Speech-makers who fail in the beginning are unlikely to succeed in the end.

So: after warming your audience, say what you are going to say. Start off with your summary.

Then remember Janner's Law: Use You's. 'You' is by far the most important word for any audience. It is the hook. Use it to catch and to keep their attention and you will be off to a good start.

4   In conclusion

Nothing so becomes a good speech as a fine ending. And nothing can be more ruinous than a weak termination trailing off into silence or into a lame 'Thank You'. Lavish as much care on the tail of a speech as you do on its top. Consider some common flops:

- Mr Brown rushes his last few sentences, gathers his notes and slides surreptitiously back into his seat.
- Mr Black ends his talk in what appears to be the middle of a sentence or at the height of an anti-climax.
- Ms Grey, who has been allotted 30 minutes to speak, runs out of material after 20, but is determined 'not to let the audience down', and says: 'In conclusion', 'finally', 'before I conclude', 'lastly', and 'to end up with', at least twice each – always rekindling false hope in the minds of her audience that she really means it.
- Ms Green thinks that she is narrating a serial story and leaves her audience in suspense by over-running her time, panicking and then forgetting to propose the resolution, which was the sole object of her speech.
- Mr Blue realizes that he is not going to conclude his prepared talk within the time available if he keeps going at the same speed. So he runs out of script and breath at the same moment, leaving his audience miles behind.
- Mr White forgets that the closing words at a peroration should be brief – and drags it out interminably, embellishing thoughts that were in the body of the speech, introducing new ideas in the guise of a summary of what he has said.

What, then, makes a really good ending or peroration? It should round off the speech. Say what you've said. This means:

- A summary of the main points of the speech, in a few sentences.
- Any proposal or resolution arising out of the body of the speech; and
- A call for support, or warm words of thanks.

If you attach the peroration to the opening, they should between them contain the core of the speech. The opening says what is coming; the closing says what has gone.

Here are some examples of good closing gambits:

13

- 'So this project does have great possibilities for our company. To succeed we must at once take the steps that I have suggested. I ask you all to support the resolution and to help put it into useful and urgent effect.'
- 'And so I have tried to suggest the appropriate action which this company should now take. If my resolution is passed and put into urgent effect, it will transform the company's finances. I hope that no one will vote against it. It presents the best possible way out of our difficulties.'
- 'So this company stands in grave peril. The only way out is clear. The actions I recommend could transform our hopes. Please do not reject them.'
- 'There is, then, no need for despair. We must resolve not only to carry out the procedure proposed in my resolution, but also to ensure that the action which must follow will have the urgent and active support of us all. I therefore move that . . .'
- 'So those are the possibilities open to us. Only one of them really carries any hope of real success. It is the duty of this Board to protect and to advance the interests of our shareholders. That duty can only be performed if steps are taken in accordance with the resolution which stands in my name. I urge that it be accepted – fully, wholeheartedly and without amendment.'

* * *

There are countless ways to construct the end of the same speech. Purge the old clichés: 'My time is running short . . .', 'So without further ado . . .', 'I see that my time is nearly up and I must close . . .', 'I have no wish to bore you any further . . .'

Instead make your summary and your appeal – for support, for money, for understanding.

Other recommended endings:

- 'And so I thank you again for your kind hospitality and wish your project magnificent success'.
- 'Ladies and Gentlemen, it has been a delight to be with you. I hope that my ideas will have been of some help in promoting your work, in which I – like you – believe so firmly. I wish you, your honorary officers, executives, members and workers, great success.'
- 'So your conference is over. It has been a pleasure to meet you all. I know I express the warm feelings of all of us when I wish you a safe journey home and every success in the future.'
- 'I know that the views I have put forward are not universally acceptable. But I know, too, that you would have wished me to speak my mind. That I have done, most earnestly. I hope that the suggestions I have made will be adopted, or at least adapted.

14

In conclusion

'But whatever decision you take, I have much appreciated the kind and courteous attention which you have given to me!'

Do not end by saying 'Thank You' or 'Good Night'. Instead, build up to a climax. A last powerful phrase, left hovering in the air – and beckoning on to the applause.

Then do not rush back to your seat and flop quickly down into your chair. Like any good trouper, wait for the applause. If it does not come, look your audience straight in the eye. Pause. Then sit down. The end of your speech should make as solid an impact as its start.

5 Files and ideas

First-class journalists (especially freelances with no access to newspaper files) keep their own careful files of clippings, cuttings, photographs and ideas, which they can later incorporate into articles, features or books. Speakers should take a leaf out of their book.

Take jokes, for instance. There are books of allegedly humorous tales for every occasion. I sometimes wonder how anyone ever laughed at any of them. But then everyone has his or her own style and sense of humour. Do not be afraid to steal the tales of others. They will be flattered. Jot them down and file them. You never know when they may come in handy.

Then there is specialist material, which you can use time and time again. Most popular speakers are invited to talk on their particular specialities. The first time, they must do research, prepare facts, unearth statistics, and make notes. If those notes are carefully filed, next time will be a walkover.

You review, adapt and update. But your preparation should be simple and brisk.

Some speakers favour a filing cabinet, others metal boxes with files inside. Still more make do with loose-leaf notebooks for stories and quotations, ideas and suggestions. The most modern store their gems on tape, or on word processors.

The object of it all is to reduce your homework to the minimum. You have no time to repeat your drudgery. So, however boring the keeping of files or notebooks may be, it is worth the effort in the present to reduce your work in the future.

Once again, the Retellable Tales in Book Three should save you time and trouble and perhaps form the basis for your own collection, as it does mine.

6   Training in speechmaking

In Britain, speechmaking is still too often regarded as an amateur art. Acquired through a combination of heredity and superior education, it finds no place in the curriculum of school, college or university.

Of course, 'the true Briton' learns to read, spell and count, but it 'not done' to take lessons in speechmaking or in presentation. Which explains why both are so commonly done so badly.

The fact that you have bought or borrowed this book immediately places you in some peril – or have you put it into a plain, white cover?

As for lessons in speechmaking – they are for Americans and other foreigners, aren't they?

There is, of course, neither educational rhyme nor reasonable logic behind this curious attitude. Speaking in private may come naturally; orating in public does not. It requires training and experience. Without the appropriate flair, no level of teaching can produce outstanding results. Without training, public speaking is likely to be a burden not only for speakers, but more especially for their unfortunate audiences.

So do not despise the lesson. If public speaking is a burden on you or on your hearers; if you need to practise in private, but with an experienced and critical audience; if you are prepared to learn from other people's mistakes, rather than from your own – then take lessons.

You do not need to advertise to your customers or clients, your friends or even your family that you are indulging in this particular form of masochism. Whether you are an experienced speaker in need of a polish; an inexperienced performer, promoted to a position of prominence where self-expression becomes crucial; a presenter of your company's products or services, needing guidance in techniques and practice in their use; or, especially, if you suffer from any form of speech impediment, a good speech therapist should enable you to avoid oratorical misery, and turn criticism into compliments.

The same principles apply to courses in speechmaking and presentation for your staff or your executives. Given even moderate material, the skilled teacher can produce marvellous changes. We believe that there is no one whom we cannot teach to be a competent presenter.

How do you find your teacher or trainer? As usual, recommendation is the best guide. On the basis of horses for courses, others' gurus may suit their needs, but not yours. So experiment.

My colleagues and I organize presentational courses for individual executives and professionals — tailor-made for the individual; or group efforts, generally for a maximum of six; and large-scale, one-day presentations of basic techniques. Our delegates take their choice!*

The more the training is angled at the needs of the individual, the greater its potential. Experience coupled with a video camera and monitor screen are our partners in perfection. The combination of seeing and criticizing yourself, together with the vision and criticism of others — outsiders and, if you wish, your own colleagues, taking the same medicine — produces dramatic results in (we find) no more than two days.

If you are prepared to lavish resources on presentations; on estimates, tenders and quotations; on promotions and on product launches; on induction and promotional training; on employing consultants to advise you on everything from organization and methods to time and staff management — why, then, do you underestimate the need to train for prowess in the marvellous art of the skilled speechmaker and the polished presenter?

Speakers in public may be amateurs at the art, but there is no reason in business or in logic for them to be untrained. If more speakers had more training, listeners would have a far more rewarding time — and speakers and presenters would reach for the stars.

---

* Effective Presentational Skills, 37 Fortess Road, London, NW5 1AD. Tel: 071-267 7792 Fax: 071-267 6394.

PART 2

Delivery

7   The confidence trick

The speechmaker's best confidence trick: Look confident. You start by looking and move on to feeling.

So how do you perform the confidence trick? Here are the rules.

As a start, recognize that if you are any good, you are bound to be nervous. That great American teacher of presentation, Dorothy Sarnoff, called her recent book: *You Need Never Be Nervous*. Sadly, that's impossible. On the contrary: You must recognize that you will be nervous – and, if you are not, start worrying. Nerves on edge set the adrenalin aflow. They sharpen your mind, your speech and your presentation.

Former Prime Minister Thatcher was asked by BBC 'Woman's Hour': 'After all these years, are you still nervous?'

'Indeed I am,' she replied.

'So how do you handle it?'

'I say to myself: "Come on, love, concentrate!" '

Another former Prime Minister, Harold Macmillan, admitted that he was nervous whenever he had a major speech to make, in Parliament or anywhere else. 'I say to myself: "Nothing else matters . . ." ' In other words: Concentrate.

As a youngster, I was a champion sprinter – a most useful attribute for a budding politician! Before every race, my legs felt like rubber. I could scarcely move. But I knew that the moment I got onto the track, I'd be off like a bullet. The best recipe for failure was: Lack of nerves. No nerves, no success.

As with sport, so with speechmaking. Recognize the need for (literally) nervous energy. See it as a miserable precursor of success. Then learn the magic of not showing those nerves to anyone else.

You start with your body. Sit or stand, upright and proud. Lift up your chin, your head, your back. Don't slouch or slump or lean forward.

In 'Yes, Prime Minister', they put the PM through TV training. He leaned forward.

'Please sit back, Prime Minister,' said his coach.

'But I want to look sincere,' he protested.

'The trouble is, Prime Minister,' came the retort, 'that it just makes you look as if you want to look sincere. You look as if you're selling insurance!'

You know the expression 'Laid back'? Do it. Lie back.

So confidence trick number one is performed with the body – up and back. The next is with the eyes – up and at the audience.

Not to look at your audience is the classic sign of fear and distress. The more fearful or distressed you feel, the more you should look your audience in the eye.

Fix your eyes on an individual – the chairman, perhaps – for about five seconds. Then move your head, your neck and your eyes to the next person. Please note: It is wrong simply to swivel your eyes. That is the way of a snake, human or reptile.

So your body looks confident; your eyes look at your listeners.

Third: Pause. Do not start until you and your audience are both ready. You have got their time, so take yours.

Confident people, who successfully persuade, look confident by stopping before they speak. Then they speak slowly – and pause while speaking.

Silence is the surest sign of confidence. Keeping silent is a trick not easy to learn, but once achieved it is the greatest. Harold Macmillan, again: 'The greatest art of any speaker . . . if you can do it . . . is . . . the pause . . .' Then he held up his hand and took breath and smiled. 'If you stop and wait, you've got them!'

Indeed. If you stop and wait, you appear confident, even when you're not.

So the trick is to stop at the beginning and then to punctuate your speech, as you would a letter or document. With commas, semi-colons, colons, full stops – and paragraphs. Taking breath.

Which brings us to confidence trick number four: Taking breath. Breathe. Fill your lungs. Do so a few seconds before you are about to begin. Take a deep breath, in through your mouth and out through your nose. Then another. Then a third. Physiologically, this will relax you. It is the finest way to drive off panic.

Learn to breathe and to relax. That way, you will produce and project your voice, not from your throat, but from your stomach – out with power through the lungs, and with confidence.

When you appear confident – in your body, your eyes . . . with your pausing, your timing and your silence . . . and you hear yourself speaking out loud, then you will know that you look and sound confident – and you will feel that confidence surge through you.

You must have that inner confidence which only comes through knowing your case. Prepare yourself and your material. That's not a trick, that's time and care and concern.

When under stress, people's mouths go dry. Their tongues flick out and they lick their lips.

If this happens to you, there's a simple remedy – a glass of water by your side. Stop. Wet your whistle. Look up and re-establish eye contact. Then start talking again.

Be deliberate in your movements and don't be afraid to pause.

Put these rules together, then, and you will soon know how to be as confident as you will look and sound. It's a trick that every successful speechmaker must master.

So let's sum up:

First: Recognize that nervous energy is essential to top performance. Greet your anxiety with expectant understanding. It will become your ally.

Next: Recognize that once you start moving, your nerves will evaporate on their own.

Third: Remember that your feelings are internal. Your audience will not know of them unless you are so inexperienced that you tell them. So:

Never admit to nerves – instead, look your audience in the face. Fix your eyes to theirs and they will concentrate on what you are saying and be far less likely to notice your mistakes.

Then: Avoid whatever form of nervous twitch is your personal affliction. To control your audience, you must start by controlling yourself.

Do so by body language, by breathing and by pausing.

Finally: Do not drink before you speak. Avoid tranquillizers. Speaking, like driving, demands a sharp mind and a clear head.

A man was wrongly charged with arson. An honest, decent person, he arrived at his trial stuffed to his eyebrows with tranquillizers. He was not at all nervous. But he never answered the questions he was asked. He was convicted and sentenced to three years' imprisonment. It took the combined efforts of an investigative radio team, of another MP and myself to get him released. Tranquillizers cost him an agonizing year in jail.

Confidence comes with preparation, practice and training, not through drink or drugs.

The more you practise, the more your confidence will expand. So:

• If you attend a meeting, steel yourself. Speak or ask questions.

- If you are offered the chance to propose a vote of thanks, accept. If a small group invites you to address it, agree.
- If you have been dealing with some new and interesting project, if you have gone on an unusual journey, or if you have something out of the ordinary to tell, then let this be known. Your club or organization, charity, political group or trade organization which has previously regarded you as a silent member will be delighted to invite you to speak to its members or to an interested section of them.
- Maybe you have a social function of your own: a dinner party, cocktail party or company lunch. This time, stand up and say those few words of welcome, of thanks or of greeting. If the speech is to be of any length then, whatever the social occasion, the rules in Chapter Thirty-eight (on after-dinner speaking) will provide you with some useful guides. And use or adapt some Retellable Tales.

Remember, the higher you rise, the more vital it is to be able to express yourself on your feet. The only way to gain experience is to get up on those feet. You will know how to handle your nerves. You will get used to the sound of your own voice, raised in public.

So speak. Your nervousness will fall away when your words emerge and your audience listens. You have learned the confidence trick – prepare, practise and pretend and no one will feel your nerves but you. And as you start to speak, your tension will fall away.

Above all, prepare. Know your subject and how you intend to present it, and you will have that inner confidence which will help you to control those outer nerves.

Then remember the marvellous story of Eleanor Roosevelt, wife of President Franklin D. Roosevelt. When she was asked how she managed to preserve her equanimity, her calm and her apparent confidence when she was nervous and ill at ease, she replied: 'I wear my invisible crown.'

So keep your head up. Wear your invisible crown. And you will not only *know* it, but you will also *show* it.

8 Be yourself

Why is it that people who are charming, friendly and articulate in private conversation become wooden and charmless, remote and friendless, tongue-tied and wordless the moment they go public? Why, when the presentation is formal, do their backbones wobble and their knees knock, even if they stay seated?

The symptoms of this personality change are almost invariable, and we've seen most of them already:

- Speakers avoid eye contact. They look at floor or ceiling, or anywhere other than at their audience. They probably swivel their eyes, appearing shifty and dishonest.
- They sit forward, elbows on table, hunched and hostile and as visibly screwed up physically as they are churned up mentally.
- If they stand, their fingers twist, their hands gyrate and their bodies jerk, with their heads sunk forward and their eyes downcast.
- Above all, instead of speaking ordinary, relaxed English, they adopt an unreal persona – not their own, but that which they believe others would expect them to be when making a formal presentation. They become pompous and formal.
- They speak fast, gabbling and rushing towards the end.

Colleagues and I teach and train all levels of business people and professionals at every level up to the very top. Our single most important, and often most difficult task? To induce them to be themselves.

If you are talking to one person, eyeball to eyeball, your eyes should maintain contact. 'All the time he was talking to me, he was looking over my shoulder,' is too common a complaint. Do not lose eye contact with your audience because the moment or the occasion is formal.

Do you sit back in the chair, relaxed and obviously at ease, when at home? Then do not lean forward when you talk to your colleagues, your board, your customers or your clients, actual or potential. You will not only show relaxed authority if you sit back but also retain the flexibility of occasional forward movement.

9 Appearance and body talk – 'the eyes have it!'

If self-presentation is an essential for self-preservation, then you must make your appearances and your appearance count. If your presentation is disembodied, take special care with your voice.

You have no other way of showing your enthusiasm and your sincerity, your confidence and your command of the subject. In person or on television, you are visible.

Start with the overall effect. How do you want to appear? Authoritative, distinguished, sound and sensible? Then wear a dark suit or dress. Relaxed and informal? Then wear light-coloured, loose-fitting clothing. The persuaders may try to influence your decision. But make up your own mind.

That celebrated caricaturist Ranan Lurie once said to me: 'Your father got his appearance right. A combination of pointed head, central bulk and above all the red carnation made him instantly recognizable. You, alas, are simply a pleasant and happy-looking individual without even a treble chin or bushy eyebrows.'

I convinced him that he should look more closely and he would see that I have at least six arms, most of them working at the same time. But I do now wear a buttonhole.

Start at the top and work down. Do you cultivate polished head or bushed hair? Do you groom your crowning glory or allow it to dominate you? Do you let your hair turn grey or white (most men) or enjoy retaining or even enhancing its youthful blaze (most women)? Do you wear your uniform (dark suit or working overalls)?

At home or on holiday you may decide that appearances matter little. But when you appear in public, you woo the public – so present yourself with care.

Study Desmond Morris's *The Naked Ape* – followed by his *Manwatching* – and your speeches should gain an extra dimension of excellence. In particular, you will learn how others give themselves away through bodily indications, and how you can avoid doing the same.

When dealing with people in any number, make your eye contact with the person in the chair or with a friendly face. Then, a few seconds later, turn your head and look to the right or to the left – then, after a few more seconds, turn your head or your eyes again to the other side – always with purpose and deliberately. And learn to watch the rest of the audience out of the corners of your eyes, no matter where you are looking.

Keep your gestures to a minimum. Let them emphasize your words, not detract from their meaning. For instance, use your hands to count numbers: 'First . . . second . . . third . . .' Or to show levels of authority – or to illustrate breadth of access, or strength of unity – or even determination. But make your gestures sincere.

Remember that story about President Nixon. 'How do you know when the President is telling the truth?' asked an opponent. 'When he does this . . .', clenching both fists, 'you know he's telling the truth. When he does this,' contorting his face and spreading his arms wide, 'you know he's telling the truth. When he does this,' bringing his hands together and clenching them and frowning furiously, 'you know he's telling the truth. Now . . . when he opens his mouth. . . !'

If you want to move around, go ahead. Involve your audience, relax your presentation or move your flip chart. The only rule: Whatever you do, it must be deliberate.

You may have back trouble, as I do. You can run, jump or climb, but not stand still? Then get a high (or bar or draughtsman's) stool, or perch on the edge of a table. Avoid keeping the table between yourself and the audience. Remove barriers. Be careful not to get stuck behind a lectern, especially if it has a microphone attached to it. Detach it or get a roving mike (see Chapter Twenty-two).

The more economical your movements, the better. Sit still and upright, with your bottom tucked into the angle between seat and the back of your chair. Stand proud. Keep your body, your chin, your eyes and your voice up.

If you stand and have trouble with your hands, rest your fingers on the edge of the table. Do not lean on them. Hold your note cards firmly and calmly in front of you. If the wrist holding them shakes, grasp it with the other hand and keep your elbows into your side.

Don't be afraid of movement. And follow another of Harold Macmillan's great rules. If you are going to make a gesture, make it from the shoulder. Don't jab your forearm. And make sure that your gesture precedes your words. Gesture. Pause. Then speak.

Introducing a guest, perhaps? Then turn around, extend your arm and then say, with grace: 'Welcome . . . John Brown . . .'

A shrug or an occasional accusing finger, a reference to the heavens or a hand pointing to the sky – all have their place in the repertoire of the skilled speaker.

You wear spectacles? Then use them as an occasional weapon. To emphasize a point, remove them, hold them still in your hand, bend forward and glare at your audience. Brandish your glasses and then return them to your nose and your speech to its theme.

Be sure that your eyes appear in the centre of your spectacles and that your eye contact is not spoiled because the top of the frame interferes with your sight.

If your spectacles, like mine, darken under bright light, you may need a second pair for speechmaking. I carry spares with me, for platforms and (especially) for television work.

If you need spectacles to read, but do not like wearing them when speaking, put them on deliberately for reading; remove them, quickly and deliberately, for talking and for eye contact.

Do not fear poor eyesight. Like other defects, it can be turned to good effect.

Generally, though, speakers should use their tongues, their faces and their minds, not their feet, their arms or their fingers. Otherwise, their listeners may take to their heels. Gestures must add to the words and meaning.

Now for some more about standing. Remember Martin Luther: 'Here stand I. I can do no other,' said he, refusing to budge. If more speechmakers would stand with authority and determination, their audiences would listen to far greater effect.

As a start and at the start, rise before you shine. Say not one word until your feet are firmly in place, your clothing and your notes arranged to your satisfaction, your audience held with your eye.

To pause before you start takes confidence and skill, but is an absolute essential if you do not wish your beginning to fall limp.

Because you are upright, you automatically dominate. Given an audience of even moderate size and the choice between sitting and standing, stand.

To stand with ease, stand at ease, legs apart and one foot slightly in front of the other. Relax the body and you can then concentrate on balance in speech. With your chest upright and forward, you can produce sound with the least effort and to maximum effect.

Watch any accomplished opera singer. Forget the modern marvels, magnified, microphone to mouth. I mean those who have been taught to produce fine and varied sound by using the instruments with which God has endowed them. You do not need the training or the talent of a great singer if your words are to live. But you cannot project your voice without using your chest as a sound box. Like Woody Allen, you may want to achieve immortality not through your work, but by not dying. If you want to achieve success through your words and to avoid oratorical death, stand up for your case.

Then move, deliberately. You are not a tree, rooted to one spot.

On the other hand, you must not turn your back on your audience, except for the occasional moment when you are actually writing on flip charts. You should never talk to your audience unless your eyes are on them. And you should move with purpose.

To create and to maintain intimacy with your audience, remove physical barriers. You may prefer to sit behind your desk while a recalcitrant employee stands in front of it. But if you are trying to present a case to listeners whom you wish to carry with you, then shift the table, the lectern or the desk. Or (more likely) move yourself around it. Perch relaxed on the edge or speak from the side.

The Canadian humorist, Stephen Leacock, wrote of Lord Ronald: 'He said nothing; he flung himself from the room, flung himself up on his horse and rode madly off in all directions!' When you stand and think on your feet, you say your piece; fling yourself nowhere; and direct your words and your body in the required direction only.

10 Voice production

The human chest is a sound box. The voice should reverberate and carry. As a stringed instrument gains its volume through the resonance of its sound chamber, so the human voice should resonate through the chest.

Try saying the word 'war'. Through your nose and voice alone, it produces a puny sound. Now take a deep breath, put your hand on your chest and sigh out the word until you can feel the vibration. Deep and resonant sound reverberates an idea to immense effect.

The opposite also applies. To attract and hold the attention of an audience, you do not need to shout at them. The dramatic effect of a whisper may be intense.

Vary and change the volume and tone of your speech, but always within the hearing of your listeners. Address the people in the back row. Imagine they are deaf – they may be!

Take special care not to drop your voice at the end of a sentence. Thoughts should rise to a climax, not fade with the final breath of a phrase. To avoid monotony, vary tone, speed and volume.

Words do not emerge from closed mouths. You may not consider this an especially brilliant observation, but if you saw how many top people whom we train in presentational skills speak like ventriloquists' dummies, you would be amazed.

'Open your mouth, please,' we implore the executive, whose confidential whispers go unheard because he scarcely moves his lips. 'If ever you lose your job, sir, you should apply for another one as a ventriloquist's dummy!' He thinks we're joking. We're not.

We explain that if you want to eat, you have to open your mouth to put food in. If you want to get an unpleasant country to do what you want – including the release of hostages – you generally have to remain in communication with it. People do not come through closed doors, nor words through shut mouths.

Take this book to a mirror. Read out a short sentence. Then repeat it several times, as naturally as you can. Watch. Is your mouth opening? Are your words coming out, loud, crisp and clear?

When you talk, you should be able to put two fingers into your mouth, together and vertically. Try it. Then modulate your voice.

So stick in the fingers for practice, but it is best to remove them when you're talking! Then modulate your voice.

Groucho Marx said of a well-known woman: 'The sooner I never see her face again, the better it will be for both of us when we meet. Mind you, I never forget a face, but in her case I will make an exception. Perhaps not: I'll remember both of them. There is only one thing wrong with her faces – they stick out of her dress. Anyway, the only way she gets some colour in her face is to stick her tongue out.'

It was said of one politician that he 'only opens his mouth when he has nothing to say'. When he wanted to say something, he would keep it closed and talk through gritted teeth. He needed a shoehorn to make a speech.

It may be true that the best way to get some people to agree with you is to keep your mouth shut. But if you are forced to speak, then please open it. Success will not go to your head until it has gone to your mouth.

Finally, and most important – know when to keep silent, and then to lift your voice. The magic pause gives emphasis to the words that follow. So stop. Wait. Then lift your voice, at the end of the sentence or so as to emphasize the key words. Pause . . . and lift . . .

Examples:

'It is my pleasure to introduce . . .' pause and then lift 'John Jones . . .'

'We must avoid . . .' pause, lift, 'unnecessary and unwanted and exceptional . . .' pause, lift 'expenditure'.

Always use this technique at the end . . . of a speech . . . of a presentation . . . or even of an intervention at a meeting . . . 'That . . . is the best way . . . to satisfy . . .' pause, lift 'this company. And all' . . . pause, lift 'of *you*.'

11   The pause

Silence please. Too many speakers who have no trouble with words fear the pause. The pause is the speechmaker's most useful weapon. Handled with confidence, it hides nerves and gives time for thought —and, above all, it is the basis for all dramatic timing.

Take your cue and your breath from the impresario: 'Ladies and Gentlemen' – pause – 'It is my honour to present' – pause – 'for the first time in this country' – pause – 'none other than' – pause – 'that most famous of all singers/comedians/boxers' – long pause – 'Mr' – pause – 'John' – pause – 'Smith!'

Refine that into the introduction: 'Ladies and Gentlemen' – pause – 'Mr John Smith!'

The pause precedes the words and the sense mounts to a crescendo at the end of the sentence.

Churchill used the pause more and better than any other great orator. 'We . . . er . . . have no intention of allowing that . . . er . . . maniac to demolish our lives . . .' Each pause and each 'er' whetted the appetite for his next attack on the Nazis and their leader.

For those of us who are not Churchill, to 'er' or to 'um' is to err! If you cannot think of what to say, keep silent. Your audience will believe that you are searching for the *mot juste*. Even if your mind is blank, look fierce, look around, stand firm. When you are ready with your next pearl, drop it.

At the start of your speech, talk or intervention, keep silent until you have the full attention of your audience. Pause.

If you are interrupted – whether by the drop of a window, the shrill of a passing jet, the intervention of a colleague, or by laughter or applause – wait again for silence before you proceed. A pause is not a sign of indecision or weakness, but the speaker's powerful technique – and the one that the inexperienced speechmaker uses too little.

The pause before a crucial word is the orator's most superb trick. 'If we do not take the steps I have suggested, I foresee only one result' – pause – look around – wait: 'disaster'.

'We all remember the terrible days of' – pause. You are only using an extension of the suspense technique, at the end of each properly constructed instalment of a radio play or soap or at the end of a chapter in a tightly written crime story. You are keeping your grip on the audience.

'After hearing all the views of this committee, I have come to my decision. We have no alternative. 'We must . . .' Wait for it . . . keep them waiting . . . then speak . . .

Of course, the pause must not be too long. Just as brevity in a pause may show lack of confidence and cause it to lose its effect, so too long a pause may appear as 'ham'. To overdramatize is as bad as to underplay. Only experience can teach you how long to pause. Only practice can show the maximum period for the best effect. If in doubt, pause longer. But like every other technique, don't overdo it.

Not long ago, a Parliamentary colleague was chided by Mr Speaker Weatherill for going on too long. 'But, Mr Speaker,' he protested, 'I have only spoken for a short time.' 'It is the pauses in your speech that have taken too long!' Mr Speaker retorted.

Prepare an important speech, rehearse it and time yourself on a stop-watch. Then make the same speech on the important occasion and get someone to time you. It will take longer. So prepare less material, and leave time for interruptions, for questions and for space.

The most common pausing times:

- The opening: Make sure that your audience have settled down and are ready to hear you – whether you are making a major oration at a rally or a minor intervention at a board meeting.
- In mid-sentence: To emphasize a vital point.
- After an interruption: Once again, your audience must settle in to hear you.
- Before your last few words: 'And now, Ladies and Gentlemen, I ask you once more to support your Board' – pause – 'so as to ensure' pause '. . . that this modest organization . . .' pause '. . . will continue to flourish.' Pause. Look around at those from whom you expect applause. Then sit down.

Which brings me to the final hint. Applause is a most helpful and invigorating leg-up for any speaker. If you did not want it, you would not speak. We all like to be liked. We all wish our words to be accepted. The 'hear, hear' or clapping is as gratifying to the speaker as the groan is a misery. It is essential to anticipate and to deal with the cheers – to fish for them and to pause after them.

Only rarely can a pause be used against the groaner. Look

around and glare at the man who has the temerity to jeer at you. Then hit back: 'You are not helping your cause by behaving like that.' Or, if kindness seems to be the best way to deal with the situation: 'I am sorry that you jeer, sir. If you would be good enough to wait a little, you will hear my reasons. And you will find that they are correct.'

Then pause. Allow the effect of the jeer to die away. Do not pause so long that you encourage the interrupter to have another go. The borderline between the effective and the defective pause is narrow. Each must be judged on its own, and immediately. Far more speakers rush forward in haste than regret the (apparently) confident wait for silence . . . attention . . . effect.

The pause is even more vital – and less of a risk – when fishing for cheers. If you are nervous, follow the sound theatrical first-night tradition of organizing your own claque. 'We must give the impression of vast enthusiasm for the new project. So when I say how confident I am . . . that it will be a . . . great success' – pause – 'clap!' (The pause gambit is even more useful in ordinary speech.)

An audience likes to know when applause is expected. 'We are all pleased to welcome our guest of honour from abroad,' – pause – 'Monsieur' – pause – 'Jaune.' Turn to your guest – pause – for applause.

'Here, Ladies and Gentlemen, is the first sample of our new product. I present it to you' – pause – 'with pride' – pause – 'I trust that you sell it, to your profit and that of the company' – pause. Look around. Someone will probably say 'hear, hear' if only to please you.

If no one applauds, you could attack them for their silence. 'The success of each of you, as well as that of the company, depends on the way you push this product. I invite you' – pause – 'to greet with pleasure' – pause – 'this new success from our research department.'

If that does not do the trick, if you cannot dredge up the applause you want, then never mind. Move on. Change your tack. Alter your approach. Try again. But do not rush. Wait. Control your audience.

Do not be afraid of the pause. Silence is a weapon as valuable as speech itself. And once you master the technique, you'll find it makes speaking much easier. After all, you have time to work out the next words you need.

Thomas Hardy remarked: 'That man's silence is wonderful to

listen to.' Sidney Smith commented on the boredom of a conversation with Macaulay, observing that it was his 'occasional flashes of silence that make his conversation perfectly delightful'! If you want your talk to be appreciated, then your silences should be deliberate, well-timed, and free from the irritating distractions of 'ers' and 'ums'.

12 Use your memory – cards, prompts and reading

You should never have to read your speech. Well, hardly ever – and then only when every word counts and it is more for the record than for your audience. So consider.

First: How do you train your memory and your tongue to follow one on the other? How do you avoid missing essential points? How do you avoid 'drying up', simply from the fear that you may do just that?

Second: If you must read your speech, what are the top techniques?

We recommend notes on cards, postcard size, and held vertically, each with 'bullet points' – the essential reminders, written clearly and in large characters or figures, so that you can see them at a glance, while talking.

Introducing a speaker? Then put the name onto a separate card and put it where you can see it clearly. When I've asked delegates for their own names, I've seen them look at their name cards – terror clears the mind of names.

Next, your opening sentence. Hopefully, you'll have the presence of mind to lead in from the chairman's introduction, from something topical, from your surroundings or from the occasion. If in doubt, do not hesitate to write in capital letters: 'MR PRESIDENT, LADIES AND GENTLEMEN . . .' – or whatever.

Then: reminders only. Each on a separate card, so that you can use and then (literally) discard.

Telling a story? Jot down words to remind you of the main idea – plus the punch line.

Following a logical theme? Then put each step onto a separate card.

That way, you can change your mind or the order of the points or shuffle the cards before you begin or even when you're on your feet. Pause and give yourself time. Cards are massive assets.

Other rules:

- Hold the cards in your hand or on the lectern, moving to the side – or on a pile of books. Or on the table, if you prefer, but . . .

- Pause when you look at your cards, which means . . .
- Never talk to your audience whilst your eyes are on your notes. Never put your head down to look at your notes, while you are talking. Eye contact and speech go together.

Once talking, the ideas should flow. You may never need to look at your cards. But if you are thrown off course by a question or an interruption . . . if you want to make sure that you are on course . . . if you need absolute precision – then pause, stop talking, look at your cards – and look up and speak again.

One important reason for using notes, as opposed to reading from a script, is that they give you freedom of movement, of manoeuvre and of speech, in response to the reactions and the mood of your audience. Any actor, comedian or other performer, including any politician, will tell you that the same joke or speech or presentation that is a winner today may be a flop tomorrow, even with the same audience in the same place. It is hard to judge mood and we all make mistakes with it. But never forget that mood matters. As they say in Parliament: 'You must judge the mood of the House'.

One time that you may have to read from your notes is if you are actually quoting. Then (again) remember Churchill: 'If you're going to use notes, brandish them!'

Don't be afraid to say: 'I'll read you precisely what she said . . .' (Or as the case may be.)

Now for the art of reading – one to be used with economy.

When preparing words which you intend to read, try the method which I am using to write this chapter. Dictate your words. Or if you feel happier sitting at a word processor, let the words flow out of your fingers. Or scrawl them in longhand or in your own shorthand, if you wish. But spoken words flow better, when spoken again.

If you write out your words – or even if you get a speech writer to do the job for you – read them out aloud. Rehearse, read, re-read, and re-write until you are satisfied with the rhythm, the meaning and the time.

Then have your final draft carefully typed out, in large characters, widely spaced and with decent paragraphs. Keep your sentences, your phrases and your paragraphs short (see Chapter Sixteen). Start a new page for a new idea.

Mark up your manuscript, using either strokes of the pen for emphasis or (if you prefer it, which I do not) pale-coloured highlights.

Or use Churchill's method. He staggered his sentences, starting one on the lefthand margin; the next, about an inch across; then the next two inches across — and so on. He would pause after each sentence; recapture eye contact with his audience; then his eyes would automatically go down to the right place. And he marked his pauses and his places for emphasis.

Know your script well enough to be able to move from it, if your audience responds — or does not. Or to deal with interruptions, or because of new ideas which leap into your trained mind, during your delivery. And if you give advance copies to the media, warn them that you may move from your script.

If the occasion is important enough and either you or your company or organization rich enough, hire an 'autocue' or 'teleprompter'. These machines throw the words up on to plastic screens which you can read but which no one else can see. They are the speechmaker's equivalent to the moving words which allow television newsreaders and announcers to keep their eyes apparently on their viewers, while they are in reality reading.

If you use this or any other sort of equipment (see Chapter Twenty-three on Visual Aids) practise in advance. Rehearse with your operator. Recognize that even the most modern wonders, like the human beings that use them, may suffer from a breakdown, nervous or otherwise.

All that said, the read speech should be the unavoidable exception to the oratorical rule: Use notes.

13   Timing

Time is the enemy. Judge and use it well and your speech or presentation should prosper.

Experienced business people are expert in time management, except when they are on their feet. Aloft in their private joy, they ignore both the minutes and the agony of their audience.

'Did I speak too long?' enquired the managing director.

'Not at all,' his host responded. 'You helped shorten the winter!'

Whether you are making a speech or a presentation, your object is to capture, to captivate and to convince your audience. This means keeping it alive, not boring it to death.

'I could listen to him for hours' is a rare tribute. How much more common is its converse: 'I thought he would never stop . . .'?

As a post-graduate student at Harvard, I debated at the famous Norfolk Penal Colony. My partner was Anthony Lloyd, now a distinguished judge. Our opponents were Bill Flynn, forger, and Buzzy Mulligan, in for manslaughter. American debating is a tough art, with strict rules on timing, and judgement on both content and presentation.

We were briefed by Flynn. 'Remember, please,' he said, 'that in this place time is served, not enjoyed! Minutes, hours and days are notched up on the wall. Your audience is sensitive. Last year, we welcomed two debaters from your Cambridge Union. The opener did not start off very well. "It is a joy," he said, "to address a captive audience!" It's no fun being one!'

So respect your audience and its immobility. In Parliament, if you overrun a sensible time you will empty the chamber, keeping only those who are themselves waiting to speak. To antagonize any other audience – especially one that is either standing, or seated in discomfort – all you have to do is to speak too long. So work out your timing in advance; adapt it to your audience; and keep in touch with them while you speak.

A vicar found only one parishioner at his evensong service. With grim determination, he followed the prayer book to the letter and included a splendid half-hour sermon. When all was over, the vicar shook the sole listener's hand most warmly. 'Even if there is only one cow in the field,' he said, 'she must still be fed.'

'Indeed she must,' replied the parishioner. 'But you don't have to give her the whole load of hay!'

In general, the smaller your audience, the shorter you should keep your speech or your presentation. Why not use the time to communicate, to listen, to invite and to answer questions, to establish and to keep rapport? Your object is to win friends and to influence business? Then do your audience the courtesy of including them in your time calculations.

You recognize the importance of time in your business? You operate that inherently inhuman 'clocking' system for your work-force, perhaps even for your junior management? You regard these measures as part of the necessary discipline of commerce? Then apply self-discipline to your utterances, otherwise you will be talking to yourself, metaphorically if not literally. And recognize that speeches always take longer to make in reality than they do in rehearsal, even allowing – as you should almost always do – for audience participation.

Start by arriving on time. I once heard a presidential candidate, Adlai Stevenson, apologizing for turning up late at an election rally. 'I am deeply sorry. There is no greater thief than a man who steals the time of another. It is the only commodity that can never be recovered.'

Plan the timing of your speech. Recognize that while time creeps slowly for the prisoner, it races for the speaker. Concentrating on your subject and your audience, you will not notice the passing minutes.

Again, always overestimate the time you need and you will seldom be wrong. If you are preparing a half-hour presentation, then plan for 20 minutes. You can always use the balance for questions.

Speechmaking? Then ask the Chair – or even a colleague or confederate in the front row of your audience – to give you a signal when you have, say, five minutes left. Do not wait for the gavel to descend or the light to flash.

A well-known politician hideously overran his time at a dinner. The next speaker whispered to the Chair: 'Can't you stop him?' The Chair lifted his gavel but it slipped from his hand and hit his neighbour on the head. As the poor man slid under the table he was heard to exclaim: 'Hit me again! Hit me again! I can still hear him!'

Why not prop up your watch well within view? Most skilled speakers have no compunction in doing that, so why should you?

I use a watch with an alarm. I set it for five minutes after my speech is due to end. I am happy that it has yet to sound off.

If you do not have a watch or clock within easy view, you must consult the time with due cunning. Your glance at your wristwatch will be noted by your audience – which is at least less disconcerting than your audience looking at theirs.

Queen Elizabeth has elevated the art of surreptitious watch-watching to its ultimate. She wears hers on her right wrist, facing inwards. When she holds out her arm – whether to shake hands, to lift her cup or even in a simple gesture – time appears before her eyes – as it should before yours.

When a professional runs out of time, you know it. The amateur rushes, apologizes and panics. A skilled operator does not admit defeat by time.

There are questions to answer, interruptions to cope with, repetition for results. Whatever the reason, the rule is inevitable – time runs out faster than you thought it would.

Moral: Always allow much more time than you think your presentation will take. At worst, you will end early. Don't worry about that. Seldom (if ever) have you heard anyone say: 'I wish he'd gone on much longer' as opposed to: 'I thought he'd never end!'

Now for audience participation and interruption and for its wish to breathe, to shift around, to pause. Take the pressure and pace off yourself. Remove the need for rush.

This is fine, provided that it works. But what are the techniques if you find that time runs out? Perhaps the previous speaker has gone on for too long . . . someone else is added to the programme . . . or you misjudged your time?

DO NOT:

- Say: 'I'm sorry, I've run out of time. I'll have to leave out a lot of what I had intended to tell you . . .'
- Increase speed and race towards the end.
- Try to pack your misjudged quart into the pint of time left to you.

Instead DO:

Sum up whatever you have said and then add: 'Which leaves me with . . . and . . .' Then summarize each topic in a few moments. (See Chapter One). Then, end 'up' – on a climax, however brief.

14 Style

For the speechmaker, style and success are synonymous. But the common idea that style will suffice without taught techniques is arrogant and ridiculous. So is the converse – the chip-on-the-shoulder, foot-in-the-mouth inferiority complex approach to public speaking in any form, especially endemic among people at or near the top.

I invited a tycoon to address a private dinner. 'Sorry,' he replied, curtly. 'Nice of you to ask. You and your friends in Parliament do the speaking. I do the work!' What he really meant was: 'I'm afraid of opening my mouth while I'm on my feet in case I make a fool of myself.'

Another told me: 'I came up the hard way. I leave speeches to you fellows with the education.'

An education does no one any harm and many top people who missed it in their youth are unashamed to learn, when their money can buy them time and tuition. Presenting yourself to the public does take courage and is certainly an acquired skill. But if you have that intangible, inexplicable magic – that style of your own – you should not fear its public display. Printers and potters produce identical replicas, good or bad. Your style is unique and rules are made to be understood, and then only broken on purpose.

Take the orator's pause, for instance – a crucial weapon in the armoury of timing. (See Chapter One.) The space between words, sentences or thoughts should not be blurred by that most awful of sounds – 'er'. To 'err' (or to 'um') is human – to pause, divine!'

The art of successful speaking is to know the case you wish to present; to understand and to use the basic skills which will enable your audience to hear, to comprehend and to accept your words and their intent; and to stamp the process with your own particularity.

It follows that you should use the services of speech writers with rare care. Unless you can find the writer who can step into your style as well as your mind, you are probably better off with a researcher. Use a ferret to produce your raw material, but knock it into your own shape.

If the speech or presentation is worth your while to make, it is also worth your own time to prepare. (See Chapter Two.) Remember another of Churchill's dicta: 'If I have to make a two-hour speech,' he rumbled, 'I can prepare it in ten minutes. If it is a ten-minute speech, then it can take me two hours.'

Stylists are as brief as their impact and their message permits. There is no reason why people who are blunt, direct and lucid in conversation should allow their speeches to deteriorate into long-winded and indirect blather, the moment they climb to their feet.

Just as there is no one successful style in business – or, for that matter, in athletics or in football, in philosophy or in politics – so those who seek success as speakers will project their personal individuality, their individual personality.

Every would-be excellent speaker needs education in the basic skills of speechmaking and presentation. They are universal. They range from voice production to microphone technique, from the skills of the construction of a speech or presentation to the art of the destruction of the arguments of others. The use of humour is also important. But training in the use of these skills should be devoted to the creation and improvement of your own style.

True education and the best training teach students – however mighty – to make the best of their talents.

No presenter of ideas or maker of speeches has ever excelled Shakespeare. 'This above all,' says Polonius in *Hamlet*, 'to thine own self be true.'

If truth is the life of style, insincerity is its death. And once you know how and get used to it, being yourself is easier.

Another technique of good style: use the active and not the passive voice. Say: 'The Managing Director told us' and not 'We were told by the Managing Director'. Or: 'He gave us . . .' and not, 'We received from him . . .'

Exception: if you wish to put the spotlight onto yourselves rather than on the MD, you could say: 'We were told by the MD that . . . but in our view . . .'

The active voice places the emphasis on those who are being active.

15   The vertical pronoun

First class speakers treat the sound of their own voices as a drug to be taken in moderation. Restrain your use of the first-person singular, but do tell stories, anecdotes and tales from your own experience.

You have probably been asked to address a particular audience for one of two reasons. Either the people wanted to hear you or they thought they ought to want to do so. These categories sub-divide.

If you have been invited to speak in the hope that you will have something interesting to tell, then you are lucky. Do not push your luck too far by retelling what you are, rather than what you know.

Leave it to your introducer to sing your praises. To do so for yourself is to court ridicule. Oscar Wilde once remarked: 'Fall in love with yourself and you are in for a lifetime of romance!' Fine, but do not do your courting in public.

If you are asked to give advice, do you really need to praise your own success? To tell tales of the trade, you must draw on your own experience and a joke against yourself may be highly successful. But you do not need to alert your listeners to your excellence. Do so and they will not believe you. Fail to do so and they may think up the idea for themselves.

Naturally, if you have been the rounds of businesses, factories, offices or workshops similar to your own, at home or abroad, and are asked to give your impressions; if you wish to express views and to make it clear that they are yours and not those of your organization or, perhaps, of your board, your partners or colleagues; if you wish to lighten the darkness of some drab subject with a personal anecdote – then go ahead. 'I once met . . . in Birmingham'; 'I was told the tale of . . .'; 'These are my views, I repeat, and if they turn out to be wrong, you will know where to place the responsibility.' All fair. Or even: 'Was it not I who said . . .'

But, 'When I last saw the Prime Minister . . .'; or 'Now, I don't like to drop names, but when I was spending a weekend recently with Lord and Lady Blank at their country estate . . .' Terrible.

Remember the story of the famous TV producer. A friend said to him: 'You know, you must be the worst name-dropper in the world.'

'I'm afraid you're right,' he replied. 'That's just what the Queen Mother said to me last week!'

Or remember the story of the remarkable Lord Montgomery of Alamein, whose first-person anecdote was accepted because of his undoubted greatness. He was telling an audience about his battle tactics. 'I could not decide what to do next,' he said. 'I thought to myself: "My God, what is to be done now?" "General," came the answer, "you decide. I have every confidence in you." So I did!'

Of course, people like to be given the inside information. Don the cloak of apparent modesty.

All this becomes even more important when you are guest of honour – which is not necessarily the same as the honoured guest. Maybe your hosts want your money . . . your support . . . your services . . . your backing. Maybe they are simply hoping to lubricate you sufficiently to obtain some useful information which, in a less cordial or obligated moment, you might never give. Whatever the reason, you are on show. So play up to it. Be grateful that you are to be honoured and not reviled. Help to keep it that way by making your speech extremely modest. Or try my father's favourite: 'After all those kind words, Mr Chairman, I can hardly wait to hear myself speak!'

'It is extremely good of you to honour me in this way,' you might continue. 'I fully appreciate that your intention is, through me, to honour my company/my organization/my entire Board [*as the case may be*]. We are deeply grateful to you.'

In the body of the speech, tell them about the work your organization is doing. Give them as much inside information as you decently can. If you are being honoured for long service, then reminisce. If you mention individuals amongst your audience, beware those you omit.

Everyone honourably mentioned is flattered. You have achieved the all-important informal touch. Your audience are your friends. The ice is melted and you are revealed as one of the people, instead of the complete egotist some had thought you were.

Then continue: 'You are indeed lucky to have in your active ranks, tonight and always, Mr Reginald Property . . . Mr James Industry . . . and that lady, famous for her good deeds, Mrs Jewel.' The guest who gives honour will receive it.

'I now close . . .' [I hope because of the time of the clock and not the time you have taken in your speech] 'but before doing so, I thank you again for the great kindness and generosity you have shown me. I have enjoyed being with you. I hope that we shall meet again often and always on happy occasions. And may this organization/

company/institute [etc.] flourish for many years to come, under your leadership.'

Turn to the chairman, bow to your audience ... You have produced a resounding ending to a good speech. Your hearers will tell you so – and mean it.

To sum up: substitute the most vital word in the English language – 'you' – for the vertical pronoun. In parliamentary language, 'The you's have it'! Janner's Law again: 'Use You's!'

16   Jargon, clichés, brevity and grammar

My shorthand is your jargon. Your jargon is my cliché. Jargon is specialized speech, understood by insiders. Clichés are once-sparkling expressions or bright truths repeated to the brink of boredom. Avoid both.

Listening to the head of a financial institution, I jotted down the following jargon in his first few sentences: FIMBRA, LAUTRO, IMRO, TSA, AFBD . . . Which reminded me of a visit to an African capital where the UK High Commissioner invited me to talk to his diplomats. First, though, would I mind if they discussed some urgent business? Of course not. I'd be interested. So, for some ten minutes, they discussed the QBP.

I was bemused. Talk swirled over well-known names, apparently to be included or excluded; delicacies to be served; British and local composers; diplomatic niceties . . .

Finally, I could contain myself no longer: 'I'm sorry to be dim,' I said, 'But would you please tell me: what is the QBP?'

Every head turned at the vast ignorance of this politician. 'The Queen's Birthday Party, Mr Janner,' said His Excellency. When my turn came, I resisted the temptation to discuss the AGM of my GMC, or the preparations for the next meeting of the CLP, the DLP or the PLP*. Meetings of the Labour Party are not tea parties, nor are they known for their diplomacy.

Anyway, there are two stages in avoiding this sort of embarrassment to others. First, recognize your own jargon. None of us notices the familiar, because habit dulls recognition. Second, once you have noticed it, use it only among your own colleagues or with others afflicted by the same verbiage. Do not inflict it on those who are strange to it.

Final hint: here is an area in which your spouse may be more useful than your secretary. In most families, spouses work and operate in different spheres and can recognize each other's jargon, point it out, chide, reprove and help to avoid. Ask yours to do so for you, or

---

* Annual General Meeting; General Management Committee; Constituency Labour Party; District Labour Party; Parliamentary Labour Party.

employ your older children in the hunt for the unacceptably obtuse. Unlike your secretary, they are likely to be jargon-free. You might even consider appropriate payment. We recommend £1 for every 'um' or 'er' (see Chapter Fourteen) or jargon spotted by a spouse; or 50p for the same service performed by offspring.

When Labour Leader, Ernest Bevin, was asked about someone's speech, he would often reply: 'Boring. Clitch after clitch after clitch!' Drive your clitches out of your spitches!

When you get bored with someone else's, jot them down. 'At this moment in time . . .', 'in this day and age' – the speaker meant 'now'. 'Let me appraise you of the situation . . .' – which should have been, 'I'll tell you what's happening'. 'We must capture the hearts and minds of the people' – if you clitch long enough, the minds will close and the bodies depart. 'No problem . . . All you have to do is to stand up and be counted . . . Just take all this on board . . .' Ugh!

English is a rich language. Consult any thesaurus and you will find that there is no need to use the 'common, hackneyed, trite or commonplace'. Whenever sentiments expressed may be 'wise, sage, true, received, admitted, recognized', you could harness that flexibility of language, that charm and originality, which can cloak even the most uninspiring and unoriginal thoughts.

Now apply these rules to some clichés particularly prevalent in the business world. Take the 'track record' of your company or firm (what 'track', pray?); and who 'heads up' your department? (It's head down, when you are at the helm of your ship of state, as you steer it through troubled economic waters.)

Some of the more pedantic rules for writing have been discarded. Freedom of expression and freedom of speech have followed. Hooray! Single words. Or two or three of them in a sentence. Sentences without verbs. All are accepted. Split infinitives offend the ears of some but are generally forgiven. Still, here are some general rules on grammar, which you should follow.

The most common grammatical error? Misuse of the first person. 'Between you and I' is wrong. So is 'Dr Brown and me were most impressed with our welcome,' and 'You and me must give some careful thought to this problem'. If this sort of problem worries you, discuss it with a friend whose grammar is impeccable. If in doubt, change the sentences around and you will soon find whether your usage is or is not correct.

If you are inclined to say: 'You and me must go,' try instead: 'Me must go' – and the error becomes obvious. Or: 'Thank you on behalf of Mr White and I for your kindness' cannot be correct when you leave out Mr White. 'On my own behalf . . . on my behalf . . . on behalf of Mr White' – but obviously not on behalf of I.

If you are not sure in doubt about the precise meaning of a word, either avoid it or consult a dictionary. Given the choice between two words, one long and the other short, choose the shorter.

The best way to avoid jargon and clichés is to choose the best words. That requires time, which means – pausing.

Next essential – brevity, the soul of success. The brief, crisp, Anglo-Saxon word is almost always better than the cumbersome alternative. Keep your sentences, your paragraphs and your speeches short.

Churchill was the master of brevity. 'Blood, toil, tears and sweat . . .' – not, 'haemorrhages, labour, lachrymose weeping and perspiration . . .'

The Judge asked the convicted villain: 'Have you anything to say before I pronounce sentence?'

'Yes, my lord,' he replied. 'For Gawd's sake, keep it short!'

Keep your sentences short. Break them up. Get rid of the 'ands' and the 'buts' – even more so of the 'in addition tos', the 'howevers' and the 'consequentlys'. Try starting a separate sentence each time with 'And', 'But' or 'So'.

Punctuate your speeches as you would your letters. Give yourself and your audience time to think.

As for the speech itself, remember the famous cartoon of the politician being carried out of the US Senate on a stretcher. 'Talked to Death!' was the caption. The corpse might as easily have been emerging from any one of the daily thousands of meetings, anywhere in the business world.

To avoid having your audience look at their watches, hold their attention. Through unjargonized, unclichéd, brief words, sentences and speeches.

President Roosevelt once complained bitterly about a sign in the wartime White House: 'Upon departing, kindly extinguish all lights when vacating the premises'. He ordered the signs changed to: 'Please switch off all lights when you leave'.

A management trainee was asked whether he needed help with a job. He replied: 'I believe that I am perfectly capable of carrying out this operation without assistance from others'. 'Just say "I can do it on my own",' his manager snapped back.

Which reminds me of the apprentice who asked his supervisor:

'What's a square foot?' 'I don't know,' his boss replied. 'But I'll make sure that you get full compensation!'

17 Wit and humour

Everyone loves a story. And anyone can be a good raconteur. What matters is to remember the four rules of that brilliant comedian, Bob Monkhouse:

- Use stories, jokes or wit that *you* think are funny.
- Make sure that your humour suits you and your style.
- Match your humour to your audience.
- Above all, do not offend.

If you are enjoying a cup of tea, a drink or a chat with friends, you will tell them tales. You will relax and laugh together. Do the same when you are on your feet.

In private, you don't tell funny stories unless you yourself enjoy them, do you? Then do the same in public. If you don't think that your wit is amusing, then you cannot hope to pass on pleasure that you yourself do not feel.

Equally, when you are joking in private, you tell the stories in your own way – and you tell the stories that fit that way. For instance, you may enjoy epigrams, puns or word play. Or you may prefer stories, putting a twist into your tales. Or you may be a good mimic or a specialist in dialects.

As in private, so in public. Use humour that suits you.

Again, when you are with friends, business companions or strangers, you adapt your humour to them, to their mood, their interests, their (literally) humour. So target your audience and do the same for them in public.

Fourth, finally and most important: When you tailor your humour to yourself and to your audience and to the occasion, avoid the offensive.

An off-colour story may suit the stag dinner, but if you introduce a blue or risqué tale into solemn or sombre occasions or, generally, with a mixed audience, you invite that awful moment of embarrassed silence, which we all recognize in the speeches of others and must try to avoid for ourselves. If in doubt, keep it clean.

Be very careful with the race/minority story. There may still be a place for the saga of the Scotsman, the Irishman and the Brit.

51

Exaggerate the accent of your own nation or ethnic group. That's
fine. To copy someone else's is a mistake. Scotsmen, Irishmen,
Blacks, Jews, Americans, Poles, Newfoundlanders, Arabs or Greeks
– each may delight in stories about themselves, but rarely when told
by others.

If you enjoy the friendship of Jewish people, for instance, you will
soon find that we poke merciless fun at our own foibles. Part of our
armour, acquired through centuries of persecution, is the ability to
make laughter shine through the tears.

I have a vast selection of Jewish stories, which I tell with relish. But
(with rare exceptions of known friends – such as Bob Monkhouse) I
don't like them being told by other people.

We cause no injury to ourselves when we make jokes at our own
expense. So if you are a lawyer, tell legal jokes; if you are an
accountant, take legal jokes and adapt them for accountants; if you
are in business, poke fun at commercial oddities; and if you want to
tell political tales, start with one against your own side and then
those you prod at your opponents will be acceptable.

'We foreigners find it very difficult to understand you English. I
know that m'i's'l'e'd spells misled. But when I pronounced t'i't'l'e'd
the same way, everyone laughed at me.'

Not great humour and perhaps it had been heard before. But then,
as one famous comic put it: 'There are basically only two jokes – the
mother-in-law, and the banana skin.' Make the joke fit yourself and
your style, the occasion and your audience – and poke the fun at
yourself.

The best humour is immediate. Extract it from the surroundings
and the people present, or from the urgent and the topical. Think on
your feet.

How do you put your humour across to your audience?

First, appear confident. Don't say: 'I was going to tell you the story
about . . .' and then tell it, half apologetically. Believe in the comedy
or you will never induce your audience to do so. Never say: 'Which
reminds me of the old story about . . .' Instead: 'Isn't that just like the
classic tale about . . .'

You'll not find the TV people inviting you to watch 'an old film'. It
will always be: 'Another chance to see that great classic . . .'

So be confident, show confidence and retain it, even in the face of
defeat. If a joke falls flat, never mind. Pretend it wasn't intended to be
funny, and carry on. Or face up to the situation and say: 'Sorry . . . I
thought it was funny . . .' – or 'Oh dear, what is it, your sense of

humour or mine?' Or: 'Sorry about that – I'll do better next time. But after a meal like we've just had, it's really the height of sadism to expect anyone to try to entertain you lot.'

Timing is all important. This means that the joke, the witticism or the humorous thrust must be well placed in relation to the speech, the content of the oratorical lecture and the mood of the audience. But it also means – the pause. (See Chapter Eleven.) Listen to first-class comedians at work. They get their effect through timing. They know when to wait . . . and when to rush forward. So listen to them, learn from them and copy. You can even borrow their jokes. As a script-writer told me: 'God gave you eyes? Then plagiarize!'

The best stories have at least one sting in their tales. The laughter should build up and the audience expect the laughs. If the first climax draws laughter and turns out to be merely a prelude, then when the real punch line hits you'll know that the story has been a success.

The formal tale has its place. But the bright phrase, the witty aside, the colourful remark – they are more important.

You have an important occasion coming up? Mull over my Retellable Tales. Use and adapt them to yourself, your occasions and your audience.

If you cannot think of or find a funny story for your needs, never mind. Humorous ideas should come as you speak. Otherwise, please make sure that your speech is shorter than it would have been, had you lightened its dullness with shafts of light and wit.

As a young student at Harvard, I sat at the feet of Mr Justice Frankfurter. Then we met at a party. He arrived late. My hostess said that she had found him sitting in his car outside.

'What are you doing, Felix?' she enquired.

'Just preparing my conversation,' the great man replied.

People say to me: 'How do you remember all these stories?' It's simple. When I hear one I like, I write it down. Then I tell it. If it makes people laugh and they and I enjoy it, then I transfer it from a notebook or envelope or scrap of paper, into a file. Then I cull them – and if they are good enough, they go into the next edition of my Retellable Tales.

Should you laugh at your own jokes? That depends on your style. You should certainly let your audience know that you are joking, or they may take you seriously. Which, on occasion, can be disastrous. 'I was only joking . . . please don't be offended . . . I never thought you'd take it seriously . . .' can presage the end of a friendship.

Straight-faced humour has its place. If it's your style, use it. But it's not for me.

18 Overstatement and repetition

Hyperbole — that is, exaggeration for effect — has its place, and is often used by humorists. There is nothing funny about a thin man; but a matchstick man, a creation of skin and bone, a fat head on a puny frame — that's different.

About the only time that deliberate exaggeration helps the presentation of a serious case is when the case is thin. 'If something is too silly to say, you can always sing it,' announces the operatic librettist. 'If logic and argument are surplus,' says the skilled speaker, 'then it's just possible that if you shout loud enough, exaggerate sufficiently, thump with sufficient force, you may numb the minds of your audience.'

This type of behaviour is the last resort of the advocate and should only be used *in extremis*. Otherwise, your exaggerations are likely to boomerang, to make people laugh at you and to ruin such case as you have. Two horrible examples:

- Reference to the speech immediately preceding: 'That magnificent and moving oration that we have just heard . . . that tugged at our heart strings and must now open our purses . . .'
- 'I only saw her passing by, but I shall love her till I die,' said Sir Robert Menzies, then Prime Minister of Australia, enthusing at a dinner in honour of the Queen. However well loved the Queen undoubtedly was and is, Sir Robert's hyperbole brought only ridicule.

Words, like drugs, may be highly beneficial in the correct quantity and dosage. Over-indulgence may cause death.

Repetition should be deliberate. Shakespeare did it best: 'Brutus is an honourable man . . .' Or remember Martin Luther King's great speech, 'I have a dream . . .'

Repeating other people's points generally spells disaster: 'Mr Jones has put all the arguments which I had wished to put forward . . .' Try instead: 'Mr Jones has put forward his case with immense skill, and I commend it to the meeting. But there are several aspects of his remarks which, I think, require further emphasis.'

'I will not bore you by reploughing the furrows so thoroughly covered by Mr Jones.' Watch out. Boredom is on its way. That sort of

Overstatement and repetition

introduction, combining mixed metaphor with cliché, is a sure sign
of impending audience distress. Leave the meeting if you can.

Then there are speakers who repeat their points in the same words.
Most well-constructed speeches should begin with a summary of
what is coming, followed by a full-blooded exposition of those
points in the body of the speech and another brief summary at the
end. 'To summarize, then: if we are to achieve success, we must take
the following steps. First . . . second . . . third . . . and, above all . . .'

English is a rich language. If you cannot think of synonyms,
consult a Thesaurus – every speaker should have one on their desk or
bookshelves. If you must repeat yourself, at least try not to do so in
current, boring clichés, which are merely a sign of speeches made
without thought, and so reveal the thoughtlessness of the speaker.

Also, always repeat lists. Your listeners will not absorb them first
time round. 'So I repeat – first . . . second . . . and third . . .'

To summarize your message into what is known as a 'sound bite' is
simple, if you remember our mnemonic – you do your PREP.

First, you state your *Position*. Then you give your *Reason*. Third,
you give an *Example*. Fourth and finally, you repeat your *Position*.

Use your fingers to demonstrate. The right gestures add variety
and meaning. And remember that if you do not repeat your list, your
audience will not take it in and remember it.

Visual aids are another form of repetition, supplementing sound
with vision. (Details in Chapter Twenty-three).

19 Tact and sensitivity

First class presenters react to their audience. They watch them with care; coax them into concentration; convince them with their themes; enthuse them with their message.

From the moment you enter the room, sensitivity is the key to stylish success. It will, for instance:

- Guide you to the top people – so that you greet them, respect them, take care never to demean them, and, where possible, flatter them – if only by asking: 'Have I covered the points that you would wish?' Or: 'How would you deal with this matter in your organization?'
- Help you steer the conversation, discussion, or presentation in the direction you wish – especially if it has veered onto an unexpected and unwanted course.
- Enable you to invite audience intervention or participation and make the best use of it. Just as any politicians worth their salt will welcome hecklers, so speakers should be pleased with interventions which enliven their task and reveal their listeners' interests and anxieties.
- Help you to avoid jargon, unexplained terminology and unnecessary complications – especially in territory well known to you, but not to any or all of your listeners. Do not presume that others have too much knowledge. After all, Mr X may be new to his department or Ms Y who should have prepared the ground before your talk, may not have done so.
- Assist in recognizing those people who would like to ask questions but are shy to do so for fear of revealing their ignorance to their colleagues. Bring out the best from the reticent.
- Help you to know when your audience are getting restless or inattentive, so that you can alter course, style or speed, introduce a story or a joke, invite your listeners to ask questions, or simply say: 'Are there any points that need clarification so far?'
- Sharpen your tact – so that, for instance, if someone asks a question which shows that he was either not listening or stupid, you say: 'I'm sorry. I am sure it was my fault. Let me try to explain again', or 'It's a very complicated concept and I am so sorry that I did not succeed in explaining it clearly. Let me show you on a chart . . .', or: 'Thank you for that question. I'm pleased to expand on that important concept.'

If you go wrong and cause unintentional offence, then apologize. An apology tells recipients that they were right and you wrong. It raises them in their own estimation and does you no harm.

Make sure that you write down any names which you may have to quote – the Chair, the managing director, the company, the guest – and that you spell and pronounce them correctly. Most people are very touchy about their names, which are themselves. If in doubt, ask them how they would like their names pronounced. I'm used to 'Grenville', 'Granville' and even 'Gretzel' – but must admit that I do prefer my own label.

Train yourself to think ahead, so that you are not only watching your audience's reaction to what you are saying at the time, but thinking towards your next sentence, idea, theme . . . or change of rhythm or style.

If your listeners look at their watches, watch yours. You will know that their time is on their minds. Be prepared to move ahead on your notes, to discard cards, and either advance to your close or involve the timewatcher. 'I am sorry, Mr Brown,' you might say, 'that we are approaching our time limit. But are there any other points which you would like me to deal with?'

I once heard a computer salesman explaining to a major company in a depressed area why it should spend money on his equipment. 'We could help you to reduce your staff by 50 per cent if you buy one of our computers,' he announced. I could see his listeners saying to themselves: 'I wonder whether I would be one of the staff that would go'. The contract was lost. Sensitivity matters.

These sensitivities apply to private as well as to public presentations – from person to person to a platform address. But when you are eyeball to eyeball, eye contact is both easier and more relaxed. The larger your audience, the greater the temptation to treat them as remote, but the greater your need to relate your sensitivities to those of individual listeners. Otherwise do not blame them if they take as little interest in you and your message as you do in them and their reactions.

If the intent of your presentation is to enthuse, then you must inject enthusiasm into your words and make them as infectious as possible. If the essence of a fine presentation lies in self-control leading into control of your audience, sensitivity is the presenter's top asset, and its absence an insurmountable obstacle to success.

So remember our Three E's: Energy, Enthusiasm and Excitement. With them, you should succeed. Without them, you are almost sure to fail.

20   Quotes and statistics

Your audience have come to hear you, but you may still pepper your speech with apt quotations from the thoughts of others. Quoting, though, is an art of its own. Perfect it.

Keep quotations short. To quote at length from memory is show. You are not engaged in stage soliloquy. To read someone else's words at length is rarely a good alternative to putting thoughts and ideas into your own words. The reading of speeches – or even lengthy parts of them – is usually an error. (See Chapter Twelve.) That error is compounded when you are not even reading your own original thought.

Quotations are only worth using if they are thoroughly apt. If your audience is flagging, do not thrust in an inappropriate quotation.

Attribute a quotation to its true author, if you can. If in doubt, you could try: 'Was it George Bernard Shaw who said. . . ?' Or if the attribution is to someone in your lifetime, you can seldom go wrong with: 'I once heard President Ford remark on television that . . .' or, 'Did you read the saying, attributed to Mr Gorbachev, that . . .' Who is to prove you wrong?

Make sure that your speech really is strengthened by putting the statement in quotation marks – and as coming from the particular author. When trying to convince a British audience to adopt an American practice, it is sometimes better to adopt the transatlantic arguments without stating their origin. Conversely, for any non-American to express a preference for candidates in an American election is to impose the kiss of death on them. By all means use the foreigner's arguments, but if you must, put them into quotation marks; try: 'A famous Marxist once proclaimed . . .' Quote Satan to condemn sin.

The best quotations come, of course, from the careless mouths of your opponents. 'Today, Mr Jones condemns amalgamation. But who was it who said, just two years ago – and I quote: "Our future depends on achieving amalgamation. We cannot survive as a small independent unit"? None other than my friend, Mr Jones!'

Avoid quotations from yourself: 'Did I not say, six months ago, that. . . ?' Or 'May I repeat what I said at our trade conference last month'. Unless a speaker has previously been accused of inconsistency, self-quotation is generally pompous and egotistical. (See Chapter Fifteen.)

If you have something to say today, say it. Let someone else point to your marvellous consistency . . . to your wisdom before the event . . . to your status as a person whose advice should be taken. The best you can do is to make that insinuation. Self-quotation, like self-adulation, is proper only among consenting adults in private . . . or as a solitary occupation.

Mind how you use statistics. Everyone knows that they are in the same category as lies and damned lies. If your presentation is to succeed, your figures must at least appear to be accurate.

A queue of graduates applied for a job with a firm of city accountants. Each was asked: 'What is twice one?' Each replied: 'Two.' The applicant who eventually got the job replied: 'What number did you have in mind, sir?'

So when you present statistics, at least indicate their origin — assuming that you are not ashamed of it.

Do not presume that others are as familiar with figures or accounts as yourself. I am amazed by the number of business people who cannot even read a balance sheet, or understand a profit and loss account. So steer your way between the cardinal sins of talking down to your audience on the one hand and attributing undue knowledge on the other. If in doubt, explain.

Recognizing that some human beings absorb by ear and others by eye, but most require a combination of both, and accepting also that your audience is far more likely to be innumerate than illiterate, supplement your words with paper — graphs and the rest — and, where appropriate, with visual aids (see Chapter Twenty-three).

21 Credits

Few speechmakers object to being thanked or resent receiving credit, even where it is not strictly due. But most get upset if their merit is not recognized or if thanks are withheld – especially if credit due to one goes to another. So good speakers are as liberal with their praise of others as they are parsimonious with their praise of themselves. Listeners who feel that you recognize and are prepared publicly to laud their worth are more likely to be receptive to the excellence of your arguments.

Here, then, is a sample, generalized opening. (See also Chapter Three.)

'First, my thanks. If it were not for Mr Brown, this gathering would never have been organized at all. If not for Ms Black, the company would be in grave difficulty. If not for Mr White, the scheme we are about to discuss would never have been born. In paying tribute to them, I thank all of you for giving them the support and backing without which they could not have put forward this essentially constructive project.

'Now, let's look at the project.' Your audience is softened up. They are ready to listen to constructive criticism from you.

Or: 'Under the guidance of Mr Green, this project has made great headway. With Mr Brown as treasurer and Ms Blue as honorary secretary, it is hardly surprising that it has gathered momentum. And now it is up to us to help them by applying constructive minds to the scheme they have created.

'I know they welcome criticism designed to advance their work. We all appreciate that their enthusiasm is increased by suggestions, coming from people like us, who only want the scheme to succeed. I am sure that they will give careful consideration to our submissions.'

Flattery? Certainly – but legitimate. Praise? Yes, indeed, and with every appearance of sincerity. Credit, thanks, tact – and all designed to prepare the ground for your message. It is not only armies that often do best when they advance from the side, and there is no shame in a swift strike from the rear.

To test the importance of these rules, listen to someone who ignores them. Beware the benefactor scorned, the doer of good deeds who goes unrecognized, the creator whose idea, invention or brainchild is attributed to another.

There exists, of course, the occasional 'eminence grise' – the spectral backroom boy who takes as much pride in praise going to others whom he has built up as does the father who basks in the reflected glory of his child's exploits. But even he appreciates the oblique reference to the power that made the throne secure, to the modest mind that 'wishes to remain anonymous but must not go without being thanked . . . Those of us who are lucky enough to realize just how and by whom the work has been done, salute our silent and modest friends – we are grateful to them.'

As an editorial mention or a praise of a product in the general pages of a newspaper are public relations people's delight – and worth more to them than the advertisement that their clients have to pay for – so the 'plug' in the course of a speech and as part of it is often more valuable to the maker and more appreciated by the person referred to than the formal and expected vote of thanks, though even that is a weapon not to be despised in the campaign to get your own way.

PART 3

Practicalities

22 Microphones

Once upon a time you had to speak to be heard. Nowadays, a whisper will do. The microphone has arrived. Know how to use it. Well employed, it is a trusty ally. Over-employed or misused it will blast away your audiences for ever.

A good voice was once a prerequisite for a singer. No more. With the aid of the 'mike', the men and women of successful music can make their fortunes without, in many cases, enough power in their lungs to fill a breathalyser. They may belt out the tune, but the nuances and expressions that the opera singer spends years learning to create are not there. The effects that brighten so many otherwise even more miserable musical moments are created by the microphone – by the tricks of the audio trade.

First make sure that your mike is switched on. Speak into it, and you will soon find out. Adjust it to a convenient height at a rake of about 75 degrees. Whether it is a standing or a table model, you will probably find a turning ring near the centre. With luck and reasonable wrist power, you should be able to fix the mike at about six inches below the level of your mouth.

If presented with a neck mike, test and adjust it so that your voice emerges at the correct volume. Then do not trip over the cord.

You may prefer, though – as I do – to use a roving mike on a long lead. You retain your freedom of movement, and the mike becomes as much an asset for you as it is for stage and television performers who hold one by preference.

However long you have to keep your audience waiting, take your time to adjust and position your microphone. With the volume and position adjusted, you are ready to begin. If your voice emerges clear and undistorted, all is well. If there is a scream, a whistle or a shriek, you are too near or the volume is too loud. If your voice emerges as if from outer space, with Martian echo or eerie ululation, then adjust. And keep your head up. Do not ever talk down to the microphone.

'Colleagues and friends . . .' Silence. Lift up your voice: 'Will someone kindly switch on this mechanical marvel'. Laughter. The engineer scurries around and flips the appropriate switch. 'Thank you.' Screams and whistles from the machine. More laughter. 'There's no need to overdo it.' The engineer tries again. 'Colleagues and friends . . .' Silence. 'Are you receiving me?' you say, smiling. 'Do you hear me at the back?' Loud cries of 'No, no' and more laughter. They are laughing with you and not at you. You have command of the situation. You are waiting until the conditions are as you require before you start speaking.

With luck and perseverance, the microphone will be put into proper order. If it is not – or if reception is intermittent or unpleasant – then you must make up your mind whether or not your voice will carry unaided. Is it better to risk being unheard than to submit your audience to squeals and screeches from the machine? Will you succeed in interesting your audience when the microphone is playing up? Have you, perhaps, a genius in the place who can adjust the amplifier, the loudspeaker, or some other unmentionable or unpro-nounceable part of this gadget? Think on your feet – fast.

'I shall do without the microphone,' you belt out. 'I hope that you will all hear me.' Applause.

Or: 'I apologize for the inefficiency of this miserable apparatus. I'll do my best with it, without it would be worse.'

You are off – to a late and unhappy start. But your audience have noted your confidence.

More major speeches are ruined because the speaker is not prepared to take time and make preparations with the microphone than for most other reasons.

Make the mike your ally. Never panic when it goes wrong. Be prepared to fall back on your own voice power, if you must. Remember that great orators of the past had to manage unamplified –and they did not do too badly – presumably because they knew the rules of voice production (see Chapter Ten).

And remember once again, to keep your head up, and lower only your voice into the microphone.

Keep your distance. Get too close and you will produce 'scream' – whine and whistle – and 'pop' – an explosion of b's and p's.

And remember that a mike is liable to be switched on, even when you think it's dead. So watch your words!

23   Visual aids

There is an art to excellence – not least in the use of visual aids. So why is this use so seldom taught? Consider – and refer to – the following points when using visual aids:

- Do not use visual aids to replace your verbal message. Charts, etc., should either:
  Provide the skeleton for your presentation, so as to attract the eye and direct the mind (later to revive the memory) and/or
  Illustrate and explain, through graphs, etc., concepts and/or detail which cannot be explained simply and/or adequately and/or swiftly in other ways.
- Which aids are best for the particular occasion? Slides (35mm) are splendid – but generally only for projecting pictures or for large audiences. Overhead slides (or 'acetates' or 'transparencies') can be switched or even amended or added to during the presentation. They should be treated with respect, their contents carefully thought out and the transparencies themselves professionally produced.
- The old-fashioned but worthy flip chart will never go out of fashion. At its simplest, it consists of a stack of blank newsprint sheets attached to a board. With pens or crayons you illustrate your words, the sheets then being flipped over or torn off.
- To avoid the blank spaces of darkness and silence between 35mm slides, you can now get what are called 'twin pair dissolve slides'. Operated with two machines, as one slide goes off the screen, another comes on it. But these prepared slides have to remain in the same order and there is no way in which you can shuffle them. Inflexibility is a high price to pay for apparent slickness.
- Transparencies, etc., should be concise, compact, uncluttered and always framed. Use abbreviations and symbols to summarize and to emphasize. Use artwork sparingly and for results, not effects.
- Keep the wording on all visual aids to a sensible minimum. Divide a mass of hard-to-assimilate material between two or more projections.
- Remind your graphics department or other aid makers to make the transparencies with backgrounds clear and light – not obscure and dark. The darker the background, the poorer the view. Green, blue and black come out well on a white background, as black does on yellow. Red on green, or green on red, are even worse than white on red, orange on black, or red on yellow. Clarity of overhead vision should never be sacrificed for artificial and artistic impression.

- If you draw on transparencies, use water-based pens, which can be rubbed out with a damp cloth – not those that require spirit for removal.
- Visual aids should stimulate interest and not simply provide a technical message.
- Beware of 'funnies'. Humour is much better presented orally, if only because you can quickly move on and away from a failed joke. If you must use cartoons, caricatures or illustrative, graphic humour, then make sure that it is thoroughly professional.
- Check your pens or crayons in advance. Break up the script by using different colours. Make sure the lettering is large enough to be seen. Use as few words as possible: for instance, do not say 'replaced by' – simply cross out whatever it is that has been replaced.
- Use variety in your visual aids – different types, colours, underlining, etc.
- To make the best of slides, overhead charts, etc, consider providing copies for all your audience – as reference to save them writing, so that they can concentrate on your presentation; and for addition to their own notes. As in the case of all other documentation, consider carefully whether you would wish to supply this in advance (not generally recommended, because busy people seldom do their homework, and often forget to bring it with them on the day); and/or at time of presentation for use during its course; and/or at the end of the presentation, to take home.
- Beware of over-preparation. An auto-cued, word-perfect script, the drama of music and lighting, the over-professionalism too often produced by specialists for the use of amateurs – avoid them all.
- Choose your overhead projectors or machinery with care. I deeply dislike projectors with fans that change the atmosphere when they come on, often do not go off along with the light, and disturb speaker and audience. Watch out especially for those that blow air out sideways, depositing papers all over the show. Better – in any event with a smaller audience – to use a modern, mirror-type projector.
- Ensure that your visual aids are properly set up before your audience arrive, ie. properly focused and with the first slide, transparency, etc., in position.
- Ensure that all the audience can see – if anyone cannot, then move the viewer or the screen.
- Do not talk while changing transparencies or slides.
- If you show slides, try not to keep the room in permanent gloom while you talk – unless you would prefer not to know when your audience slide off into slumber. Maybe you can place yourself to one side or under a spotlight, or at least turn the light on when the slides are off.
- The first transparency or slide should generally provide an overall summary – to which you can return, filling in the detail with your further projections.

Visual aids

- Talk to your audience, not to the machine – and even if you are reading out what is on the screen, do not turn your back on your audience or put your face down to the machine.
- Minimize your own movement and that of the visual aids; do not distract from the content.
- Watch good schoolteachers using blackboards, then transfer the techniques to your transparencies, slides or flip charts. They will ask their audience questions while they write, never remove their eyes from the class for more than a few seconds, and turn sideways when writing, never turning their back more or longer than absolutely necessary.
- Be deliberate – do not jog, jolt or jiggle an item on the screen.
- Changes of transparency should be slick. Hold the replacement in your right hand; remove the existing transparency with your left and put the new one into its place, all in one movement; and practise until you can put the replacement into a firm, central position without fiddling. To recognize a transparency, put its title at the top of its frame; then lay out all of them on your table, with the title of each sticking out above the next.
- To point at a slide, you must use (and have ready) a stick, or other pointer or a touch-arrow. For a transparency, you have four possibilities, which can be used in combination, for variety as required:
  Point with a pencil, pen or even a finger on the slide itself, casting the shadow of the pointer onto the screen.
  Put your pencil or pen down on the transparency. Do not hold it, or the slightest jiggle or movement will create a major flicker onto the screen.
  Use pointer or finger on the screen itself – but beware of casting the shadow of your body onto the screen at the same time; and/or
  Use a sheet to cover up that part of the transparency that you do not require the audience to see – and then move it. Use the masking technique sparingly: it irritates audiences who find themselves wondering what is hidden, rather than thinking about what is revealed.
- When pointing at a flip chart – as at a transparency – use your nearer hand or arm, so as not to have to twist your body and turn your back on the audience.

24   Prepare your venue

If you can choose the place where you make your speech, the most important rule is to pack them in. The more packed the venue, the better the atmosphere. The emptier the room or the hall . . . the higher the ceiling . . . the more separated your audience . . . the more arduous your task.

If the choice is yours, choose a room with a few less seats than the audience you expect. If you get more, they can stand around the side, and come earlier next time. If there are fewer, move the troops up to the front.

Theatre owners 'paper the house'. They give free seats to teachers, firemen, students . . . to old people's homes . . . to anyone who will make an otherwise empty place seem full. They know that there's nothing worse than to play to an empty house.

The same applies to speakers. For instance, after-dinner speeches are hard enough on their own (see Chapter Thirty-eight). To make them to an audience across a dance floor . . . around tables, far apart . . . that's the worst. It's cabaret, without mobility.

A good idea is to get a small, raised platform set up at one side, so that you can see the people you address. Or try to arrange that you are seated – and will stand, when talking – with your back to the wall. You will not only keep your victims to the front, but at least some of them will turn their chairs around to make eye contact with you.

When preparing your venue, check on the acoustics. Will you need a microphone, and if so, will it be the type you want and in the best position? (see Chapter Twenty-two.) Will you have the right people at your side, to give you advice or guidance?

Will you need a table, lectern . . . visual aids . . . documentation. . . ? Preparation is vital for its own sake and for yours, and especially so that you can best perform the confidence trick (see Chapter Seven).

If you do not choose the venue, you may at least be able to ask your hosts to cater for your requirements. If they do not know what microphone you prefer, where you want to sit and with whom, whether or not you require a table or a high stool, what documentation you will want put out before or handed out during the meeting, whether you would like to sit in a particular position . . . well, you won't be able to blame them if they do not look after you.

If you do find yourself with a sparse audience, do not panic. Suggest to the organizers that they ask all those present to come right up to the front. People hate being at the front, preferring to tuck themselves away in a nook near the door, the better to make their exit if they get bored; and it is not only speakers who are sometimes shy. Still, a capable Chair can wheedle most people into 'helping our distinguished speaker'. If he or she is inexperienced, then (having obtained permission) you can ask your audience to 'gather round'.

It is often better to abandon the platform, draw the stage curtains and come down to your audience. If the formal gathering has failed to draw in the crowds, then at least ensure that you have an informal chat, so that your audience go home satisfied with their evening. It is most unlikely that they will be, if you regale them from above with an oration more suitable to a packed and cheering hall than to an empty room. Someone overestimated the audience in the first place and created your unfortunate situation. You must make the best of it.

If the room is too hot, stop and ask for a window or a door to be opened. Your audience will bless you. If it is too cold, speak to the organizer and see whether they can warm the place. If they cannot, at least your audience will know that you are thinking of their comfort.

If there are aeroplane noises overhead, stop until they pass. To speak on regardless is a sure sign of inexperience. If a carpenter is banging next door, ask someone to use influence or pressure to get silence for you. Then wait.

Do arrive early. Get the feel of the place and check out the venue – position, amplification and the rest. If you are being introduced, then you can brief the introducer, explaining what you would like to be emphasized or omitted. If you are one of a list of speakers, you may be able to choose your place in the queue. Last is generally best, with first the next choice – unless you want to speak after a particular person, so as to counter the arguments you confidently expect.

So one part of the art of preparation lies in organizing your own speech, asking and answering the four questions, and preparing your material and your notes.

The other part? Sorting out your venue, as best you can, or if you can't, then at least getting acclimatized to the place and to its atmosphere. To command your troops successfully, you must feel in command of the battlefield.

25   Advance organization

In Italy, opera singers employ claques. They pay the organizers who then ensure that the star receives the appropriate (or even inappropriate) applause, at the right time. If any star sees fit not to pay, then (as one of a member of the claque recently remarked) 'We are quite capable of whistling and cat-calling instead.'

Those who speak in public may also have a claque – paid or unpaid. It can do no harm to ensure that you get off to a good start, or that your words appear to be treated with such delight that (with luck) your opponents may prefer to stay silent.

People are like proverbial sheep, especially in public. They want to follow the flock. Few have the courage to speak their minds openly in the face of a vociferous majority. 'What's the good of it?' they say – not realizing that if they did only speak, they might well win. They might discover that the noise-makers were no more than a loud-mouthed minority.

The most inoffensive type of claque work is easily organized. 'Please show me some support,' you say to your friends. 'If you do not give me some loud "hear, hears", I shall stop trying. I refuse to be shot at on my own.'

Or: 'This is going to be a difficult audience to warm up. If you would be kind enough to start the clapping when I am called to speak, I shall remember you in my will!' It only takes one or two people to clap the speaker for the rest to join in.

Again: 'I am going to tell the story about the . . . So laugh!'

You may carry your claque along with you because they are under some obligation. Maybe you employ them, or are the kind benefactor on whom they rely.

In that case, no preparation should be needed. Wise lawyers soon learn to laugh at judges' jokes – and whenever possible to produce any of their own ideas in the guise of words of wisdom dropped by the Bench.

Advance 'softening up' of an audience may often go far deeper than this. If you have a case to advance, do your best to sound out your audience. If you have a resolution to propose, make sure that someone will second it. Proposers without support are miserable creatures and, in most cases, would have been better to keep silent.

Good speakers prepare not only their case, but also their audience and supporters.

Of course, this preparation should not show. One reason why inexperienced speakers often take too little care in the preparation of their material is that they have seen how apparently easy the experienced speaker makes it all seem. Be not deceived. In general, the higher the polish, the greater the elbow-grease; the more relaxed and effortless the style, the more careful the preparation.

Natural speakers may need to take less care than the rest. Follow them around and you'll soon note how their performances vary. Those who stumble, repeat themselves, go on for too long, break the basic rules of good speaking and start to bore their audience have probably not prepared their speeches.

If you are in the chair, make your preparations with care. If there is to be a question time, prime someone to ask the first question – otherwise the silence may be embarrassing and spoil the occasion.

If you have to appear neutral but need to espouse a particular viewpoint, get its best proponent ready with his or her speech – and someone else available to do a later mopping-up operation. If preparing a team, the basis used by most athletes for relays is helpful. The anchor – your best – goes last. The next best goes first. The third does the third leg. The worst goes second. Or you may want to put your anchor first – particularly if there's a right of reply.

If you are not in the chair, but are especially interested in a particular topic or anxious to speak on it (or if you have to leave early or arrive late) do get the arrangements set up in advance with the Chair. Most people who chair meetings will oblige if they can. They will probably be glad to have advance notice of your intentions, so that they can plan operations accordingly. Planning is the partner of success.

PART 4

Handling your audience –
problems and solutions

26   Audience handling

Experienced speakers look around for kindly faces. Even in the most hostile gathering there is usually someone from whom you can extract a friendly or tolerant smile. Start by talking to that person. Then turn your head and your eyes on to others.

Speakers who look over the top of their audiences, out into space, indulging in soliloquy, are only a mite better than those who keep their head lowered and mumble into notes.

Audiences are people. They want to be entertained. They have come out of interest or curiosity – if not in what you are going to say, then in what the meeting is about. Keep their interest by talking to them, and not over their heads, literally or metaphorically. Look at them. Speak to them. Target your audience. (See Part One.)

Are they skilled or unskilled, simple or learned, well versed in your topic or new to it, likely to be friendly or hostile?

If you were working on a private business deal you would tailor your talk to the nature, personality, interests and sensitivity of your hearer. Only common sense? Well, if more public speakers would apply that same sense to their audiences, the market for public speaking would not be spoiled as it is. People would go to meetings, instead of preferring their television sets. And speakers would be a great deal more successful than most of them are.

Whatever and whomever your audience may be, watch them while you speak. See whether they are concentrating, or shifting around in their seats. If you have held them still for some time, stop. Pause. Take a sip from your glass of water. Fiddle through your notes. Give your audience the chance to relax and then to resettle. No one can concentrate for any lengthy period of time without a break.

If your audience is restless when you want it to be still, restore your hold on it. If you have been serious, then throw in a joke, a story, an anecdote. If you have been speaking at high volume, then switch to a confidential tone. If nothing works, then wind up – either permanently or for an extended question time.

There is no more important rule for public speakers than to keep a hawk-like watch on their listeners. It is different, of course, if you are talking to yourself. Ignore this rule and you soon will be.

One of the speaker's problems is where to look. Facing your audience and fixing them with your eye is a problem. Why? Know the reason and the problem becomes easier to beat. Consider a paragraph in Desmond Morris's *The Naked Ape*.

A professional lecturer takes some time to train himself to look directly at the members of his audience, instead of over their heads, down at his rostrum, or out towards the side or back of the hall. Even though he is in such a dominant position, there are so many of them, all staring (from the safety of their seats), that he experiences a basic and initially uncontrollable fear of them. Only after a great deal of practice can he overcome this. This simple, aggressive, physical act of being stared at by a large group of people is also the cause of the fluttering 'butterflies' in the actor's stomach before he makes his entrance onto the stage. He has all his intellectual worries about the qualities of his performance and its reception, of course, but the massed threat-state is an additional and more fundamental hazard for him.

There it is. We fear those who stare at us. If you want to lift your head above the crowd, you must expect people to stare at it. Learn to stare right back.

If you want your audience to be hooked into your theme and to accept your message, then involve it – from the start. Think and talk about 'You'; identify the individuals and their interests with your words. Insert the hook and keep it tight, through audience involvement techniques.

The first and most important: Ask questions. These may be either real or rhetorical.

When you address an audience, however huge, you can always ask them: 'How many of you are (*for instance*) company directors . . . lawyers . . . members of. . . ? Please would you raise your hands if you are? Thank you. Now consider how this problem could affect each of you, individually . . .'

Or: 'So we're talking about the law on health and safety. How many of you have never seen a fatal accident on the road? Is there anyone? Please put up your hand, if you never have? Not many . . . So whether on the roads or at work, accidents are not other people's problems. They are ours . . . yours . . . mine. And it's up to us to try to prevent them, isn't it?'

So you began with the real and you ended with the rhetorical – a question that people are meant to ask themselves but are not expected to supply an answer for.

When lecturing on the law on dismissals, this is how I almost always begin: 'You have been sent here by your companies, your organizations, or your businesses – at minimal expense – so that you may learn how to dismiss lawfully, fairly and at minimal cost. That's why you've been sent.

'Now, why have you come? It's so that you can learn how you can get the most money out of your employers, when you are dismissed from your job! Now, isn't that right? Knowing one or two of you as I do, I think you had better pay attention, hadn't you?'

If you want to rivet your audience from the start, that's the way to do it. 'Use You's' – plus questions.

Remember as always that human beings have a concentration time of not more than a couple of minutes. So you bring variety into your speech by changing pace, by pausing and by introducing anecdotes and stories. But do you also involve your audience, for the same reason and purpose?

Try to avoid the normal, lazy way of proclaiming at the start: 'I'll talk to you for about 20 minutes and then take your questions.' You are articulate and you know your subject or you would not be making the speech. So why not stop after each area or theme or part of your talk and say: 'Now, have I made that clear?' Or: 'Has anyone any questions on what I've covered so far?' Even if no one answers, everyone will be pleased to have been asked. And anyway, you've used audience involvement to break up your talk and to lighten the darkness.

Next: personal allusions. Refer and sometimes defer to individuals in your audience. Thus:

'Mr Brown, you're Chairman of this Company. What do you think about that suggestion?'

'Mrs Brown, you had a case like that, didn't you? What happened was that . . .'

'The real problem has been: how to get others to follow the route so well and carefully laid out by Tom . . .'

'We salute Jane, John and Albert, for the way that they have . . .'

There's no end to the possibilities. Just be careful not to offend, either directly – by allusions that will upset those individuals or by referring to some, who will be flattered, at the expense of others whom you do not mention and who will be upset. As usual, pre–planning is a great help.

Next: you can often actually involve individuals by asking them to make specific contributions to the discussion. 'Mr Green, you've handled this sort of problem. How did you cope with it?'

Or you can bring people into the laughter, by gentle teasing. If you know the audience, that's easy. If you do not, then ask in advance: 'Who's a good sport? Who's happy to join in with a laugh?'

As a speechmaker, you have (by definition) a live audience. Keep them living by involving them, using them, enlivening your talk with their concerns, their interests and their voices.

To summarize: Be sensitive about time. If your listeners look at their watches, watch yours. You will know that time is on their minds. So move on . . . discard cards . . . move to your close. Or perhaps involve the time watcher: 'I'm sorry . . . but we are coming up to our time limit. Mr White, are there any other points which you would like me to deal with?'

Always remember the vicar who said to a parishioner: 'I don't mind you looking at your watch during my sermon, but when you take it up to your ear and shake it. . . !'

Finally, and above all, research. Understand and defer to the sensitivities of your audience. (See Chapter Nineteen.)

27 Coping with questions and confrontation

Making uninterrupted speeches is one art. Coping with interruptions, questions and confrontation is another. For most speechmakers, it is equally vital.

The secrets are preparing the case; knowing the subject; and then understanding and practising the techniques and tricks of the trade. These include specially: coping with other people's anger or irritation.

First: Preparation. As with all other presentations, this involves answering the usual four questions, in adapted form:

- *Who* are your audience? Identify the individuals in the group, their concerns and their interests, their bias, their prejudice – what they will like and appreciate, dislike or disdain. As in any other adversarial pursuit, if you can study and know your opponents, do so. Recognize and respect their strengths and unearth and exploit their weaknesses. Establish your moderate, central stand, on ground that you share with your audience. Cut out the ground from under your questioners by determined courtesy.
  Also, where will you be working? Try to picture the place – the boardroom, conference room, hall – the audience and its setting.
- What do *they* want? To win them over to your viewpoint, you must understand theirs. What are their objectives? What are they after? Can you deflect them in your direction, through cunning or through compromise?
- What do *you* wish to achieve? What is your message? How can you make their interests move towards your own?
- *How* can you win? What methods should you use? What allies can you harness, brief and prepare? Conversely: what opponents can you neutralize or even win over in advance?

I asked a Chief Whip of a ruling group in an especially controversial city council how he managed to keep his troops in line. 'Deal with them in advance,' he replied. His weapons? Mainly flattery, threats and listening to their point of view.

'What about trying to convince them with yours?' I asked.

'That's usually useless!' he replied. 'Self interest, that's what matters . . .'

Like the classic tale of the employer who showed the company accounts to the union convenor and begged him to moderate his demands for wage increases. After a morning's argument, the union chief remained adamant.

Finally, the employer simply said: 'If you don't agree, George, we're going to close down the plant and that will be the end of your job – and everyone else's, including mine!'

'At last, a reasoned argument!' George replied. 'I'll put that one to the troops . . .'

Your own authority and confidence depend upon knowing your case in all its detail. Rehearse your arguments. Get your colleagues and allies to cross-examine you on the questions you would least like to be asked and to rehearse the answers.

Next: coping with questions.

If you are asked a question, answer it. Whether you are on stage or at a private meeting, or facing a press conference, radio or TV interviewer, there is nothing worse than evading the question you are asked.

Try to separate differences of opinion from those who express them. As Lord Acton wrote: 'It is an accursed doctrine that makes a difference of opinion a matter for personal hatred.'

Still, you may be up against someone who really does equate your case with you, and who has a personal and emotional dislike for both. Then you must look to your weapons.

Once again, the first is – knowledge and preparation. The next: aim at the throat, the gut, the groin. Avoid personal abuse, especially if it is defamatory. Use calmness and courtesy. Make your opponent's task as difficult as possible.

That worthy object is often best achieved through damning with faint praise or praising with faint damns.

'I have always regarded your company with respect – so I do not understand how you can now say . . .'

'Mr Green is a skilled and experienced debater, but perhaps he would have put his case rather better had he simply said . . .'

'Mr Green must forgive me if I do not fall into his trap. He knows, as I do, that the truth is . . .'

Reply to that sort of approach in kind.

'It is good of Mr Jones to recognize the repute of my company. Its good name is precious to us. So it is doubly surprising to hear him allege that . . . Not a new allegation, of course – but one which competitors have put about from time to time.'

Then show that you take criticism seriously.

'We have fully investigated the matter . . . We have followed the advice of independent consultants . . . and when we present those results to him – then, knowing of the high repute of his organization – I hope that he will withdraw his allegations.' Hope breathes eternal in speechmakers' breasts!

When under attack, do not forget the basic skills of presentation. Look your adversaries straight in the eye. Then sweep your eye contact to your audience. (See Chapter Nine.)

Sit or stand upright, still and with dignity.

Do not show nervousness by fidgeting or rushing. Instead, pause. Give yourself time to think of your answer, your riposte, your retort.

Then answer the question directly if you can. If not, provide an answer that is both true and acceptable. Parry the thrust – then strike back. Say 'yes' or 'no' – then add any qualifications. Then demand an answer to your questions. Fight back with flair.

Do not be bullied by interruptions. Insist on finishing your sentence or your point and then give way.

Bring in friends and allies if you can. 'You ran into that trouble, didn't you Mary? Then will you please tell John how we dealt with it – so very successfully.'

Or turn to your audience and say: 'You're not going to allow that sort of suggestion to go unchallenged, are you?'

To win a confrontation means persuading the audience to be on your side. If they start against you, then win them over. Keep your eyes on the opposition – and fight. At worst, if you lose the argument, you will at least win respect.

Do not be afraid of nerves (see Chapter Seven). The larger or the more important the conference, the audience or the occasion, the more crucial it becomes that your adrenalin sharpens your mind. The top technique for facing confrontation? Concentration.

Now suppose that you are faced with an angry response. How can you deflect it or turn it to good account? The answer is simpler to set out than to apply. Putting the principles into practice requires prodigious self-control, self-restraint and self-effacement.

There are four basic rules for coping with the rage of others:

- Listen – don't argue
- Empathize – and apologize
- Offer alternatives
- Follow up

Never argue with an angry man. The angrier the protagonist, the less you should argue. Instead: listen. Give the person a hearing. Communicate your understanding through your silence.

If the person is normally passive, listen with abnormal care. Beware the anger of a patient man.

When the volcano has blown itself out, show and express your understanding. Think how you would feel if you had been in the same position. Even if the entire misery is based on misunderstanding . . . is not your fault . . . is open to explanation or even to challenge – wait. Your time will come.

Meanwhile, try a variant on the following:

- 'You are right. I know exactly how you feel.'
- 'I am so sorry. I do understand.'
- 'Yes, it should not have happened. I am very sorry.'
- 'If that had happened to me, I would feel exactly as you do. I am sorry.'

Then the alternatives:

- 'I know it's not the same, but I wonder if it would help to . . .'
- 'Look, I know that nothing can replace your time lost, but we would be very glad if you would be our guest at . . . accept a complimentary copy of/session at . . .'
- 'Let me try to fix an alternative which will be at least as good/better in the long run – and which I will make sure will cost you less/will not cost you more.'
- 'Let me try and put things right for you. May I suggest . . . How about . . . Perhaps you would like to . . . Why not try . . . Maybe it would help to . . . ?'

Finally: follow up.

You have staved off the confrontation or even won your way? You have won agreement to resolve the disagreement? Then confirm it in writing – and reaffirm it by carrying out any duties or obligations which you may have yourself accepted. Your adversary already has a chip on his shoulder. Make sure that he does not become like the 'well-balanced man' – with a chip on each shoulder!

So: start by watching for the signs of dissatisfaction – the gestures or grimaces of irritation, turning to anger. Listen to the fury and let its winds blow. Like the boxer, weave with the punches, sway and bend – and do not allow your temper to break.

Psychiatrists, psychologists, skilled cross-examiners – all will tell

Coping with questions and confrontation

you that unless you wish to provoke greater hostility, you must meet aggression with calm and with understanding. Relate . . . empathize . . . then apologize, even if you have no real cause.

Then offer your alternatives. One or more is acceptable. Then check up to ensure that your accepted offer turns into reality.

Meet confrontation with concentration, with concern and with courage and the conflicts are yours to win.

Passions must be felt, recognized and controlled. Allow your mind to cloud with passion and your performance will collapse.

Studied calm is a powerful weapon. Let your audience share your feelings but know that your mind guides your heart, or you will not influence their ideas, their votes or their cheque books.

You may wish your audience to feel sorrow with you, but they must not feel pity for you. You want them to laugh with you, but if they laugh at you, you're lost.

Direct your words at your theme and not at your own feelings. Conclude with a thundering peroration, or an icy blast, but preserve your speech as a well-constructed, carefully presented offering.

Passionate eloquence has its place in the pulpit, but rarely works at a company meeting, an organizational gathering or a public conference. Open emotion displayed in public seldom succeeds.

28 Interruptions

Interruptions are to the skilled speaker as raids to the commando – a challenge to draw on resources and to test the mettle. Handled properly, hecklers can rouse the audience and put them on the speaker's side. The unexpected break should add variety to a dull occasion.

From the platform or top table, the speaker has a total advantage. Used properly, the interruption should bring or keep the audience in sympathy.

To reap the benefit of useful interruption, you must be alert. Tied to a script – written or memorized – you will be thrown off balance. If you cannot think on your feet, stay seated.

Consider some common examples. Take the shareholder who comes to a company meeting to criticize. He shouts interruptions. How do you deal with him?

Maintain your dignity. Make quiet but firm appeals for a fair hearing: 'I appreciate that you have a point of view to express and you will have your chance to do so. Meanwhile, please have the courtesy to listen.' Or: 'I ask you to give my viewpoint the same fair hearing that I have given to yours.' Or: 'I listened to you/your case without interrupting. Please accord the same courtesy to me/mine.'

You could try: 'If you would be good enough to listen to what the Board/the company has achieved and is now proposing in the present difficult circumstances, you will learn something to your benefit.'

If the moment has come to attack, try: 'If you would listen to me, sir, instead of to yourself, you would be doing both of us a favour.'

If you are coping, the Chair should not intervene. If the meeting gets out of hand, then he or she must do so. At best, this will bring calm; at worst, the interrupters will be asked to leave. Still, a wide-awake speaker can usually keep the audience in reasonably good humour and win a hearing without the use of force.

Some interruptions are healthy and helpful – whether or not this was the intent. Humorists' outcries can often be turned against themselves. The scream of a jet engine overhead may drown you for the moment, but gives you the opportunity to draw some moral about the point you are making. Even a friendly remark addressed to a member of your audience arriving late may save you both from embarrassment, as well as giving you the opportunity you may in any event need to sort yourself out, to vary the pace of your talk, or to give your audience the chance to relax for a moment, to shift about in their seats and to prepare for the rest of your speech.

You must show self-confidence and self-command to achieve command of the situation and of your audience.

If you are needled by interrupters and are tempted to panic – pause, smile, retain control. The rowdier the meeting, the more disconcerting the interruption, the more aggravating the break in your train of thought, the more important it is for you to demonstrate to your audience that you are not to be thrown off your balance. Lose control of yourself and all is lost.

Go to first-class political meetings and watch accomplished politicians at work. Listen to them provoking then downing their hecklers. Observe as they prompt their audience to turn on the interrupters. A few inefficient hecklers will do their work for them, rouse their supporters, bring the uncommitted to their side and enliven what might otherwise be a dreary occasion.

The more spontaneous the reply, the wittier the retort, the speedier the counter-attack, the more effective the speaker and the speech. A weak riposte now is better than the brilliant barb that you afterwards wish you had thought of at the time.

Do not let interrupters put you off your stroke. Use them.

29   Under the skin

Your sensitivities lie very close to your skin. If you want to save it (your professional skin, that is) you must know how to recognize where you will least like the needle to be inserted, and learn how, if necessary, you can extract it with the least possible pain, and, especially, without losing control of yourself, of your case and of your audience.

An example from a presentational skills course, where we were teaching accountants how to pitch for a major job. I took the role of the interviewer and questioned one of the senior partners about the professionals' least-loved subject, their fees. The encounter went like this:

Janner: 'Now Mr Brown, how much are you proposing to charge us for this work?'

Brown: 'That will depend entirely on the nature of the job and how much time is spent on it and by whom.'

Janner: 'But you must be able to give us some sort of idea.'

Brown: 'Not at this stage. But we do charge at an hourly rate.'

Janner: 'What is your hourly rate, then?'

Brown: 'That depends on who's doing the job.'

Janner: 'Of course I see that. But tell me what your hourly rate is.'

Brown: 'That really depends.'

Janner: 'On what? Why are you being so coy about it?'

Brown, reluctantly: 'Probably, £175 an hour.'

Janner: 'Is that negotiable? It seems very high to me.'

Brown, exploding: 'I didn't come here to be cross-examined about our fees. This is not what this course is about.'

Janner, after long pause? 'Really? I thought you wanted to know how to make presentations under pressure. I've just put you under that pressure, perhaps a little unfairly – but now look and see how you reacted to it . . .'

We played back the exchange, explosion and all. And then we went through the routines of how to control anger in public.

First: recognize, pinpoint and target weaknesses. In our clients' case, their weakness was their sensitivity about their charges. Yours may be something quite different – anything from your relationship with colleagues to some theoretically lawful behaviour which you would still rather not find highlighted on the front pages of the newspapers.

Second: list the sensitivities, bring them out into the open, discuss them and decide how best to handle questions about them. That will give you confidence. If the nasties do arise, you will know how to deal with them. If they don't, then at least you will enter battle with your nerves under better control. Preparation is essential for the confidence trick (see Chapter Seven on looking and conveying authority and certainty when you don't feel it).

Third: if you are hit with unpleasant questions, pause and take breath. Give yourself time to think.

Fourth: the more hostile the question, the more collected your answer. Do not argue with an angry client or customer. If your interviewer leans forward, lean back. Respond to hostility and aggression by being calm and cool. (See Chapter Twenty-seven.)

If you do get angry and you regret it, then apologize. On the way out of that notable session, Mr Brown (not his real name, of course) shook my hand warmly. 'Sorry I lost my temper,' he said. 'But you were right to make me do it and I've learned my lesson.'

Well, I hope so. If not, then at least he'll recognize his anger, if it hits him again.

30 In tight corners – and the arts of response

If in trouble, choose your words with special care. To borrow from the world of boxing – if you have been hit below the belt, are out for the count, or in a tight corner, you have three alternatives: you can throw in the sponge, trade blow for blow, or duck smartly under your opponent's fist and leap nimbly away.

You are proposing a toast to the bride and groom? The bride's father is dead. The groom's parents are divorced. What do you do? You can surrender by making no mention of the parents. This is abject cowardice, and generally regarded as such.

You may neatly duck the situation with a few carefully chosen sentences: 'The bride's father . . . we wish he were here not only in spirit . . . but he would have been proud and happy today . . . How pleased we are that our groom's parents are both so well – and here, together with us all, for this grand celebration . . .'

Or you can start with the same sort of comment, and then extend it into the appropriate eulogy. 'Let us face the blunt truth, Ladies and Gentlemen – no occasion is completely perfect, no life without its problems. How sad we are that the bride's father is not here . . . but we admire her mother doubly for the fortitude with which she bore her loss and especially for the courageous and splendid way in which she brought up the bride . . . The extent of her triumph is revealed by the radiance of our bride. We rejoice too that the bridegroom's parents sit joyfully together with him, united in his happiness and good fortune . . .'

There are plenty of equivalent situations in business. Victory may be achieved by an apology. The counter-attack is explained in Chapter Twenty-seven. Methods of ducking away from trouble will depend on circumstances. Here are some useful opening gambits:

- 'We fully appreciate the circumstances which have led to your anger and disappointment. But there is another side to the story and we do hope that you will give it your earnest consideration . . .'
- 'You are, in theory, correct and fair but . . .'
- 'I do see your point of view – but I'm sure that you will give consideration to mine . . .'

- 'Yes, we made a mistake – but in good faith. The situation nevertheless remains that . . .'
- 'We see your viewpoint. Now do please consider ours . . .'
- 'You have set out your case admirably. It is only courteous, then, for me to set out as fully as possible the situation as we see it . . .'
- 'We believe that your complaint is based on a misunderstanding. We do see that . . . but we would urge you to consider . . .'
- 'No, we do not agree with you. But still . . .'

Have you noticed that people who use words as weapons employ similar tactics to those of the fencer or boxer? You give way a little so as to attack a lot. You retreat gently, so as to counter-attack with firmness. You at least pretend to see the other person's viewpoint, so that he or she will be prepared to consider yours. Alternatively, you politely disagree – and then show your magnanimity, good sense or goodwill by offering a compromise or by giving in on some point, however small.

Try these gambits when desperate and able to deliver:

- 'If you see fit to make these allegations to third parties, we shall have no hesitation in putting the matter in the hands of our solicitors . . .'
- 'In one last attempt to remedy a situation which, we repeat, is not of our making, our Mr Jones will contact you and try to arrange some convenient time to visit your office . . .'
- 'Your threats are empty, their premise groundless. If you wish to take the matter further, we refer you to our lawyers . . .'
- 'We regard your allegations as both impertinent and groundless. If they are repeated, we shall take such steps as we are advised by our lawyers, to protect both our position and our good name . . .'
- 'If you are so ill-advised as to carry out your threats, then please direct all future correspondence to our lawyers . . .'
- 'Our lawyers will be in touch with yours . . .'

Debaters who content themselves with making their own speeches without referring to those which have gone before, deserve to fail. Many discussions – in public and private meetings of companies and in organizations of all sorts – are in reality debates. Skilled speakers must study the art of reply. This requires alertness to what has gone before, and a keen eye and ear for the most effective response.

Proposers of motions or resolutions normally have a 'right of reply'. They open the debate or discussion and, before the vote is taken, they have the privilege of closing it. Their second speech should not be a mere repetition of their first. They should deal – courteously, clearly and firmly – with the intervening debate.

Respondents should thank those who have spoken in favour of the resolution. Directly or by implication they should congratulate them on their perspicacity. 'I was not surprised to have the warm support of that respected businessman, Mr Brown – but I was nonetheless . . .'

'Mr Green is highly experienced in the trade, and I do hope that everyone here will give his words due weight . . .'

'Ms White comes to us from a different side of the industry. So it is all the more significant that she approves of this resolution . . .'

'Mr Green is, as you will all know, an extremely skilled and public-spirited lawyer. We must all be grateful to him for the careful analysis he gave to our problems – and for the legal light that he cast upon the dangers of action suggested by those who oppose this resolution.'

Skilled respondents demolish their enemies. 'I am sorry that Mr Diamond has not appreciated the warnings given by Ms Black . . .' 'If Mr Stone had really considered the argument that . . . I feel sure he would have come to a different conclusion . . .' 'Mr Ruby is wrong. The facts are not as he suggested. The true position is . . .'

Then sum up your arguments once again, in a few brisk, crisp sentences. Commend your resolution to the meeting – and hope for the best.

Use notes when replying. No one will expect you to remember all that has been said. Once again, the card system is best. (See Chapter Twelve.) You may, if you wish, deal with the questioners or opponents in turn, but it would probably be better to rearrange the comments and criticisms to suit your argument and its structure.

Remember, a reply is a speech like any other. It needs a good opening, a sound body, and a proper end. Some suggested openings:

- 'Thank you for allowing me to reply to some of the points raised . . .'
- 'I suggest that nothing that has been said against the resolution has in any way destroyed its essential validity . . .'
- 'We must all be grateful to those who have taken part in this debate. Even those who oppose the resolution do so in the interests of the company. But, as we have seen from the speeches of Mr Brown, Ms White and Mr Black, its opponents have not really grasped the advantage of the course of action suggested – and the risks of following any alternative . . .'
- 'The differences between us have been fully aired. Every possible

alternative has been thrashed out. But, at the end of the day, are we not still left with only one real possibility? The resolution must be passed.'

Some of these rules also apply to many responses to toasts. Do not ignore the speeches that have gone before. Do deal with any points of criticism or suggestion raised by previous speakers. Do not fear to use notes to remind you of the words of others. And do make certain that your speech is properly constructed.

You have one great advantage over the person replying to a debate. His or her speech is bound to be extempore. Yours may be carefully prepared, provided that you cover up that preparation by reference back.

31 Persuading – the art of advocacy

Barristers, said Dean Swift, are 'bred up in the art of proving that white is black and black is white, according as they are paid'. He left out of account, of course, the ethics of the legal profession, which may require its members to keep faith with the court, by acting and if necessary, speaking against the interests of their clients.

Advocacy is an art: deception an evil. Still, the Swift aphorism is too good to forget. Business, professional or any people may be forced to propound or to defend public policies or decisions with which, in private, they disagree.

It is not only the Cabinet that must stand by majority decisions. The same normally applies to the board of a company, to the partners of a firm, or to the committee of an organization. Either you accept democracy – allowing your views to be overruled when the majority of your colleagues are against them – or you resign. If you remain in office, then you must stand by your colleagues. This may mean engaging in their public defence.

So advocates may have to propound not only views that are unpopular with their audience, but even some that they themselves dislike. Business people attack lawyers and politicians as sophists and word-twisters. But just listen to that executive trying to make the creditors' meeting 'see sense' . . . the chairman trying to get himself (and possibly the company secretary) out of trouble . . . the sales director, drilling his sales force about an unpopular (and perhaps not very satisfactory) product.

There is little art in persuading the convinced, preaching to the converted, or keeping your team behind you when they all agree with your views or policies. To argue a difficult case – or even one that seems impossible – is a far greater challenge. You may take many a lead from the brief of the skilful lawyer-advocate.

Start with the quiet, sincere but firm approach. Call it 'the soft sell' if you like, but the studied lack of histrionics lies at the root of the modern persuader's art. Gone are the days of the ranter, the arm-waver, the loud shouter. Theatrical tuggers at the strings of the heart may still have their place in a revivalist meeting or chapel, but they are strangers to the court of law and should be equally so to the company or organizational meeting.

The more your audience starts against you, the greater the importance of moderation, especially in your opening. Here are some well-tried gambits, for when you are in a minority:

- 'I fully appreciate the difficulty of my task in convincing you that ... but I hope and believe that if you will be good enough to give my case a fair and full hearing, you will be as convinced as I am that ...'
- 'Mr Black, who has just addressed you, is an experienced advocate and has presented the case against ... with skill and eloquence. But there is another side to the picture. Before coming to a decision, I am certain that you would wish to hear both sides of the story fully explained ...'
- 'Many of us were saddened to hear the vehemence and even the venom with which the case for ... has been put. While many of the attacks have apparent validity, when you go beneath the surface, all is not as some of our friends have suggested. I am sure that this committee/organization/ meeting would not wish to take any decision on such a very important matter without having had both points of view put before it. I shall put mine, as briefly as possible; but I would be grateful for your indulgence if I take a little time to explain my case ...'

Now for some of the traps to be avoided:

- 'Does anyone really think Mr Y has cheated the company?' Cries of 'Certainly ...' In these circumstances, rhetorical questions are a menace. Thus:
- 'Could it conceivably be in the long-term interest of this organization to follow the line proposed by Mr W?' Shouts of 'Yes!'
- 'Does anyone really think that I do not know my job after all these years?' Loud cries of 'Yes' – and laughter.
- 'I am ... a man ...' pause. Shouts of 'No, no ...' The pause is a vital weapon – but watch where you place it.
- 'You may think that the statements you have just heard from Mr Z are about as untrue, misleading, ill-conceived and plain stupid as one could ever envisage.' This sort of attack – especially by someone in a minority – can only lead to vituperation, and defeat.
- 'I am furious ...' Then do not show it.
- 'I could weep when I hear such extravagant attacks.' They all know that tears are not in your line – so away with the crocodiles.

It is nearly always a mistake to walk out of a meeting, but there are occasions when there is no decent alternative. If decisions are taken that you regard as illegal, dishonest or so contrary to the welfare of the body concerned that you must dissociate yourself publicly from them, then you may have to leave. Otherwise, stay and fight.

Your chances of winning from without are far less than of working your colleagues or audience round to your way of thinking from within. If you leave, you are not likely to be invited back. The dramatic exit may be required for the diplomat whose country is publicly attacked in his or her presence. It is seldom an answer for the spurned orator.

The threat of resignation is a powerful and sometimes a valid weapon. It must not be misused or over-employed. If your colleagues or the meeting would be happy to see you go, then do not offer to provide satisfaction.

'If this decision is to be made, I hope it will not be taken amiss if I say that I shall have no alternative other than to reconsider my membership.' Fairly put.

'I have worked for this organization for many years and am anxious to continue to do so in the future. I would not wish to sever my ties nor to be forced into a position where I would have no alternative but to do so. I do beg you to reconsider. Or, at least, please do give me a fair hearing for the other point of view. I would put it like this . . .' You should get that fair hearing.

Avoid: 'If you do not change your minds, then I shall resign.' You invite the retort: 'Go ahead.'

32 Personal attacks and assertive responses

A 'gentleman' is 'a man who is never unintentionally rude.' Mature speakers never intentionally lose their temper. They also try to cause offence only by design.

Outside politics, most wounds are both regrettable and regretted. 'The moving finger writes and, having writ, moves on: Nor all thy piety nor wit shall lure it back to cancel half a line, nor all thy tears wash out a word of it.' In one off-guard moment, you may acquire an enemy for life, unnecessarily. The spoken word can no more be erased than the written.

Humour and wit are vital to the speaker. But many a jest, however kindly meant, has been taken amiss. There is all the difference in the body of wit between pulling legs in private and tweaking tails in public. The same joke that went down splendidly at the dinner table may be a disaster when told from the platform. (See Chapter Seventeen.)

No section of the public is more concerned with its own dignity than the world of commerce. Lawyers may be pompous, but they recognize the bitter court battle as part of their trade, with no effect on personal friendship outside court. The private jest is seldom resented, but the adversary whom you attack in public may not wish to speak to you in private.

It follows that apart from the laws of defamation, it is best to keep discussions on ideas, not personalities. If you do attack opponents, be sure of your ground. Make certain that their discomfiture is intended and that it has a reasonable chance of leading to the results you seek. Whether you are speaking at a comparatively small meeting or a mighty gathering, be careful. You are not alone. If your attack is ill-chosen, you soon may be.

If you must attack a personality, then prepare your case well. Gather your documentation: letters, quotations, firm facts and witnesses. The more bitter your resentment, the quieter and the more apparently reasonable your tone should appear. Lose control of yourself and you will probably, and deservedly, also lose control of both situation and organization.

Find out in advance whether your words are likely to be well received. There is no worse time to be shouted at or voted down than during a personal attack.

If the moment arrives for a personal vendetta, select your time and place with assiduous care. By launching an attack, you invite a counter-attack. By mentioning the names of your opponents you may give them the publicity that they seek plus – in the eyes of those who believe in fair play – the moral right to reply. Instead of being in sole occupation of the platform, you may have to surrender it to an opponent whom you would prefer to lurk unseen and unheard.

If your opponents descend to personal attack, it is rarely wise to lower yourself to their level. Your object, after all, is to win your case – to convince your audience of your rectitude, of the usefulness of your activities, of the excellence of the way in which you are running the business – or, conversely, of your opponent's error. The sharp intellect is a better weapon than the rough tongue. When the theme is laced with incivility, the audience may suspect a lack of factual backing or of self-control – or both.

Instead, try:

- 'I am sorry that Mrs Jones has seen fit to deal with this serious matter in such an unpleasant way . . .'
- 'If Mr Jones would be good enough to listen to what the board has achieved, I think he'll regret the way in which he has referred to it . . .'
- 'We are all here for the same purpose – to advance the business. The sort of remarks that have just been made are likely to send it into retreat. They can give comfort only to our competitors . . .'
- 'We will answer each criticism, in turn. We will ignore the personal and regrettably offensive way in which we have been attacked.'
- 'If Mr Black really is, as he says, concerned for the welfare of this organization, I hope that he will listen to the case for the steps which he has so bitterly criticized. He should then not only have the good grace to withdraw those criticisms, but also to apologize to those whom he has inevitably hurt. I am sure that this was not his intention.'
- 'Mrs Green is, as we all know, a kindly woman, and we all appreciate what she has done for the company. We know how deeply involved she is, emotionally and otherwise, in its success . . . and no one will bear her the least ill-will because she has spoken her mind . . . But . . .'
- 'We all appreciate, I know, the customary frankness with which Mr White has dealt with this resolution. But we do not appreciate his personal insinuations. These can only detract from the genuineness of his case, and the real concern with which he and those who support him – and, indeed, many of us on your board – view the circumstances he discussed . . .'

Hostility breeds hostility, and an aggressive approach invites an aggressive response. The converse also applies. Surprise your critics with your moderation, understanding, sensitivity and by listening with care and respect, and their views may mellow. Anyway, it is an approach more likely to succeed than the frontal attack.

Once you have let rip with your hostility, not only have you discredited future friendly relations, but you may even have over-looked the chance that the critic was really on your side. Some apparently hostile questions are asked at meetings to obtain answers for the benefit of people whom the questioner wishes to convince. 'All right, don't listen to me . . . We'll ask George White . . . He'll tell you a thing or two . . .' Blast the questioners as idiots and you obliterate friends or confirm foes in their enmity.

If you must lose your temper, then at least do so with deliberation. Choose your moment and your words with equal care. If you must tear at your opponent, do it properly.

A judge once said to a famous advocate: 'What you are saying to me is going in one ear and out the other.' To which the lawyer replied: 'That my Lord, does not cause me any surprise, having regard to what lies in between!'

Most of us think of the best repartee when the occasion is past. While swift retorts often produce acclaim far beyond merit, the rude, unkind, offensive or angry outburst, the facetious, sarcastic, ironic or spiteful suggestion, breeds contempt, derision, stony silence – and defeat for the speaker, not for the individual towards whom the words are directed.

PART 5

Occasions

33 Pitching – and 'beauty contests'

Winning business against competition means beating your competitors. To do that, you must study, practise and excel at the art of 'pitching' – often in what are now known as 'beauty contests' or 'beauty parades'.

While at one time you could perhaps have sat back and waited for business to flow in to you, today you must go out and get it. That means convincing prospective customers or clients that your products or services or both are better, more cost-effective and more attractive than those offered by your competitors.

Cost and quality are, of course, still crucial. But the less the difference between yours and those of your competitors, the more personal or individual the service which you are offering must appear to be. To win, you must present your company, your product or service and – always – yourself, to best effect.

The secrets of winning 'beauty contests' are spread out in this book. They cover everything from preparation to presentation, from using visual aids with skill and economy to aiming your speeches at the right targets.

In every beauty contest there is, of course, an important element of chemistry, which you may to some extent adjust. There is also an element of luck: some you will win, some lose, but you will certainly win more if you follow our rules. For those you lose, we have some suggestions for lifting yourself off the canvas and back into the ring.

You may think that politics is an unpleasant business, only indulged in by politicians. 'A statesman', goes the classic definition, 'is a dead politician!' Well, a non-political businessperson is a dead entrepreneur. There is as much politics in business life as at Westminster or in local authorities. Winning competitive pitches demands political acumen, skill and cunning, and we show you how to develop and use your political skills. Every competition – from childhood examinations to parliamentary elections, from major business beauty parades and pitches, to private gatherings or one-to-one efforts to win orders or arguments – requires courage, determination and methodology.

'Pitching for business' comes outside the main scope of a book on speechmaking. It is the entire purpose of my sister-volume, by that name.

34 Conferences and seminars

Business and professional people are often dragooned, shamed or enticed into presenting themselves and their wares at conferences or seminars. To this also there is an art.

Your approach to success depends upon the purpose of the occasion. Is yours, for instance, a promotional exercise, designed to introduce new clients or customers or to stiffen the loyalty of old ones? Do delegates come to learn from those who are trained and qualified to teach? Either way you are in show business.

There is absolutely no excuse for a dreary conference. However dull the subject, it can be enlivened by visual aids (see Chapter Twenty-three), relaxed by wit and brought to life by enthusiasm.

Individual speakers should follow the usual rules of good presentation. In particular, they should know and prepare their material, communicate with and according to their audience, speak with style and demonstrate with skill.

Whether dealing with a small-scale teaching seminar or a larger assembly or conference, the best presenters will respect their audience. If they wish to return, they will also entertain them.

The fact that so many conferences are dull and disastrous is a denunciation of those who organize and of those who address them. They not only harm their own cause, but they also spoil the market. They forget that while schoolchildren are tied to their desks and to their classrooms, conference delegates can opt for the bar. Hence the modern and musical disease of 'conference syncopation' – staggering from bar to bar!

The speechmaker's success depends to a vast extent on the conditions created by the conference or seminar organizers. Check these in advance, preferably before you agree to speak. If, for instance, the room is to be vast and the audience small, the acoustics echoing and the amplification minimal, or the delegates crowded and unhappy and the food inedible, then do not attach your good name to their bad feelings.

Otherwise and in any event, arrive early enough to check your atmosphere and your apparatus, your audience and your audibility. Consider especially:

105

- Are the stage, platform and/or table as you like or need them?
- Stuck as you now are with the amplification arrangements as they are, how can you make the best of them? For instance, will you be able to remove, adjust and/or stroll with the microphone, or is it fixed – and if so, is it at your height or at that of a pygmy or a giraffe? (See Chapter Twenty-two.)
- Is the overhead projector or other equipment for your visual aids in proper order and position? If you need assistance, perhaps in the showing of slides, is it available? (see Chapter Twenty-three.)
- If you need arrangements for your comfort and convenience, will you get them? These may range from water for a dry throat, to (in my case) somewhere quiet for a lunchtime nap and battery recharge. The same applies to the provision of pre-meal drinks or intermission tea or coffee.
- If you are to be paid a fee for your speech, are the arrangements clear, recorded or confirmed in writing and followed through? If these are to any extent on a commission, bonus or other basis that depends upon the success of the event, then how will you find out what you are owed, and will you need to send an account or an invoice?
- Should you require smokers to remain at the back or to one side or do you want to mix the chimneys with the abstainers? Or how about banning smoking from the hall?
- Always try to fill up seats from the front. If you are not sure whether the room will be filled, can you insist that no one sits in the back rows until front and centre are full?
- Will you avoid interruptions from the clatter of crockery and cutlery, before and after breaks? Separate reception and coffee rooms will help, but thin partitions destroy the best of plans.
- If you are to be introduced, has the introducer adequate and correct details of what you would like him or her to say about you? Who will introduce or sell your products or services? Have you made arrangements for details, samples or goods – or order forms, brochures or other documents – to be properly and prominently displayed?
- How will you achieve a climax at the end, so that your delegates/audience will leave happy?

35 Travelling tongues and speaking to foreigners

If you are blessed with equal facility in the language of your audience and your own, your problems in addressing that audience are minimal. You only have to follow the rules laid down in the rest of this book and all should be well. Subject, of course, to cutting your cloth to the style of your overseas listeners, there is no essential difference between rousing, holding, interesting, convincing – or boring – an audience of English or French people, Russians or Greeks – whether abroad or in the UK.

Melodrama goes over rather better in the United States than in Britain. The florid oratory that went out of fashion in Britain many years ago still thrives in parts – and with some audiences – abroad. In general, if you play up to the image expected of you – if you give your audience a touch of urban wit, rather than uproarious slapstick –you are likely to come across best.

Stick to your own style when in America and you have every chance of a friendly welcome. I once toured the United States, talking about Britain, the Welfare State, and even what they choose to call 'socialized medicine'. I met a certain surprise that this Englishman was not cold, reserved, humourless, upper-crust and frosty. The image of the icy Anglo-Saxon who will only speak when introduced – and, preferably, when well warmed with alcohol – dies hard. So the friendly, humorous opening acquired an extra significance and importance. Establish rapport and you are well away.

Once your overseas listeners know that you really do intend to entertain as well as to instruct – to talk across, not down – they are even more ready than your compatriots to give you a warm welcome. The best tip for heating the atmosphere? Start in your hosts' language.

Are English and American the same? In general, yes. Still, the idiom differs and so do the allusions. The American speaker in Britain who takes the trouble to look at the daily newspaper and to joke about the current crime wave, strike outbreak, political disaster or other local misery does well. When you are talking to overseas listeners, return that sort of compliment.

A simple, well-tried opening in the USA: 'You will be relieved to know that I am not about to launch into discussion of whether or not that which is good for General Motors is good also for the country as a whole . . . of the merits or otherwise of the political efforts of the Cabots, the Kennedys or [here insert names of local politicians currently in the news]. If I am asked whether I support the Yankees, the Redskins or [here insert name of the local baseball team], I shall refuse firmly to enter into your local politics. We British have enough trouble trying to run our own affairs, without risking another Boston tea-party. No. I shall confine myself to a discussion of . . .'

Another invaluable story. 'I have been asked to comment on your current commercial crisis. I must respectfully decline. You may know the tale of the dying man who was visited by his priest. "My son," said the priest, "do you renounce the Devil, now and for ever more?" "Oh Father," said the dying man, "this is no time to be making enemies – anywhere!"

'Ladies and Gentlemen, as the solitary Englishman in your ranks, I wish to make no enemies – anywhere – so I shall tell you about our troubles – rather than venturing to discuss yours.'

Once you have established friendly relations with the overseas buyers, suppliers or fellow traders, if you stick to subjects which interest them, all should be well. They are as anxious to pick up profitable tips from you, as you are from them. Provided that you assume a cloak of modesty, they will wish to hear of your achievements. After all, that is why you have been invited to speak. So do not be shy. Talk freely of your doings and the effort may prove more profitable than you had expected.

Now suppose that you are forced to launch into your speech in front of people for whom English is not their mother tongue. There are two main possibilities. Either you address them in English and hope that they will understand. Or you speak in the foreign language. The second is preferable, provided that you can cope without making horrendous errors.

If you are really talking business – putting across facts, figures, theories or ideas in respect of which words must be given their precise meanings; if what you say may create misunderstandings if the words are not used with their correct nuances; if shades of meaning matter, then stick to English and if necessary work through an interpreter. (See Chapter Thirty-six on interpreters.) It is no tribute to your bravery if you venture into foreign seas without a lifebelt.

On the other hand, it may be that this is an occasion when it would be worth preparing your speech beforehand and having it translated – and then reading it. Make a friendly, impromptu opening (or one which is apparently not read) and the audience will just have to put up with what may not be an oratorical masterpiece but which will at least be accurate.

In that case, do all you can to mitigate the misery by looking up from your speech; talking to your audience, whenever you can; pausing from time to time, to throw in a joke in English, or an apology for having to read your script.

If you are going to make your speech in English, then prepare a few words, right at the start, in your hosts' language – or, if you are the host, in that of your guests. It matters not how badly you mispronounce the words. That adds to the fun. Nobody cares if you make a hash of the grammar or even if you manage to make a ghastly boob which gives words their wrong meaning. What does matter is that you make the genuine effort to speak to folk in their own tongue. You pay them the compliment of making what is obviously a brave attempt to be friendly – and in the most genuine possible way.

Start with your usual opening, in English. 'Ladies and Gentlemen, fellow workers in the — industry . . .' If you then break into the foreign tongue, you will produce just that element of surprise which should give rise to a very friendly reception. 'You did not know that I was learning Greek/Spanish/Hebrew/Chinese . . . did you?' (This, of course, in the language concerned.)

'After I'd met Mr . . . in . . . who speaks such marvellous English, I was shamed into trying. I am only sorry that my efforts have been, as you hear, so very unsuccessful. To avoid any future misunderstandings of what I have to say, I hope that you will forgive me if I return – very gratefully – to English!' All that in the foreign language. Memorize it if you can. Otherwise read it. The fact that you will have got the information and the translation from one of the nationals of the country concerned is irrelevant. The compliment you have paid your audience will be appreciated.

There is an alternative. You can launch right into the 'Ladies and Gentlemen . . . How are you? Welcome to Britain — we are very happy to have you and hope that you will have a very good time.' All that in the foreign language will delight your audience.

End with 'Farewell – and come back soon,' in the language of your hosts or guests. Then add: 'Jai Hind' or 'Vive la France' or whatever 'hail' is appropriate in their land. As usual, if you get the start and finish of your speech right, the rest will fall into shape.

Naturally, if your audience happens to be a mixed bag, then these rules will have to be modified. I have heard a very successful opening: 'Ladies and Gentlemen, Messieurs, Mesdames, Senoras y Senores, Meine Damen und Herren . . . welcome to you all – and if I have managed to mispronounce even the few words in your language which I have ventured to speak, I know that you will appreciate why I am going to make the rest of my speech in English – I think it will be easier for us all.' Pause while the audience nod, smile and chatter.

Misunderstandings created by speakers – especially by politicians – who stick to their own tongue are only exceeded by those who have the temerity to create vast international misunderstandings by murdering the languages of others, and murder is a crime in every country in the world!

36   Interpreters and translators

William Davis, the distinguished editor and writer, told me this story. The first time he visited Japan, he had to make an important speech through an interpreter. He started by saying: 'Good morning'.

The translation of this apparently brief introduction took half a minute. He later challenged the interpreter: 'How could it take you so long to translate "good morning"?'

The interpreter explained that had he simply translated those two words, Mr Davis would have appeared to be discourteous, which he certainly would not have wished. So the interpreter had translated the greeting into the form in which a Japanese gentleman would have wanted it to appear!

If you are speaking through a skilled interpreter, then, you may properly expect your intent as well as your words to be properly translated. Do not presume that your interpreters – nor, indeed, those supplied by others – are making or remaking your speech because of the time they take in translation. Equally, you cannot guarantee that your words will be translated with the nuance or even the meaning that you intended.

Take, for instance, the famous UN Resolution 242. Dealing with land won by Israel during the Six Day War, the English version refers to return of 'territories'; the French to return of '*the* territories'. The difference between the two is contentiously obvious. And as the Israeli statesman Abba Eban once remarked, the best thing about the Resolution is that it reads the same in both directions, thereby providing a link between people who prefer to read it in Hebrew or in Arabic, rather than in English or in French!

You can, in the vast majority of cases, assume that interpreters are doing their job honestly and to the best of their abilities. Those abilities vary; and the differences should be recognized.

How can you check on an interpreter's efforts?

- If you have no knowledge of the other language, listen carefully to the translation and if in doubt, you can either interrupt and say: 'I don't think that's exactly what I meant, is it?' Or you can make sure by repeating your statement or opinion in other words, so as to clarify or emphasize your meaning.

- If possible, get a colleague or a friend who has a command of both languages to check for you.
- Put both your speech and the translation 'on the record' – onto a recording machine. That's evidence.

To avoid mistranslation or misquoting, even in his own language, that canny and experienced politician, Tony Benn, always records interviews with journalists. Not only can he prove what he said and what he did not say, but (he claims) the fact that his interviewers know that he has the evidence makes them much more careful about the words that they put into his mouth or the views that they attribute to him.

Another advantage of the tape recorder is that you can (as Benn does) play back your speech; listen to those parts that go well; and on future occasions, avoid your errors, your gaffes and the arguments that fell flat. Disadvantage: it destroys the informality of the occasion and tenses up the interviewer.

Next: Timing. Translation takes time.

Most presentations take longer than you expect, so you should always prepare for less time than you have. Translations take twice as long and are at least ten times as boring for those who have to hear and understand the same tune sung twice over.

Remember, too, to allow breaks for translation. Stop after every paragraph. If in doubt, stop more often. Do not allow your speeches to deteriorate into alternate mighty swathes of incomprehensible sound.

In any presentation, brevity means sanity. Keep it doubly short, if you are at a translator's mercy.

Humour. Most jokes are what the French call 'jeux de mots' – plays on words. Which is hard enough in your own language; doubly difficult in anyone else's; and invariably impossible to translate. So don't tie up your interpreter by playing with words. Instead, use whimsy, ironic, good-natured stories or anecdotes. (See Chapter Seventeen.)

Other jokes: as always, poke fun at yourself, your own nationality, community or religious group. Mind how you tread on the toes of others.

If you are blessed with simultaneous translation, your audience will be wearing earphones; their eyes will be on you; but their reactions will follow between ten and 30 seconds behind your words. So you tell a humorous story. No reaction. You follow it with a sombre sentence, then your audience laughs. Your fault, because you did not leave enough pause between your changes of mood.

Simultaneous translation, is of course, is the modern art of the international conference. One to one or in small groups? Then you will have to put up with the interpreter, translating as you go along. Large groups in modern settings provided by well-heeled companies or organizations? Then the simultaneous translators work busily in their booths.

Do not forget to turn on the microphones and to talk into them – slowly, please. Treat every microphone as if it were alive. It may be, and your unguarded frankness may be translated into four languages. Remember that at any major gathering, nothing is effectively off the record. During the lunch-hour break in a European Conference, during the icy days of the Cold War, the organizers 'swept' for bugs. Under the table of the Polish delegation, they found a microphone. The chairman protested to the Head of Delegation.

'Oh come,' he said. 'You know that we have to report back on what goes on here. At least let us ensure that it is accurate!'

Tapes like that get translated later. Your words are on the record, and whether you know it or not, they are often recorded.

During the Second World War, Britain was plastered with posters, claiming: 'Careless words cost lives'. When talking to those whose language is not your own, double your care; halve your speed; and multiply your chances of success.

Sometimes, this burden can be reduced. If, for instance, most of your audience speak English, it may be enough for your translator to summarize your theme, your argument or your words.

I have a reasonable grasp of some half a dozen languages – at least sufficient to be misunderstood in each. Speaking to an audience in one of those languages, I try to avoid an interpreter by occasionally translating myself into English – and always doing so when I have the least doubt as to whether I have expressed myself accurately.

The old saying: 'I'd rather be red than dead', can be translated for international speeches: 'A read speech pronounces a sentence of death on your relationship with your audience.'

But if a speech *must* be read out, learn the techniques (see Chapter Twelve).

37   Ceremonial and commercial

With a roll of drums and a fanfare of trumpets, the Chair marches to the centre of the platform. Behind, high on a screen in the darkened room, flash the name and logo of the company. Speaking from invisible notes on the autocue, executives tell their story, proclaim the company's successes, acclaim winners of awards, and present greetings, salutations and gifts to the worthy.

These expensive flourishes turn prosaic conferences into modern spectaculars, audio-visual experiences (see Chapter Twenty-three, on visual aids), professionally produced and royally rendered. If it is properly prepared and well delivered, the speech is the centre of the message. The rest is vivid illustration. If it is delivered in an embarrassed monotone, its deficiencies are exaggerated by their unhappy contrast with the brilliant audio-visual effects. Conversely, many an excellent speech has been ruined by inadequate, unsuitable or inappropriate slides, by over-amplification or too obtrusive music, or by visuals that are intended to aid but in fact hinder.

I once joined over a hundred colleague MPs at a dinner, put on by a famous firm of City accountants. The opening cocktail reception went well. The victims were then duly herded into the dining room and seated at their tables, one host executive at each. The presentation was horrific. We endured a series of speeches, read by the Chair and two of his colleagues, against a background of lush, logoed slides.

Our hosts should have been asked our classic four questions, as described in Chapter One:

- *Who* are our audience?
- *What* do they want from us?
- *Why* are we here? What is our message?
- *How* do we best put that message across?

They had answered question three. They wanted to show us the size, strength and structure of their set-up – to convince us of its heritage of excellence. They had decided to spread their message orally, by their top people, and visually, by modern techniques. They had answered question one: they knew who we were, and how to attract us. Question two, which is the most important, they had ignored.

After all, why should such a large number of busy people wish to spend an evening with them? We would all enjoy a good meal and most would happily swallow a few drinks. But few of us were totally undernourished or dehydrated.

What we wanted was to tune in on our hosts' view of the market, their explanation of past events, their visions of the future. We wanted our questions answered, even if they went unasked. Instead, we were served up a droning monotony of voice, to a background of well-produced irrelevancies. Not one of us cared about their pyramid of management strength, the growth in turnover, the monumental architecture of their new premises.

So they wasted the opportunity and their company's money; modern technology destroyed the communication, the presentation and the speeches.

By contrast, I enjoyed a brisk presentation by an hotel company. Drum rolls, fanfare, name and logo, flashes of hotels – all were there, along with a succulent buffet. Both speakers were spotlighted; they spoke well, voices and eyes raised.

The Minister of Tourism spoke briefly and clearly. He presented flags to the hotel managers. The three E's flowed through the event – Energy, Excitement and Enthusiasm.

The combination of classic speechmaking and technological miracles can produce high impact. Misused, it can destroy.

Our City hosts would have done much better to stand on the stage, to ask what questions we wanted answered and then field them with skill and authority. Instead, they killed off their occasion.

38   After dinner

A captive audience, well wined and amply dined, should be an orator's joy. Unfortunately more often than not speakers are too apprehensive to enjoy the food, and instead make a meal of their speeches. Which is unnecessary, if they would only follow a few basic rules.

First, wait for silence. When you have it, look around amiably and begin: 'Ladies and Gentlemen . . .' or as the case may be. Those few words are useful. You discover that you have not lost your voice after all. Your audience (at that stage at least) is ready to listen – and to be entertained.

However heavy the dinner or the company, however important the occasion or mighty the listeners, no one wants a dry lecture on top of a wet repast. So however important your message, do your audience the courtesy of exercising patience. Start with a joke, a witticism, a story.

The best jokes are usually impromptu. A friendly reference to the Chair, the restaurant, the food, or to the headline in the evening papers (those of the audience who have read it are delighted to be in on the joke). Otherwise, there are many good opening gambits such as:

- A few moments ago, the Chair turned to me and said: 'Would you like to speak now – or shall we let them go on enjoying themselves a little longer?'
- Not long ago, an after-dinner speaker was greeted by a woman, at the evening's end, who said to him: 'Mr Jones . . . that was a terrible speech!' He composed himself as best he could – and was then greeted by another woman who said: 'I'm awfully sorry about Mrs Brown . . . She has such a long tongue . . . and she's such an idiot – she hasn't got a mind of her own. She only repeats what she hears other people saying'.
- 'Thank you for your hospitality to my wife and to me. In the words of the proverb: Behind every successful man stands an amazed woman!'

However weak the wit, dry the humour or wet the joke, provided that you put it across with verve, courage or at least a friendly smile, you are on your way to establishing a rapport with your audience. (See Chapter Seventeen.) They will settle back into their chairs, relaxed and be either receptive to a continuation of merriment or, at worst, better braced for such message as you decide to give.

Now launch into the speech. Keep it short. The lower down you come in the toast list, the greater the premium on brevity. So why do so many of the most nervous speakers find it necessary to be the most long-winded? Do they think they can make up with length for their lack of wit, their terror or their dearth of wise words?

You may argue your bank manager into submission, stifle your competitors by talking them into the ground, or exhibit superb salesmanship by making it clear that you are not going to leave until you get what you want. But all this is in private. Enter into the public arena in general, or the dinner table in particular, and you must be brief (see also Chapter Thirteen on time management).

The after-dinner speech requires the same careful construction as any other. It needs a flow of ideas as well as of words. The more the words are laced with wit, the more likely that their wisdom will strike home.

Watch your audience. If they drop off to sleep, either tell them a joke or sit down. If they jiggle the cutlery, wind up your sermon. If you want to be asked again, do not outstay your welcome.

As you approach your end, remember what it is you have been called upon to do. If you are responding to a toast, you should start by thanking the person who made it and complimenting him or her on its wit and wisdom.

Finish where you began – by rehearsing, once again, your delight at having been asked . . . your pleasure at the privilege of responding to the toast . . . and your good wishes to the organization which has asked you.

More important, if you are making the toast – do so. Nothing is more discomfiting than for the Chair to have to say: 'And now, kindly rise and drink with me . . .' That is your job. Do it.

The standard formula? 'Ladies and Gentlemen, I invite you to rise and drink with me a toast to the continued success and prosperity of . . . the health and happiness of . . .' or as the case may be. By all means vary it, but do not forget it.

One toast which should never be varied is that to: 'Her Majesty, the Queen'. If you are privileged to propose the loyal toast, then do so – in those words. No one wants a speech from you, extolling the beauty and majesty of the monarch – still less a defence of hereditary peerages, royal privileges and the like.

The presence of an ambassador calls for a toast, to the head of his or her state – but unless this is one of the non-formal variety, reserve your eulogy for some proper occasion.

No one should smoke until after the loyal toast and others of the formal, national variety. This explains why some hosts call on proposers of these toasts when the waiters are collecting the soup. Alas!

39   Votes of thanks

The formal vote of thanks to the speaker is a mark of courtesy, as necessary as the word of gratitude to the hostess at the end of the evening. You may not have enjoyed your meal. The company may have been excruciatingly dull. Like the fabled hostess who was said to have made her guests feel at home even when she fervently wished that they were, you will still thank her as you leave and no doubt compliment her warmly on the excellence of her cooking and the pleasure you have had in the company of her other, well-chosen guests. Because the compliments are apparently unrehearsed, they may be believed. Anyway, they must be given.

So it is with guest speakers. They must be thanked. In America, it is normal to make handsome payment to speakers, even to Rotary Clubs, friendly societies or business or charitable organizations. The guest speakers are given appreciative thanks, in tangible form. In the UK, the audience considers that it is doing speakers a favour by listening to them!

When your guests say: 'It was very kind of you to invite me to this splendid, peaceful Highland resort,' they probably mean: 'I wish I had thought of some way to refuse your invitation to trek up to your God-forsaken, Arctic, barren development area slum!' So at least bathe them in the warmth of your thanks.

Incidentally, have you remembered to offer to pay your speaking guests' expenses? They would probably be too embarrassed to ask for them and may even refuse your offer. But to beg for and receive the benefit of the time of busy speakers and then to expect them to pay for fares or accommodation is a typically British stupidity. All speakers know the wretchedness of being dragged many miles for a few minutes of speech to a minute audience. That is one of the hazards of the trade. When they do so entirely at their own expense, in money as well as in time, their irritation is understandable.

What, then, of the vote of thanks itself? How should you put it across?

Sincerity, once again, is the key. To achieve it in a vote of thanks depends on a genuine (if possible) and topical (certainly) assessment of the positive and helpful aspects of the visitors' speeches. Refer to their wit and wisdom . . . to the full and frank way in which they dealt with the subject . . . to the particular interest that you had in those portions of the talks which dealt with . . . Elaborate on a point or two, to show that you have really taken it in – or that you have been taken in, as the case may be. Do not use the occasion to launch into a tirade of your own. Your job is to thank. Do it.

A vote of thanks is a mini-speech. The general rules apply, in abbreviated form.

Write out your first sentence and the skeleton of the speech (see Chapter Twelve on notes). To have the whole speech written in advance is a travesty. 'We have all been extremely impressed with the wise words of Mr Stout,' the speaker reads from a typed card. 'He gave us a very clear exposition of the subject. We have much to think about as a result.' Terrible – an impromptu effort not worth the paper it was written on. Of all the speeches which should never be written out in advance, votes of thanks head the list.

'We are very honoured to have had Ms Slim with us this evening. We realize and appreciate how far she has come. We know and understand the effort that it has cost her. And I know that I am expressing the feelings of everyone here when I tell her how deeply grateful we are to her.' Pause for applause. If you rush on your audience will not know what is expected of them. There will be a few embarrassed hand-claps and the speaker will not be complimented.

'We listened with great interest to Ms Slim's views on . . . I was especially impressed with the concept of . . . If my own company does not take steps to put this system into effect, it will not be through any lack of enthusiasm on my part, nor any failing on the part of our distinguished speaker. She has paid us the compliment of laying out before us in the clearest terms the essence of the organizational method which she has distilled through years of trial, error and experience.

'The greatest tribute which can be paid to our guests will be through our adoption of her ideas.' All speakers like to feel that they have sown good seed on fertile ground. Treat their words as pearls and they will not think of you as the proverbial swine.

'Perhaps our greatest delight has been in the way in which Ms Slim has succeeded in bringing her somewhat recondite subject to life. She has proved that to tell a tale of . . . need not be dull. She has enlivened our evening with wit and humour.

'And so, in thanking Ms Slim for her good words this evening, I can only hope that we shall have an early opportunity of hearing her again. We wish her every success. Thank you, Ms Slim, very much indeed.'

Thank you, too, for a terse, appropriate, sincere, friendly and well-constructed vote of thanks. Just think that the audience inwardly groaned when you were called upon to speak, worrying in case you were about to make the late hour even later, cause them to miss the last bus or train or to lose the services of their aggravated drivers — or, possibly, embarrass them by saying what they really thought about their guests. So they were pleasantly surprised and are likely to invite you to perform the same service again. Or maybe they knew all the time that you would perform this underrated chore with aplomb, which is why they asked you to do it. In that case, their trust was not misplaced. Thank you, indeed.

40 Presentations and awards – as giver and receiver

You may view presentation or award speeches from two angles – that of the giver and that of the receiver. In either event 'a few words' will be expected of you; in either case, the keynote of the speech is sincerity and that the words are indeed 'few'.

Everyone likes to be honoured. The art of the well-turned compliment is appreciated more than almost any other. Flattery given freely and wholeheartedly is always welcome – but in moderation.

'Mr X is the most brilliant businessman, straightforward and sweet-tempered, a paragon of commercial virtue . . .' Rubbish. No one will believe it – not even Mr X, in spite of his bias.

Compare this: 'On the one hand, Mr Smith has been the head of a large and successful commercial concern. He has had to see that his business became and remained thoroughly competitive. He must strike the hard bargain, ensuring that his business is tough and competitive, enabling the enterprise to flourish, in spite of economic circumstances, the bitter and fierce rivalries within the trade, the battle for skilled staff and for shrinking markets.

'On the other hand, Mr Smith has preserved both the good name of the company and its good relations with its suppliers, with its customers and competitors and with its own staff.

'That he has succeeded in building up the business without destroying the foundations of goodwill; that he promoted the economic welfare of the business without demoting or undervaluing the honour and integrity of the Board; that he has earned such a warm regard not only for the company but for himself – those are the reasons why we are delighted to honour him this evening, and why we are so sad at his impending retirement.'

Or take the manager, the foreman or the operative leaving after long service, or receiving an award for distinguished, long-term conduct.

'We were thinking of presenting Mr Jones with a watch. But we do not believe that our staff really want to know the time just when it has become least important to them. So we felt that this . . . would be more appropriate and much more useful. It comes with the thanks and admiration of the company – and its gratitude.

'It is also given with the affection and goodwill of his fellow members of staff. They have contributed towards it and I know they hope, as much as I do, that it will remind him – and his wife and family – of the affection and esteem in which we all hold him, and of our thanks to him for his loyal service.

'We all wish Mr Jones, together with his super wife, a long and happy retirement, blessed with the very best of health. And we hope that he will visit us often. He will always have the warmest of welcomes from all of us, his colleagues and friends.'

No flowery insincerities. No 'schmaltz', no overdone compliments. Just straightforward, sincere and sensible words, bound to be appreciated by the person concerned.

Sometimes the presentation of an award is really an excuse to encourage people to come to a dinner or other function, knowing that they would not wish to offend the recipient by being absent. With this sort of award or presentation it is expected that the toast to the recipient will be coupled with a eulogy of the organization he or she represents – and/or of the virtues represented by the organization conferring the award. This sort of excuse for an oratorical jamboree is becoming increasingly common, and is a not altogether welcome transatlantic import. The public relations people have created a new vehicle. If it comes your way, be prepared to steer it.

'In the new and expanding sauna industry, we are proud of our pioneers. This dinner is in honour of Mr Finn, whom we are all delighted to welcome to England.' Hear, hear!

'Ms Finn has helped to put our industry onto the British map. Close on the heels of the central heating boom has come the realization that sauna treatments bring health and true family relaxation. While no public authority should be without one, there is an immense, untapped demand for them in the larger private homes throughout the country.' (The press start scribbling.)

'What better occasion could there be than this to launch the great new drive for British-built saunas? We shall create a home demand so as to build up an economic export potential . . . And we wish to express our admiration and thanks to our honoured guest, Mr Finn, to whom I am delighted to present this gold pin, in the shape of a sauna, as a token of our respect and gratitude.' Loud cheers. The audience rises. Cameras flash.

This is only a mild exaggeration of the sort of award occasion that occurs somewhere, every day. If you are the presenter, the more fatuous the occasion, the less deserving the recipient, the bigger the publicity hoped for, the more your sincerity becomes vital, if the occasion is not to deteriorate into sickening slush.

How do you appear sincere, even when you are not? By playing down. By avoiding exaggeration. By excluding melodrama, theatricals, tears in the eyes or choking in the throat. 'I am so moved that I can scarcely speak . . .' Then don't. 'Ms Jones is fabulous, fantastic, magnificent . . .' Superlatives are seldom either sincere or accurate. A few, quiet words of praise are worth paeans of adulation.

With luck, you may be at the receiving end of an honour, an award, a presentation or a toast. Praise may be heaped on your receptive shoulders. How do you cope with it?

'I am very grateful to Mr Smith for his most generous obituary,' said Adlai Stevenson.

'There is one difference between a speech of this kind heaping praise on the living, and a funeral oration, extolling the dead,' said Israel's first President, Chaim Weizmann. 'In the former case, but not the latter, there is one listener who is ready to believe in the truth of all that was said.'

More common: 'I would first like to thank Mr Jones for his very kind references to my wife and myself. We are deeply grateful – and only wish that half of it were true.' Or: 'I am grateful to you, Chairman, for the very generous way in which you have referred to my organization and to myself. We shall do our best to live up to your high regard.'

Just as it is vital for the maker of the speech of praise to be patently sincere, so the recipient must be clothed in decent modesty. It would be ungracious and insincere to say: 'It's all true . . . you shouldn't have said those things . . .' You could hardly say: 'Every word is an understatement . . .' You may be immodest about your wife: 'All that's said about my wife is true. I am very proud of her – she's a gem!' But then you must go on: 'I only wish that I could believe the same of the words about myself. Still, I am most obliged to Ms Smith for having spoken them. Maybe she convinced my wife of their truth, even though she left me in doubt.'

Then return the compliment by speaking well of the individual or organization that has had the good sense to honour you. 'I have been very lucky to serve this company over so many years . . . It has been a privilege to work with you all . . . I shall miss you . . . I hope that we shall meet again, very often . . .' Or: 'Whilst this fraternal organization has been good enough to make an award to me, I should in fact have been making a presentation to the organization. The honours are flowing in the wrong direction. I shall try to redress the balance a little by saying why it is I regard the work of this organization to be of such enormous significance, especially in the present state of . . .'

Or: 'It was very good of Mr Smith to speak so well of me. As everyone here knows so well, most of the virtues that he was kind enough to attribute to me were in fact his own. This company is fortunate to be led by a man of his calibre . . .'

Sincerity and the nicely turned compliment should not be the sole prerogative of the giver.

Finally, the conclusion. 'And so my speech – like my time with the company – has drawn to a close. Thank you, Mr Smith, once again for your very kind words. Thank you, my colleagues, for your goodness to me – and for your most generous gift. My wife and I will treasure it always – as we shall the memories of our association with you. Good luck to you all.'

Or: 'And so, in accepting this award, I thank you all for the compliment you have paid to me – and through me to my organization. My colleagues and I are all happy to have been able to carry out our work – and we undertake to attempt in the future to exceed our past achievements which have caused you to honour us in the present. Our thanks to you all.'

The sentimental anecdotes you have slipped into the body of your speech; the reminiscences, memories, tales with a moral – all of which go down so well in this sort of situation – these are all rounded off with a final word of thanks. End, where you began, with your gratitude. It has been a fine occasion – and an excellent speech.

41   Funerals, feasts and epitaphs

You may be called on to 'say a few words' on funeral or on festive occasions, involving family, friends or colleagues. In general, similar rules apply to those outlined for the after-dinner orator – and elsewhere in the book. But here are some special suggestions.

There is no speech that is harder to make than a farewell. Nor is there any more worthy duty in the eyes of God or man than a salute to the departed.

If you face this responsibility, the key rules are:

- From the start and to the end, you must neither lose your composure nor break down under the weight of emotion. You must achieve detachment.
- Do not declaim. Speak slowly, clearly, simply.
- Avoid pompous and insincere language. Instead, choose short, simple, Anglo-Saxon words.
- As for content, remember that the people who usually matter most are the immediate family; the widow or the widower, parents and children. Friends come next, far behind.

So start, by addressing the family by name: 'Mary, George, Richard . . . we have all come here today because we loved . . .'

On the principle that I am addressing the bereaved, I always ask them what they would like me to say.

Keep your speech structured and brief. Say what you are going to say. Start, 'With sadness but with pride, I pay the tribute of us all to . . .'

Then say it. Set out your points in order. Try to catch the essence of the person, as you remember him or her and as their family would wish you to.

Then the family itself. 'We are also here because of our affection for . . . we admire them for their . . . we love them because they . . . we are with them in their grief, which we share.'

Then say what you have said. Sum up your message. 'And so we shall remember . . . – with affection, with joy – and with thanksgiving, because we enjoyed and shared in the warmth of his friendship. We shall miss him.'

In your few moments, then, you must try to conjure up the happiest of memories of the deceased. Avoid platitudes and clichés.

And if a touch of humour fits, use it. A whimsical, smiling recollection of a joy brought into your life by your friend . . .

Finally, remember that people eulogized may have had faults while alive, but they must have none visible, now they are gone.

There is an ancient Jewish tradition that someone must say good words at a funeral. So after David Cohen had been buried, the Rabbi asked: 'Who will perform this holy duty? I cannot do so because unfortunately I can think of nothing good to say about poor David . . .' Silence.

'Please, someone must find something to praise, in David's life?' Silence.

'I beg you . . . someone . . .'

'I'll do it,' said Sam. He came to the front, faced the audience, and proclaimed: 'His brother was worse!'

If you must pay your respects to the departed, you will certainly be able to do better than that!

Happily, whilst every lifetime contains the seeds of its own sorrow, there are far more joyful occasions than sad ones. Births and baptisms, christenings, confirmations, barmitzvahs and first communions, engagements, weddings, anniversaries and birthdays: each is the occasion for a word of congratulations at the start of a meeting or speech – or for a celebration at which a speech is required.

Of the full-blown variety, the after-dinner speech may form the model (see Chapter Thirty-eight). Perhaps the best advice of all is contained in the saying: 'The secret of talking to the public is the same as that of speaking to your spouse. Keep your tongue in time with your thoughts: if either gets ahead, you are done for!'

42   Appeals and fund-raising

The art of extracting money from listeners requires careful thought and ready adaptation. The Chancellor of the Exchequer may have political problems, but at least he can enforce his financial requirements. Speechmakers trying to raise funds for a favourite charity, for a trade or industrial benevolent fund, or even for some less apparently altruistic outlet, must win the cash. How? That depends on the audience and the cause. Here are some suggestions.

There are those who give out of pure kindness of heart. Guilt and self-interest are usually more powerful motives.

There are those who work hard for a charity – and others who do not. The latter may contribute money earned while not striving for the good cause. In their own way, they can do as much for the needy as their more apparently energetic colleagues. Tell them so – by implication.

'There are those of us who are in the happy position of being able to spare time to work for this important charity. There are others who find it impossible to do so. May I make a special appeal to them? Give us the means and we will do the job. It is a job that desperately needs every penny that you can spare – and more . . .'

What, then, of enlightened self-interest? Maybe it's a question of insurance. The charity deals with the aged, infirm, ill or needy? And the young, middle-aged or at least fit? That's now. What happens if *you* get dumped on the scrap heap . . . sacked . . . struck down by (Heaven forbid) some fell disease? You have a pension? Well maybe the company will not be in a position to pay it or it will not satisfy the needs of the spouse you leave behind. So, now, when you are in a position to assure your own future, do so.

This is seldom said. The better approach is this: 'I ask you to give as an expression of gratitude for the fact that you do not need to make use of this great trade charity for yourself. I hope that none of us will need at any time to occupy a bed in this convalescent home; to receive a payment from this fund; to rely on the benevolence of others in the industry . . . But who knows?'

Pause, significantly. 'And even if, as we all hope, we escape the need for help of this sort, we can be proud that those who do require it can look to us. They have given good service; they have earned every penny that comes to them; they have been smitten by the ill-fortune that we have managed to avoid . . .'

And so on. We all spend money on insurance, don't we? Well, this is a healthy and helpful form of outlet for the same intelligent response to potential misfortune.

Consider always the best way to confer a bargain. This is generally done with the kind aid of the Revenue. If business people feel that they can lawfully and properly give more by paying less, you are far more likely to get your money, to have a bed endowed in the trade home, to acquire your 'Smith House' or 'Jones Hall'. So check on current covenant schemes, charitable trusts, and tax-deductible donations.

'Think of it, Ladies and Gentleman. All those who pay income tax at the current standard rate can confer a benefit on this charity out of all proportion to the amount which they have to give up from their own spending. Here are some examples . . .' Then say how much a gift of £X or $Y per year will mean, gross, to the charity.

Remember, of course, that when a charity receives covenants, these can provide good security for loans, if it needs the money at once. It is sometimes possible to get people to give a lump sum on the basis that it will be grossed up for tax purposes over the years. The charity's accountants should know the rules.

Then, remember that lawful blackmail is the charitable fund-raiser's most potent weapon. You phone your supplier. 'Jimmy,' you say, 'we've had such a tremendous call on our benevolent fund that we simply have to raise an extra £50,000. Can I count on you for a thousand?'

Jimmy groans inwardly. 'Certainly, Bill,' he smiles. 'Shall I send an advertisement for the Ball brochure?'

Use the same tactic in public speech. Look at Jimmy when you ask for funds. He may turn away his gaze, but he may not dare to keep his cheque book closed. After all, when he came to the function or the meeting, he realized that the skinning knives would be unsheathed. Or, even better, corner him in advance. Find out how much he is willing to give. Announce it – as a bait for others, or to shame them into raising their donations to an appropriately announceable level. If you have goodwill, then use it for the benefit of the less privileged. No one will ever tell you of the resentment they feel. It's all in a good cause, isn't it?

Of course, whether you can use this sort of direct attack or whether you have to be more subtle, whether you can announce donations at the meeting or have to let the word go round from mouth to mouth, whether you conduct a mock auction at inflated prices, a raffle, a tombola, all depends on all factors in the charitable case. But one rule applies to nearly all: you cannot afford to be bashful, or to worry about rebuffs, if you are looking for money from the pockets of others. Anyway, why should you be embarrassed? You are not asking for yourself.

The best time to attack is when the mind is weak through the stomach being overloaded, or the heart touched by your words. If you have people in a happy, receptive and giving mood, then (literally) cash in. Either ask them for their donation at the time – and pass round the appropriate banker's or covenant forms – or at least write to them the very next day saying: 'It was very good to see you last night . . . I enclose a banker's order . . . I am sure that I can count on your support . . .'

I reproduce with appreciation an interview in which a successful appeal-maker gave away some of his secrets:

'I know plenty of people who can make an excellent speech, but not an appeal. The technique is quite different. The man who makes a speech can create the right atmosphere for someone to follow on. The appeal-maker must not waste time making speeches. He needs a couple of minutes to say what it is all about. And, of course, an appeal-maker must never be satisfied with his audience. Whatever he says, he must have the people in a frame of mind when they want to give. He should know when to stop.'

An audience should be 'like a juicy orange – you squeeze, but not until the pips fall out. When you stop is a matter of psychology or intuition.'

When you have finished your appeal, can you tell whether the audience is still with you?

'If they applaud you as loudly when you sit down as when you got up, you can be happy with the job done.

'An appeal-maker must never read a speech. What he has to say must be spontaneous. It must come from the heart. He must never embarrass people but make them feel happy about their giving and leave them in a good frame of mind, thanking him for a successful job. People recognize the sincerity of the appeal-maker.

An appeal-maker must be somebody who sincerely believes in the cause he puts forward . . .

'Finally, the appeal maker must set an example in giving.'

Give and the world gives with you . . . the mean person is not an appealing figure, in any sense of the word.

43   Panels

Curiously, even prominent people are prepared to take part in panels. The audience gets at least two views for the price of one evening. Speakers – who might otherwise resent the competition and the feeling that the audience really should be satisfied with an evening of one of them – agree to participate out of delight at not having to prepare any set speech. Some or all of the speakers are often fooled into accepting because they think that the others on the panel have already done so, or they turn up because they have been asked by someone whom they cannot refuse.

Whatever the circumstances, most speakers have to perform at panels or 'brains trusts' at some time or another. So here are some suggestions.

The organizers should provide each speaker with a pencil and pad. Too often, they don't. Never arrive at any meeting without pen and paper, least of all for a panel discussion.

When asked a question, jot it down. Alongside, put your random ideas. If you have none, indicate to the Chair that one of your colleagues should open the batting. Something will come to your mind while your colleague answers. If it does not, then say: 'I agree,' or 'No comment on this one, thank you.'

There are questions that may provoke all sorts of possible answers, none of which you wish to give. Do not be browbeaten into words you may later regret, especially if the press are there.

Each answer you do give should be a small, neat speech. It should have a beginning, a body and an end. Do your PREP (see Chapter Eighteen). It must be concise; and precisely because it is extempore, you may find it considerably more difficult than the ordinary, set effort.

You may have to cope with interruptions from your colleagues or from the chair. Take them in your stride. React to the informality of the occasion. Do not be afraid to break your train of thought – or, if you cannot return to it, say: 'Now where was I, before Mr Brown's witty intervention?' Someone will remind you. (See Chapter Twenty-eight).

Conversational informality is the key to successful brains trusting. You are performing at a dinner party, with an audience to play up to?

Make use of your powers of showmanship. React to your audience. Fish for applause and laughter. Relax and enjoy yourself and your audience will do the same.

Well-chosen panels include people with different backgrounds, viewpoints and ideas. Friendly teasing or gentle jibes go down well. Smart retorts to points made by other speakers seldom go astray. The tradition is that of the dinner party and not of the political tub-thump. So avoid aggressive and unfriendly rejoinders, rude or unkind rebuttals, personal remarks to or about other speakers which hurt, whether or not they are calculated to do so. The object is to demonstrate your brains, not to tear out those of the other panellists.

44 In the open

You may have to make an open-air speech at the factory gates, at the dockside, or (more likely) at some open-air trade show or speaking event. Perhaps it is only a vote of thanks at your local sports day or a talk or lecture on site; or maybe a speech at a rally in Hyde Park, or Trafalgar Square or at your local war memorial? Wherever the place and whatever the circumstances, there are basic rules on open-air oratory that should help you succeed out of doors.

Human voices carry poorly in the open air. So the prime essential for the outdoor speaker is to be heard. If you have a microphone (see Chapter Twenty-two), use it. The chances of outdoor amplifying equipment going wrong are far greater than with their indoor brethren. The variety that hooks on to a car battery is especially vulnerable. Listen to the politicians next election time. Pity their attempts to be heard – especially when a crowd is all around them and the amplifying equipment points only to the front.

If you do have a microphone, remember its outdoor limitations. For instance, if ever you have to speak in a moving vehicle – perhaps from the front of a car or the back of a truck – talk very slowly and distinctly and urge the driver to move as slowly as possible. People like to hear what is being cried out at them from a moving object and they get aggravated when it darts past without giving them the chance to pick up the words, however banal or trite those words may be. Usually, there is time for a slogan only. 'Today's the day . . . come to the carnival . . . 12.15 p.m. at the park . . .' Then you are gone.

Most outdoor speaking is stationary. Mike or no mike, many of the indoor rules go out of the window. For instance:

- The outdoor speaker can be far freer with movement and gesture.
- Old-fashioned oratory – rabble-rousing – is more effective and appears less insincere when out of doors.
- Instead of having an audience ready-made, you may have to collect it. Whereas indoors there is no point in speaking to yourself, outdoors you may have no alternative, so the louder and more provocatively you rant, the greater your chances of an eventual audience.

In the open

Some rules of indoor speaking require special emphasis out of doors. For instance:

- Don't be afraid to pause . . . to wait . . . to give every possible indication of complete calm and confidence.
- Never panic, no matter what may be thrown at you – even if this is more than mere words. Remember always that speakers on the platform have a vast advantage over their audience. If they are firm and refuse to be ruffled, they should win.
- Make certain that your voice carries. If you use a battery-operated hand megaphone, pull the trigger tight. As my Harvard professor used to say: 'Take your voice and throw it against the wall at the back of your audience and make it bounce off.' If you get hoarse as a result, do not worry. You have joined the professionals. Lose your voice and it will come back. Lose your audience, and it is gone forever.

45   While others speak

Part of the price of the pleasure of hearing your own voice is the need to endure the speeches of others. You may, of course, be lucky. If you are the sole guest speaker you will have only the introduction and vote of thanks to sit through. During the former you will think of your speech and – if you take the advice given in this book to heart – try to find something in the words of your introducer to quote, adapt or answer, and so establish a rapport with your audience. During your vote of thanks, just try to believe that the words spoken of you are true.

Inevitably unlucky are after-dinner speakers, no matter what their places in the toast list. The Chair of a committee may be able to regulate the speeches of others, but the rest must put up with them. If you happen to be a Member of Parliament, you may be able to escape from the function after you have spoken, perhaps blessed with a three-line whip. ('Mr Jones must now return to his parliamentary duties. We appreciate all the more that he has spared some of his valuable time to be with us.') Heaven help anyone else who leaves before the other speeches are complete.

So cultivate the art of enjoyable listening.

In private, the good listener is generally credited with fine powers of perception, intelligence and even eloquence. In public, to fall asleep whilst others speak is the height of bad manners. How to avoid it?

Every practised speaker is a skilled doodler. One handwriting expert is alleged to make his living largely by interpreting the doodles of the famous. Much more constructive? The writing of those neglected letters.

The dinner is too dull? Too bad. You must try to get your neighbours to talk about their speciality and you may find that they are more interesting than you had realized. The after-dinner speeches are a misery? Then use the back of the menu, toast list, guest list or brochure. Take out a pen and write your correspondence. Look up every now and again at the speaker. No one – least of all the speakers – will suspect that you are doing anything other than paying them the compliment of noting their words. My relatives always know when I have been cursed with dull speeches to hear. They receive missives on agendas, minutes, pads . . . anything that happens to be handy.

Of course, you could instead be jotting down notes for current work. In the unlikely event of the speaker sparking off a constructive chain of thought, make a note of the idea before it flees for ever. If you hear a good story, write it down. If all else fails, and you can fight off slumber no longer, then you must do your best to organize your forty winks so as to attract the least possible suspicion.

I have a friend who, through long years of practice, has learned to sleep whilst sitting bolt upright and with his eyes open. Most of us must be content with the head rested on the hand, the elbow on the table. Alternatively, the head droops forward and the notes, brochure or agenda are in front of you so that it may (with luck) appear that you are reading – or at least engaged in deep thought.

Speakers should learn to amuse themselves during the unamusing speeches of others, without any appearance of flagging attention or lagging concentration. Spare a thought for diplomats and the royals, who must do it all the time. And remember that politicians have been defined as 'people who speak while others sleep . . .'

46 Impromptu

The impromptu 'few words' are a speaker's most daunting challenge. Here are some hints on how to meet it.

First: Don't panic. Keep cool. Take a deep breath and use our 'confidence trick' routine (see Chapter Seven).

Second: Take as much time as you can get. Sneak away for a few moments, if you can. Nip off to the loo or step outside the building and snatch a moment to reflect.

Third: Grab a pen and paper, a card or a menu. Jot down your ideas.

Then:

Fourth: Think, fast. Do your PREP (see Chapter Eighteen). State your *Position*. 'I am delighted to thank our host and hostess for this marvellous party . . .' Give your *Reason*. 'They have lavished their hospitality, their kindness and their good company on us, and we are very grateful.'

For *Example*: 'What a marvellous banquet . . . band . . . show they have put on, haven't they?'

Then restate your *Position*: 'So please join me in drinking a toast to John and Jane – to the good health and happiness of our host and our hostess.'

Fifth: Keep it crisp and brief. Lack of notice is no excuse for a boring ramble.

Those are the general rules. There are variants on them. If, for instance, someone asks you a question and you have to give an immediate response, gain time for asking for the question to be repeated. You could grab even more moments by writing it down.

Finally, some major don'ts.

- *Don't* apologize, saying: 'I'm very sorry that I haven't had time to prepare this talk as I would have wished, or I'm sure I'd make a better job of it.'
- *Don't* blame someone else. 'I'm really cross with Paul for not giving me time to prepare this speech . . .'
- *Don't*, above all, show any of the tell-tale signs of the amateur. Don't rush, gabble, lose eye contact, slouch. Instead, use measured speech, and wear your invisible crown.

47   Handling the press

You may make your speeches to audiences you see. But if they have commercial importance, your words may be quoted. So this chapter is for public speakers – the speechmakers whose words have public interest and who *should* use, *must* beware of and *will* do best if they know how to handle the press.

Not long ago, the *Mail on Sunday* commented on recent and monumental moans about the mauling of Ministers by the BBC's Today programme. 'It is Ministers' responsibility to prepare themselves sufficiently to deal with them. If they don't or can't, they should not blame the BBC or others for their own shortcomings.'

Correct. And if speechmakers want a good press, they must know how to set about getting it. Those who suffer at the hands of newspapers can usually blame only themselves.

As a start, do unto the press as you would have them do unto you. With rare exceptions, reporters and editors respond to good will and to frankness. Treat journalists as enemies and they will respond accordingly.

For instance: with only the rarest of disreputable exceptions, journalists will honour 'off the record' communications. A typical example: The telephone rings. It is John Brown, from the newsdesk of a national paper. He asks for a comment on a problem concerning one of your clients.

You could refuse to say anything, in which case the paper would be entitled to publish: 'When challenged, the company's accountant, Mr Green, refused to comment.'

A much better way is to say: 'Do you want to talk to me on or off the record?'

Brown: 'On the record, if possible.'

'Well, on the record, I can tell you . . .' Then you say what you are prepared to have quoted.

Brown: 'And off the record?'

You can then give the background, the explanation or the information you wish, so that the journalist will understand the situation. Provided that you have made it plain that you are providing unquotable background, 'off the record', you can expect your confidence to be honoured.

The press need stories. They depend on your good will. Equally, you should know that editorial content is far better advertising than any you can pay for – provided that it is acceptable. So how do you project your image through the press? What news can you make, create or organize? How best do you spread the good word? Whether you are dealing with the professional, the national or the local press, real news is welcomed.

As a start, study your markets. Who are the people you really want to reach? Which newspapers are most likely to take what story? Which editor or reporter has a personal interest in the particular theme or idea?

So you are opening a new office, launching a new product, organizing a new service for your clients, or preparing or unveiling a research project, of public interest? Then try a press conference to promote the news, real or apparent. Or choose a particular outlet and give them an 'exclusive'.

To plant or to place an article or story, you must know your market and who controls it. Perhaps you should start with a query letter, offering the idea, or kick off with a telephone call, lunch or a drink? Or maybe you can respond to an important, current story?

Or you could use a press release – a document sent out to the press or other medium, saying what you would like others to read or hear about your services, your project or your idea. Before preparing the release, decide to whom you should send it, when, and the message you want to convey. Select your recipients with care or you will waste resources, or (worse) misjudge your market.

Put the release into journalists' language. Keep it brief, pithy and to the point.

If your information is aimed at different markets, you may need separate releases. Either way, put them out professionally, on your company notepaper and with 'News Release' printed at the top. Date it. And if you do not want it to go out too early, mark it with an 'embargo' or release date, at the top.

Attach any enclosures, correspondence or other documents to which the press release refers. And add the name, address and/or telephone number of a contact from whom further information is available.

If you decide to send out the wording of a speech to be made in the future, be especially careful with the embargo. Then make sure that the speaker follows the script or otherwise carefully informs the media who have already received the release of any deviation from it. Mark the key passages which you hope will be prominently reproduced.

Headline your message at the start; elaborate it in the middle; and repeat it at the end. Use the classic structure of the presentation – say what you are going to say; say it; then say what you've said.

If you decide to set up a press conference, make sure that you have a real story to tell. Choose your time, place and victims with care; bring them in by a telephone or written invitation or both. Make sure the venue is easily accessible.

Consider preparing a press kit and sending it in advance – or at least have it available at the time. When fixing that time, check with the journalists whom you most hope to attend, to make sure that it suits them.

Do not ever invite the press to receive hard news at your conference and then give one of them the jump on the rest. Embargoes must be honoured.

Keep press conferences short. And provide modest hospitality and sustenance.

Always do a follow up – a telephone call or a further meeting – with everyone of importance to whom you made your presentation. Then hope for the best.

At that stage, much depends on the competition for space. Journalists are always hungry for stories but short of pages in which to publish them. So you take your chance and hope that you will not be ousted by some more pungent story or (perhaps) by some unhappy scandal.

So much for your chasing the press. What if they are after you? In biblical words: 'Respect and suspect'. Respect them because they have power which can be used for or against you; suspect them, because it is their duty to report, and they may do you or your clients much harm.

A journalist's duty is to extract as much information as possible from you. So start by listening to them. Where are they from? Why are they interested in the information sought? What are they prepared to tell you about what they know, before you decide whether or not to respond and if so, then how?

Can you get time to prepare? It's always better not to say 'No'. Instead, try: 'I'll be pleased to speak to you, but I can't at the moment because I'm just going into a conference with a client. Would you like to call back this afternoon?'

Then, armed with as much information as you can get, prepare – by asking the same four questions that you should use in preparing any presentation.

QUESTION ONE – Who are they? Identify the newspaper and individual.

QUESTION TWO – What do they want from you? What is their angle, their purpose, their object?

QUESTION THREE – What is your message? What do you want to put across?

QUESTION FOUR – How? What method should you use to explain your case?

Once you have answered the four questions, you can consider whether to invite the journalist in to see you, on your ground; whether you are better to organize a quiet lunch or drink; or whether you are prepared to deal with the matter by telephone.

You can consult with your colleagues and decide whether (for instance) you should provide any, and if so what, documentation. Remember that journalists are busy people; all prefer to get better results with less work; and some are lazy. So feed through your material or your message in the form most likely to be published in the way that you want.

We teach speechmakers and other trainees how to cope with television or radio, in the comparatively few and precious seconds which will be given to them. It's the same with the press. Do your 'PREP'. (Compare with Chapter Eighteen.)

State your POSITION – 'Our firm is providing a new service for its clients.'

REASON – 'because . . .'

EXAMPLE – 'For instance, I have been able to . . .' Then back to the

POSITION – 'So we shall expand this service, so as to cover . . .'

In radio or television terms, they call it a 'sound bite'. It's a compact, structured and concise summary of what you want to get across.

If the press does the dirty on you, what can you do? As a start, try going direct to the paper's editor and complaining, bluntly and frankly, of the way that you or your clients have been treated. If you are lucky and the editor is fair, you may even get an apology.

You could try the Press Council, especially if there has been any improper invasion of privacy.

Otherwise, you could take your revenge by refusing to deal with the individual journalist or with the paper. But this is a last resort.

Philosopher Bertrand Russell refused to grant interviews after he had been seriously ill in China. A resentful Japanese newspaper reported that he had died and refused to retract the story, even when he telephoned them.

When he was passing through Japan on his way home, the press tried to interview Russell. The secretary handed out printed slips to each reporter, reading: 'Since Mr Russell is dead, he cannot be interviewed!'

Newspapers take live stories and, in general, are friendly sources.

Not everyone would agree, however. In the words of Lord Longford: 'On the whole, I would not say that our press is obscene. I would say that it trembles on the brink of obscenity!'

Which brings us back to the 'suspect' principle. It is the job of journalists to ferret out the truth. They are entitled and bound to ask the appropriate questions. If they feel that you are evading or dodging a question, they will probe until they consider that they have received a fair answer.

If you have nothing to hide, then you can be open. If you are prepared to reveal what it is that you must hide and why, then go 'off the record'. But if evasion is essential, for whatever reason, you must acquire and practice the art, with professional skill.

So regard and treat the press as human. Understand what journalists are after and try to provide it. Then give of your best and hope for the best and if you are lucky, you will win better reports than you sometimes deserve. Conversely, if you are cavalier with the press, you will probably get what you deserve.

48   Radio – the sightless wonder

Ask any experienced radio producer or interviewer which are the best and the worst categories of performer. The best? Professionals, like most actors or politicians – especially trained and experienced politicians, because they are skilled at making up their own scripts as they go along. The worst? Executives – industrialists and business people. Believing that their success in commerce qualifies them to harness sound without sight, they mumble and ramble and 'er' and 'um' and prevaricate and make the worst of themselves and of their case.

So if you must make a radio appearance, how can you avoid joining the ranks of the awful? Here's a good concise victim's guide.

Start by arriving on time. If you are late, you will either miss the show or never be asked back.

The ultimate in reporters' lateness provided me with one of my few and cherished chances to enter the *Guinness Book of Records*. I had arrived my customary few minutes early for a local radio recording session. The reporter was late. After half an hour of waiting, I made my revolutionary proposal to the man in charge: 'Let me interview myself!' I suggested. I promised to ask myself only the nastiest and most probing questions, and to give myself the most brilliant answers. 'You can dub in the reporter's voice when he turns up!' To my delight, he agreed.

I carried out the interview with immaculate courtesy, but dug away at my own weak points, being sure, of course to supply succinct and appropriate replies. When the interviewer turned up, with the judicious use of the razor blade he duly dubbed his voice into the question. And no one noticed.

Next, approach radio with a touch of paranoia. Whether you are asked questions by telephone ('down the line') or in the studio, unless you are certain that your words will not be broadcast, take care.

President Reagan was to make a crucial 'state of the nation' broadcast. The producer said to him: 'Now, Mr President, please will you say something so that we can have some sound level. Tell us what you think about our United States economy?'

'I must tell the nation,' said the President, 'that our economy is in one hell of a mess!' Unfortunately for him, the studio had already been linked up to loudspeakers in the White House and Press Room. Despite the frantic efforts of the President's advisers, his words were beamed around the world, to the huge delight of all those who take pleasure in someone else's awful error.

So concentrate. Ignore the interviewer sipping coffee, news flashes on a monitor screen, people through the glass in the control room or busy 'cutting' tapes in the next studio. Allow your mind to move off your subject and you are in trouble.

The best help to concentration is: posture. Sit up.

If your piece is recorded, do not worry if you 'fluff'. 'Sorry,' you say. 'I'll repeat that.' Then do – and leave it to the interviewer or editor to slice out your initial and muddled effort. They will not hold that against you. They have too many miseries of their own to correct and they are professionals.

Do not be bullied. A good interviewer asks questions and lets the victim get on with answering them. If you do not get fairness, complain. If you need time to think out the answer to a question, ask to have it repeated. If you cannot properly reply, say so.

Sincerity is vital. Only your voice can convey it. Be concise and relevant. Answer the questions you are asked – briefly, accurately and to the questioner's point. Then elaborate or qualify your reply.

Brighten your broadcast with stories and analogies. Talk to the interviewer as though you were engaging in ordinary chat, with no one else listening. Concentrate on the interviewer and forget your audience.

Take care what you wear, for the sound it can make. Radio broadcasters are heard and not seen. A young woman deafened listeners with a crackling roar every time she breathed. A particularly sensitive directional mike picked up and magnified the rustle of her new dress.

Avoid noisy bangles, beads or leather jackets. Do not click ball-point pens or fiddle with paper clips. Above all, do not rattle paper. If you work from a script or from notes on separate sheets, do not turn them over. Lift each gingerly and silently from the pile.

Avoid drinking too much 'hospitality coffee' before committing yourself on air for any length of time. Mother Nature often destroys the best of presentations.

Keep off alcohol. Many careers have been ruined by that most hazardous marriage of broadcast and booze.

Nothing is more daunting in prospect, more challenging in reality or more lasting in memory than a broadcast confrontation. If your interviewer gets nasty, keep cool. You lose control of yourself and of your audience at the same moment. Lose command of yourself and you cannot command the argument.

If they want to turn you into a human sacrifice, don your armour. If they wish to make a meal of you, ensure that you are thoroughly indigestible.

Remember, an interviewer's job is to produce good radio. So if you suspect trouble, try threatening to 'dry' if your interrogator is unfair.

If you are faced with guest opponents, battle for your fair share of precious time. And always try to commandeer the ending.

After a particularly bloody radio confrontation, a supporter of mine said: 'You did well – but not well enough. How could you let that (expletive) get the last word?'

So be courteous but firm. Find out in advance how long your piece will last. Is it to be pre-recorded, in which case your 'fluffs' can be removed but also your best arguments edited out? Or will you go out 'live', so that your errors cannot be erased?

If offered an invitation to speak ill of some other person, as opposed to criticizing their opinions, remember that broadcast defamation is libel. Keep awake and take care.

Finally, make sure you are off the air before you relax and speak your mind. Concentrate until you are sure that you can no longer be heard.

49   TV – your head on the box

Television is every other sort of presentation writ large. It is the ultimate challenge for the speechmaker or other presenter, with (in general) a maximum audience for exploitation and error alike. Add the dimension of sight to sound and errors can pile high.

Every TV second counts and must be cherished. Compare the cost of buying, say, a ten-second 'plug' on commercial radio as opposed to the same amount of time on TV. The higher cost of television reflects its potential power and impact.

Every peril in radio presentation is concentrated, condensed and made visible. Politicians and business people alike are made and broken by the oblong screen. So if you have the chance to project yourself, your company or your cause on the box, follow the same rules as for radio, plus:

- The make-up person will take charge of your face, but you should adjust your own dress. Remember that the box magnifies the most minor blemishes: tie askew; white label sticking up from the back of dark jacket; dandruff on the shoulders; dangling shirt tail, drooping socks, laddered tights.
- Dress in clothes suitable to the image you wish to present and in colours and patterns that do not move, shimmer or 'strobe' on the screen. Checks or narrow stripes on jackets or (especially) dresses, suits or ties are the major culprits.
- Avoid 'flashy' jewellery, in either sense of the word. Best colours are pastel shades; worst, black, white and red.
- Fix your eyes on the interviewer or at your fellow gladiator, thrown into the same ring for the pleasure of the public. Eye expression is crucial for contact, confidence and conveying sincerity. Victims who surreptitiously swivel their eyes – perhaps for a glimpse of the audience or the clock, or a peep at the monitor screen – are done for. Immediately, by chance or by malicious design, the camera switches to them and they look shifty, cunning, wicked . . .
- If you are to be interviewed in a separate place or studio from your interviewer, ask for an 'eye-line'. Find out where to look so that you appear to be fixing your eyes in line with your interrogator.
- Keep gestures to the minimum. The rarer and the more sparing, the greater the effect. Watch amateurs on the screen – the unconscious scratchers, twitchers, lip-lickers and nose pickers, the finger-waggers,

147

arm-wavers and (even more disastrous) pounders of fists and strummers of fingers – but copy the professionals.

- Sit up and keep still. Animation should come from your face, eyes and speech, and not from your body. Treat your interviewers with kindness and – as they are probably human – they may return the compliment.
- Smoking will probably be forbidden in the studio.
- At the start of the interview do not smirk. Instead smile – and then look at your interviewer.
- If you read from a prepared script, you will be helped by a 'teleprompter'. Be not afraid. It is controlled by the performer and the operator will go at your speed.
- Do not look at the clock. The studio manager – probably the person who led you to your seat – will stand within view of the interviewer and relay time signals.
- The time to dive in with your capture-the-last-word summary is when the 'come to a close' hand windmill signal starts. If it means interrupting someone else, go ahead – courteously but firmly.

To succeed on the screen, you must project your personality, radiating relaxation without relaxing, confidence without appearing smug or superior and sincerity without gush: the same qualities, in fact, that apply to personal presentations, but with far greater tact.

So how to achieve these evidently desirable aims? Take training. Watch yourself on a video screen. Get as much practice as the media will allow you.

You cannot practise for an interview, but you can follow the crucial rules. Prepare. Listen to the question; have it repeated if you do not understand – or if you want extra time to think; then reply to that question, not to some other one that you would have preferred to hear. Then add whatever you wish.

A Cabinet Minister was lost while driving through the countryside. He stopped at a village and wound down his window. 'Where am I, please?' he asked a passer-by.

'You are in your car, sir,' he replied, unhesitatingly.

'That,' replied the Minister 'is a perfect parliamentary answer. It is brief, accurate – and adds nothing whatever to the sum total of human knowledge!'

So try to add a touch of information, a spice of wit or a modicum of common sense or your TV presentation is hardly likely to sparkle. But do so by addition. 'The answer to your question is . . . But perhaps we could ask a different question?' Or: 'The answer is yes – but please remember that. . . .' First answer, then add.

In a confrontation or debate keep calm. Do not underestimate your opponent. If you are defeated, announce that you will fight back. Or flick away the defeat like a fly from your shoulder, hoping that it does not matter.

If interrupted say: 'May I finish my sentence please . . .' or 'If you don't mind, I'll just finish this point then give way . . .' Then wrap up your argument as swiftly as you can.

Above all and again – concentrate. Forget the millions of viewers. A moment's distraction may spell disaster. Lose concentration and you lose all.

Follow instructions, and if you mess up your performance then at least it may be someone else's fault!

The joy of television is that everyone both hears and sees you and trouble can only be a fraction of an error away. So sit back. Pause and think. And the best of luck to you.

Period 1

PART 6

Chairing

50   Winning from the chair

Speechmakers must know and practice the techniques of chairing. Whether you are controlling a meeting of your own partners, colleagues or employees or coping with clients or with creditors, the success or failure of the meeting will depend on you. You are both the master of ceremonies in charge of ceremonial content and the compère. You decide not only whether or not you speak and if so, about what – but also who else speaks, when and for how long.

So how do you get your way when you are in charge? Chairing meetings is both a science and an art, and needs to be taught and learned. Here are the basic rules.

Start with preparation. Your meeting should be based on a carefully plotted plan, formalized into the agenda. You must decide on the order of business, to suit your purpose; and accept responsibility for the operation of the agenda, as you do for the meeting itself.

In practice, deviations may be essential. One participant arrives late, another must leave early . . . one item must be reached, another could be left . . . But explain the structure to the participants and then you can reasonably hope for their co-operation, based on their consent.

As with the meeting as a whole, so with its individual parts. Consider:

- Which are likely to be troublesome. Do you put them at the beginning to get them out of the way – or at the end, when you hope that the participants will give way, so as to get away?
- What is your time balance? Have you too much for the time available – or so little that there is not enough meat for the meeting?
- Does the order of business suit your convenience and that of your allies? Who (for instance) will need to arrive late or to leave early?

Next: collect, inform and prepare your allies. Many major decisions at well-run meetings are taken before they begin, but without the participants feeling that they are rubber-stamping.

Look at contentious issues; decide on the results that you wish to achieve; target your allies and discuss tactics and strategies with them; and get your team into order.

Make sure that you yourself are fully briefed on all issues. As with all other presentations, you must appear and then be confident – which is only possible if you are thoroughly briefed.

So your meeting begins. You are in the Chair, with the agenda before you. Your company secretary, assistant, appropriate partner or other ally is beside you. What qualities should you cultivate and show?

To start with: fairness. The Chair must be fair.

If you can get others to put forward your viewpoint, do. If you decide to speak, do so clearly. As a well-known accountant once began: 'I will now give you the benefit of my well-considered bias!'

Fairness includes:

- Giving all points of view a fair hearing, which means:
- Calling on those who disagree with you and giving them fair time.
- Listening to others who disagree with you – they may be right.

Next: to control others, you must start by controlling yourself. The more turbulent the gathering, the greater the stress, the more difficult the problem, the more urgent the circumstances, the more poignant the attack, the greater the need for calm.

Any loss of temper must be deliberate. There are many occasions when you will feel anger and few when it is appropriate and helpful to show it.

Then: in the Chair, you need swift, clear and objective reactions. You must sift out the reality of a problem, burrow into the depths of an argument and find the real issues – sort out, recognize and advocate sensible solutions.

Concentrate – all the time. Once you have spotted the key problems and solutions, target them.

You may wish to steer the meeting away from a point. That also requires an ability to stand back, to assess the problem and to act or to avoid acting accordingly.

Next: the Chair is in charge of compromise. Where the object of the current exercise is to reach a decision which is acceptable to the gathering, it is for the Chair to steer the meeting towards consensus. Edmund Burke once said: 'All government – indeed every human benefit and enjoyment, every virtue, and every prudent act – is founded on compromise and barter.'

Acceptable compromise is the prime objective of the Chair, a goal that is often difficult to reach without much patience and bargaining. You offer alternatives which move back and forth, sometimes during the course of a speech, during a debate, or even over a long series of meetings. A middle ground must exist. Your job is to find it.

As usual, you start by listening. No one is prepared to climb down unheard. Contestants who believe that they have been granted a fair fight may not begrudge an adverse decision, and if they can save at least part of their case from the wreckage, they may believe that their time was well spent, their meeting well run.

For this purpose, you are the referee or the umpire. Depending on the organization, the rules and the occasion, you may be entitled or even expected to put your own view. But if this view is to prevail, you will have to listen to those of others.

The American Declaration of Independence proclaims that governments derive their just powers from the consent of the governed. Any person in the Chair who loses the consent of the meeting may forfeit the right to govern that assembly.

It may be that the decision must be specific, firm, without doubt or movement. But compromise – each side giving some ground at the side, to achieve agreement in the centre – is the ordinary route to negotiated settlement. And do not hesitate to back down if you have little to gain but much to lose through confrontation.

It is better to compromise your argument than yourself, your position, or your authority. Retreat and compromise are partners in discretion. To do so with grace is the mark of an experienced and sensible Chair.

In his famous *Tom Brown's Schooldays*, Thomas Hughes wrote: 'He never wants anything but what's right and fair, only when you come to settle what's right and fair, it's everything that he wants and nothing that you want. And that's his idea of a compromise. Give me the Brown compromise when I'm on his side.'

We all know the Brown compromise. It means giving way. If the other side is the one who yields, it is for the Chair to provide the unsuccessful contestant with a decent chance to save face. If dignity is preserved and humiliation avoided, he will return to argue another day. Only if you wish to get rid of him for ever should you see a contestant ground down and out. In the process, you may create in him an unquenchable thirst for revenge. That is the loser's price for total victory, apparent and real.

When it comes to deciding whether or not you dissolve a business or an organization, to buy or to sell, to hire, to fire, the answer may have to be yes or no. Even then, perhaps you should dissolve only part of the set-up, adjourn rather than destroy, buy or sell a part, rather than the whole; give notice, rather than dismiss summarily; hire fewer, rather than none.

General Eisenhower liked to say that decent people travel in the centre of the road because on either side there is a gutter. You should steer your meetings into the centre. On either side there lurks ill feeling. Equally, you must be able, where necessary, to lead your meeting into taking an unequivocal decision, allowing no doubt. The Chair is as much in charge of that firm resolve as of a collective compromise.

Most people who come to meetings want the Chair to succeed. There are exceptions. How do you deal with them?

When deciding how to handle a meeting, you must always assess your audience. When planning how to cope with potential trouble-makers, you must treat them as individuals, on the basis of their particular objectives, style and potential.

Sometimes, people will resort to mischief for the fun of it. Most of us have a touch of mischief in our nature and taking it out on the Chair is an acceptable pastime, especially if either the Chair or the occasion or both are dull.

Treat Mr Mischief with his own medicine. At best, join in the fun. Exchange quip for quip, insult for insult, thrust for thrust. But keep cool and smiling.

If your good nature becomes too stretched, the audience will probably by then be on your side. They want the meeting to get on with its business. They will support you if you chide or reprove the individual or eventually tell him in plain terms to belt up.

The same person may try to achieve the same disruption by attacking your colleagues – the company secretary, perhaps, or the speaker. In general, that requires far more firmness from the Chair. Experienced speakers may actually welcome heckling. You may let them get on with their own defence. Otherwise, you can say:

'Please direct your observations to the Chair.'

'I am sorry, but I cannot allow this discourtesy to continue.'

'I am sure that you do not intend to be discourteous, but I cannot permit attacks on a member of our staff. I am responsible.'

This acceptance of responsibility by the Chair is itself responsible, expected and respected. Even where the fault is not yours, you may have to accept it, especially if you are Chair of the organization and you operate on the Civil Service basis that those elected to office carry all political cans.

Do not allow the mischief-maker to take over your meeting by direct or indirect attack. Some opponents will try to take control by bending the rules – raising endless points of order or using some long-forgotten procedure. Democracy requires firmness from the Chair. Your sense of humour may be your greatest asset, but it must be backed by the meeting's knowledge that you will, if necessary, assert the authority that your colleagues or audience have given you, or which you have assumed because of your position.

Watch out for operators trying to twist the meeting, via the Chair. Their efforts and stratagems may be aimed at all or any of the following:

- To avoid discussion of later items by provoking prolonged argument over earlier ones.
- Conversely, to rush important but controversial items through, with little or no discussion – either so as to win on that matter itself, or intending to reach an item lower down the Agenda; perhaps one which you had placed at the end, hoping it would slide by in the home straight.
- To induce you to call on people on their side or to interrupt or silence their opponents.
- To force a vote they believe they will win – or to avoid one, if they expect defeat.
- To fill the sea of discussion with red herrings so as to destroy the effectiveness of the meeting.

To cope and to control, you must know the procedures of the organization and how they are by rule or by tradition operated and made acceptable.

Dealing with a company or with an insolvency meeting? Then you must study the rules as laid down by law. Chairing a meeting of any organization? Look to its rules and procedures.

Amongst the rules there may be some requirement about when the meeting ends. Even if there is not, watch out for time management. Your participants will expect you to get through the business of the meeting swiftly and efficiently and to get them out and away on time. So over-estimate the time you will need. Leave plenty for discussion, argument, and for calling on participants who may have much to contribute but be too shy to volunteer.

Watch your audience. If it becomes restless, either wind up or change tack or momentum. Use humour. And follow from the Chair the same basic rules of presentational skills as you would if you were trying to win meetings from a platform or a lectern, or from a chair at the side or the back. Pause and use silence; make and keep eye contact; speak clearly and with deliberation.

51   The chair as compère

When you chair a meeting – any meeting – you set the tone. If you are dull, the meeting will be boring. If you are in a lively or contented mood, the meeting will be of good cheer. If you are long-winded, members of the audience not bound to stay will disappear. If you are angry, aggravated, tactless or unkind, this will soon be reflected in the atmosphere. You dare not be off your guard. You are the compère, the life and soul of the gathering – or its death and decay.

Consider the ordinary variety programme. The compère is the link, holding the show together. The same applies to anyone in the chair.

To keep a meeting in good humour, here are some suggestions.

- Do not allow yourself to get aggravated. The more difficult the gathering, the more important it is for you to keep your self-control and your pleasant manner.
- Set the tone before the meeting begins. Try to do your colleagues or your audience the compliment of arriving on time. Spare a few minutes before-hand, if you can, to iron out difficulties and to prevent personal affronts.
- If the meeting is a small one, try not to ignore people who come in late. 'Good evening. Thank you for coming': worthwhile words to make a guilty latecomer feel at ease – and obliged to you. Or at least smile a welcome.
- There is no need to take too literally the old warning: 'Stand up, speak up and shut up.' But do try to let others do as much of the talking as you can. Introduce them, invite them to speak, ask what they think. Link the speakers together and provide the channel through which they communicate. But as for yourself – talk only when you must.
- Let your audience feel that they have had their say. Do your best to allow time for adequate questions.
- Cajole your speakers into brevity and (usually) into agreeing to answer questions at the end. The audience that has its questions answered is almost always satisfied. No one wants to be a rubber stamp.
- Where the session is a small one – a committee or board meeting, for instance – the same principle is even more vital. Let the others put their views before the gathering. Try not to choke off discussion before it comes to an end. Wait until you get the feeling from the meeting that the time has come for the particular debate or argument to be wound up.

Watch others chairing and learn from them – hopefully from their skills, but otherwise from their fumbles. Study the techniques and the cultivation of that confidence which brings style and control in its wake. And if you need training, get it.

Watch your audience. Keep your voice up. At major meetings, use a microphone, and learn how to do it professionally; and judge your volume so that you are heard at the back, even by people who are hard of hearing.

So harness, massage, encourage and promote the interests of those whom you wish to win. Their desire for the success of the meeting, together with your preparation, skill and talent should guarantee success.

52   Debates and procedure

Before you take the chair, study the rules of debate. Your duty: to enforce them. Chair and speakers must know the rules, either to follow them or to attempt to evade them.

When you are in the chair, you are in charge. You have been elected or appointed to your position and you are expected to guide and control the meeting.

When you stand, everyone else is expected to sit and to be silent. If you cannot get order by rapping your gavel and demanding silence, you may have to adjourn the meeting.

Unless the meeting is closed, you are entitled to speak whenever you wish and to prevent anyone else from doing so unless you wish. You have the agenda, but you may vary it.

You should rule by consent. For instance, if you decide to change the order of business, you should explain your reasons. If the bulk of the meeting objects to the change, then you should revert to the original order. You are not a dictator. Forget this and expect rebellion.

Normally, each item of business should be discussed separately. If there are steps to be taken – or even if it is to be resolved to take no action – a resolution or motion will be 'put'. This can be done informally, where there is either no opposition or a general consensus. If discussion does not lead to agreement, there should be a vote.

Where the formalities are being preserved, a motion will be proposed and seconded. It will then be thrown open to the meeting for discussion. The Chair will try to call on people to oppose the motion. After discussion, the proposer will normally exercise the right of reply. Then comes the vote.

If the motion or resolution is not on the agenda, the proposer should be asked to phrase it as concisely and clearly as possible. The Chair who has to put a resolution which even the proposer has not put into sensible English (and into words that can be put into the minute book) is in a bad way. The motion should be clearly stated either by the proposer or by the Chair before it goes forward for debate.

The length and number of speeches will depend on the Chair. But

161

anyone may 'move the closure'. A show of hands will indicate whether those present have had enough of the subject or whether they wish to debate the matter further. If the Chair is in doubt as to whether or not the debate should be closed – or if it would appear partisan to terminate it – then it is easy to test the feeling of the meeting, if necessary by asking whether anyone wishes to 'move the closure'.

If it is agreed that the question 'be now put', then that is what happens. The meeting votes on the motion.

If a motion is carried that the meeting moves on to 'next business', then no vote is taken. It is often better not to reveal the split in the ranks. Or all sides may prefer to avoid a vote that no one is confident of winning.

Some organizations allow the moving of 'the previous question'. If this is passed, it means that the discussion on the current topic terminates and all reference to it is expunged from the minutes. No vote is, of course, taken on the matter in question. There are times when people feel that it would have been better for the organization or meeting had the discussion not taken place at all. 'The previous question' is a useful procedure.

Again, someone may move that the entire meeting be adjourned. It is not only the Chair who can terminate the proceedings. If those present at the meeting wish to put an end to it, they may normally do so. But, of course, there may be debate 'on the adjournment'.

While a debate goes on, participants may interrupt. One common device: a 'point of order'. Anyone is entitled at any time to raise a point, which (in theory at least) concerns the order or conduct of the meeting. A participant is only free to query whether the procedure in hand, what the speaker is saying, or the Chair's ruling . . . is 'in order'. No one should stray away to deal with side issues or use the occasion to deal with substantive issues. Skilled interrupters, though, can often disguise their disruptive attacks as 'points of order', and so insinuate extra speeches where none would otherwise be allowed.

In some meetings, the custom is for speakers to give way on 'points of information' – but generally, it is a matter for them (the speakers themselves) to decide. The Chair cannot force them to give way if they decline to do so. But if the Chair addresses the speaker, the latter may remain standing but (like anyone else at the meeting) must accord the Chair the right to speak – and while he or she does so, must remain silent.

The speaker, then, must 'obey the Chair's ruling'. No one who 'has the floor' may occupy it in the teeth of objection from the chair.

If all motions were proposed, seconded, opposed and voted on as they stood, the job of the Chair would be moderately easy. Too often, there are amendments. In general, motions to amend a resolution must (if seconded) be allowed. They should be considered individually and voted on if necessary. If accepted (whether or not after a vote) they become incorporated into the original motion, which must then be put, as amended. If rejected, they die. An amended motion, once put, can then be the subject of further amendment, with the procedure as before.

Often a skilled Chair can induce the mover of a resolution to vary or extend its terms so as to incorporate the amendment. A peaceful meeting is a Chair's delight.

If an amendment is really no more than an effort to kill the resolution, the Chair may rule it out of order and require the proposer of the amendment to put forward his or her views in opposition to the substantive motion.

The Chair must ensure that all participants are given a reasonable opportunity to express their views, but should not allow a minority to dominate. The Chair is entitled not only to select the speakers but also to sort out the resolution and the amendments, so that the feelings of the meeting may be tested in the fairest way.

Once the meeting has had a reasonable opportunity to express its view, the Chair may – with the consent of the meeting – close the debate and put the motion to the vote.

Additional points:

- Unless a Company's Articles (for the constitution of the organization in question) require motions to be seconded and/or submitted in writing, neither is strictly necessary.
- No one has any right to speak more than once on any motion or amendment – although the proposer of an original motion (but not usually of an amendment) will generally be given the right to reply.
- Once a motion has been defeated, it should not be allowed back before the meeting under some other guise.
- No amendment can be proposed after the original motion has been passed or rejected.
- An amendment cannot be proposed or seconded by those who performed that service for the original motion; but they can, of course, accept (or speak on) the amendments proposed by others.
- If you wish to frame an amendment, usually the best way to do so is by moving that the words you have in mind be added to, omitted from, or inserted into (as the case may be) the motion or resolution.

Meetings are usually governed by consent and common sense. Keep your head and never panic. Speakers should help you, unless you have shown yourself unwilling to act impartially. In that case, the battle is on.

53 Handling speakers

No area of the duties of the Chair is so potentially hazardous as handling the guest speaker. Here are a few hints:

- If you are not sure how your guest pronounces his or her name, ask. Then write it out, phonetically, and keep it in front of you on a card, clearly visible at all times. If it is to be put in a programme, toast list, brochure or other document, check the spelling. Many people are very sensitive about their names.
- Find out in advance as much as you can about the speaker. Members of the royal family are renowned for their splendid memories. They come into a room and promptly recognize people and even remember where they last met. This is partly because they are blessed with good memories, but mainly because they do their homework. The best way to flatter your speakers is to remember all about them. The surest way to antagonize them is to be indifferent to them and to their past achievements.
- If they have incurred expenses, ask them to let you know.
- Remember to say thank you – and to write and repeat your thanks afterwards. You can never express gratitude too often, provided that you at least sound and appear sincere.
- While trying to ensure that the speaker gets a fair hearing, be careful not to interrupt too often. Competent speakers can handle their own audiences and prefer, where possible, to do so. The Chair should exercise authority with moderation.
- Prime speakers on the length of time you want them to speak: always give them at least ten per cent less time than you are prepared to accept. Ask them whether they would like to be reminded when they are a few minutes away from the appointed end. Most speakers will gladly agree, and will not then resent a reminder. If necessary, push a note in front of the speaker, with '5 minutes please', in large letters. Do this without pre-arrangement and you may upset them.

Much of the Chair's job is done before the meeting begins. If you read this book beforehand, you should do better at the time. Otherwise, bring it with you.

So all that remains is to wish you – in the role of speaker or in the Chair – the very best of luck. However experienced and able you may be, however carefully you follow the rules, there is no substitute for good fortune. May you be blessed with luck, skill and success on your feet, both in and out of the Chair.

BOOK TWO

Draft speeches

PART 8

Model speeches

54   Openings

Prominent people are frequently invited to declare functions or occasions open – from trade exhibitions or fairs to sales conferences, from new premises to the same old annual garden fête run by the local church or by the trade benevolent society.

The opening pronouncement may be one of two varieties, which must be carefully distinguished from each other – the formal opening and keynote speech. Either way, you may be asked to speak because of your eminence; because of past usefulness or benevolence; in hope of future service or cash; or because of a mixture of all of them. If you want to be asked again, though, you must do a good job this time.

The following are examples of brief openers, plus skeletons of keynote speeches. By their nature, these presentations are expected to be longer and fuller, and likely to provoke thought or action rather than an atmosphere of generalized goodwill.

Opening a trade fair

Ladies and Gentlemen,

Some ancient peoples had disgusting habits – like examining the entrails of animals to see whether the auguries were satisfactory for some proposed enterprise. I have taken a much shorter and pleasanter route – to the greater oracle of this organization, Mr . . . He tells me that the preparations for today's gathering have been carried out swiftly, in harmony and without a whiff of industrial ill-will; that advance orders already total half as much again as those received at this stage last year; that we are expecting one of the biggest gatherings in the history of the trade.

What a delight it is, then, for me to sound the tocsin and to proclaim in advance the value, the importance and the success of this year's vital exhibition.

On your behalf as well as my own, I thank our organizers, Mr . . . and Mrs . . . and Miss. . . , as well as . . . and their staff. If the arrangements look smooth and simple, it is because the organizers have worked so hard.

Now – in anticipation of good companionship, top sales and a continuation and ending to the fair which will be as successful as its inception – I have the greatest pleasure in declaring the fair – open.

Opening an industrial exhibition

Madam Chairman*, Ladies, and Gentleman,

We are not as wasteful in this industry as our colleagues who build ships. We will not smash and spill good champagne on the side of our machines (*or furniture or equipment – or as the case may be*). Instead, we will use the wine to drink a series of toasts.

First, we salute the prosperity of our trade/industry/company. Today's effort is of vast importance to it and so to us all.

Second, we salute the health of those whose efforts have created this exhibition – from our chairman/chief executive/organizer (*etc.*) at the top of our trees, to the carpenter, the electricians and the cleaners who have firmed down its roots. Our warmest thanks to them all.

Third, we salute the future of our great new product, the . . . (*here give details*).

This is an exhibition of machinery/equipment/furniture (*or as the case may be*). It is designed to exhibit products – and to help design exhibits. Its success depends on orders and cheques, not on words – however warm or well meant.

Symbolically only, then, I am proud to launch this exhibition. By its end, I hope that at dinner tonight we shall drink a toast to the beginning of a new era of prosperity for our trade/industry/company.

Madam Chairman, Ladies and Gentlemen – I declare the exhibition open.

Opening a new building

Ladies and Gentlemen,

Like most of us here, I have survived many happy, successful but hideously cramped, cribbed, cabined and confined years in our old premises. It is therefore with delight that I can declare this new building open.

Think what we can now do. Each of us can swing as many cats as we wish; turn around in our chairs without being accused of indecent

---

* Horrid? Yes, but still common. Better yet, use the Chair's name: 'Mrs Brown . . .'

assault; drink a cup of coffee without worrying whether we have swallowed our neighbour's sustenance.

Seriously, we can now expand our business and, inevitably I hope, our profits – so bringing delight to our bank manager, to our shareholders and to all of us who are a proud part of our enterprise. We hope that we will pack our custom-built building with more and more satisfied customers. Certainly we shall be able to do our work not only with greater economy and speed but also in greater comfort – and that is important because the environment of our workforce has taken priority in the plans for our new structure.

Ladies and Gentlemen – this is a time for building. The bricks, the mortar, the cement, the steel – all is in place. We must now build the business – and have done with the words, mine or anyone else's. I thank the architects, Messrs. . . ; I thank all of you for putting up with the inevitable discomfort involved in the move; I thank those who have organized this reception and, in particular, our own Miss . . . I most happily declare this new building – open.

Opening an old people's home

Friends,

A sage once divided charity into categories of merit. At the bottom came gifts where the donor was known to the recipient and the recipient to the donor. At the top were those where neither knew the other. This old people's home has been created by the generosity of the trade/industry – individuals, firms and companies – each giving so that others may enjoy their old age.

There is far too much clap-trap talked about old age, isn't there? Autumn years . . . senior citizens . . . well earned years of pleasurable rest . . . Well, that's how they should be. Unfortunately, they are too often years of loneliness and poverty.

But not for the residents of this home. Here they will have privacy in their own rooms, companionship in the communal rooms, relaxation in the gardens, peace when they want it but kindly supervision and help when they need it.

Your committee has had more trouble in selecting residents than it has had even in the raising of the money for the building. With hundreds in need, how do we select the tens who get help? Who are we to select who are to live here in happiness and who to die alone? All have served the trade/industry; all deserve service from us.

So my function is two-fold. First, I join you in looking back with pride and thankfulness to what has been achieved – and in thanking those responsible. Our special gratitude to . . . and . . . and . . .

Second, we must now service and expand the home.

I once went to a very rich man and asked him for the money to create a building for a certain charity. He replied: 'How are you going to run it . . . to staff it . . . to pay for it once it is opened? I am tired of giving buildings and then having the same people come back to me and saying: "What's the good of giving the building without the running costs?" '

Well, we have the building – given not by one person but by many – our thanks to them all. We have enough to keep the place going for . . . months. Did you know that it costs about . . . to pay for each resident for each year?

So in thanking you all for your kindness and generosity . . . for your presence here today and for your presents to this home in the past – I ask for your support in the future. We close one era when we open another.

It is with the greatest of pride – and in the hope and confidence that this home will provide a great comfort and joy to its residents – that I declare the building open.

Keynote – sales conference

This Company lives through sales – and we all live through the Company. It is by building the sales that we can ensure a prosperous future not only for the organization but also for each one of us here. We are part of the same enterprise. This conference has been carefully designed to help us all in our work.

I am happy to introduce to you not only the conference but also our new season's range/tremendously successful line/new equipment, specially designed for our market by . . . (*or as the case may be*).

(*Description and explanation of product/service, etc. follows.*)

The key to this conference, then, lies in expanding our territory and our sales – but with the help of our new lines/products/equipment (*etc.*).

My introduction marks the beginning of two/three days/weeks of intensive discussion/instruction/conference – which I am confident will herald the start of a year of distinction and prosperity.

The conference will also enable us to get to know each other socially and to enjoy that good companionship that is so much part of the atmosphere of this organization. On behalf of your board/ directors/chairman, I wish you good days and fruitful discussions – followed by brisk and burgeoning sales and continuing success for the company and for all of you. I am happy to declare this conference duly opened. Good luck to you all.

Opening an exhibition

We are honoured to be holding in our shop/factory an exhibition of paintings by Martha Smith and of sculpture by Roger Jones, drawing their inspiration from our trade/industry.

You will all have seen the brochure/catalogue, designed by our own Walter Brown. One half, read from the top, sets out the work of Martha Smith; the other half, reading from the bottom of the page, lists the sculpture of Roger Jones.

I know that our two guest artists will not be offended if I say that the hanging committee felt a little like the brochure – not quite sure which way up to hang some of the pictures or to stand some of the sculptures. No matter. The shapes are glorious and the colours superb.

You will, I am sure, be as delighted as I was to learn that each of the artists has offered to donate one work to our trade charity. This is immensely kind of them and we are very grateful.

I am told it took Martha Smith about a week to create each painting and Roger Jones took nearly as long with his larger sculptures. Still, it is not the time that matters but the spirit.

Many years ago, when a pound was twenty shillings and worth a sovereign of gold, the painter Rex Whistler claimed £500 for a portrait in oils, commissioned by a client. No price had been agreed and he sued on a *quantum meruit*, claiming that £500 was reasonable and right.

Counsel cross-examined him on behalf of the client. 'Mr Whistler,' he said, 'how long did it take you to paint this portrait?'

'Three days,' the artist replied.

'Then are you asking my client to pay £500 for three days' work?'

'No,' retorted the painter. 'I am claiming £500 for a lifetime of work which enabled me to paint this portrait in three days.'

It was not the time that was taken by our generous artists which is the dominant matter – it is their lifetime of skill which has made each of them predominant in his or her own sphere. They are giving us of their own best works. I offer them on behalf of all of us our warmest thanks.

The time has now come, then, for each of us to browse, to look and to learn. There may be some of you who are capable artists – I have trouble in drawing a circle with the help of a compass. A cynic remarked: 'He who can, does; he who can't, teaches.' We might say: 'He who can't visits exhibitions and admires those who can.'

We have an exhibition now and here. I thank the artists for bringing that collection together and enabling us to enjoy it at our leisure. I have much pleasure in declaring the exhibition – open.

55   Guests of honour

To the disabled

Some people are obviously disabled because they are missing a limb. . . , because parts of their body do not work properly. But I know plenty of people whose bodies are in excellent shape, but who never use their heads. I congratulate this organization on its work because it helps disabled people to make the best possible use of their assets – and encourages people here, who have absolutely excellent heads, to use them, and to compensate for their physical disabilities.

We must each make use of the assets we have. This organization helps its members to recognize and to exploit them to the full.

Far too many disabled folk are left bored and lonely at home. You help to get them out into society, so that they are part of the world, making their contribution and enjoying doing so.

Your committee are themselves disabled – but by their work they have not only brought new and vigorous life to others, but have – I know and they know – enriched their own lives in the process.

I congratulate the committee for their efforts; I welcome so many members here today; I am delighted to be your guest of honour – and to give any impetus I can to your efforts, today and every day – and I thank you very much for inviting me.

Now, my friends – on with the party . . .

Note: This approach is, of course, designed for the physically handicapped. A variation for the mentally handicapped follows.

For the mentally handicapped

Our object must be to enable each member of our society to make the best of his or her assets.

When I went into the Army, many years ago, my closest friend was a postman's son. We had sat our aptitude tests together.

I found the verbal reasoning and intelligence test easy. The first question sticks in my mind: 'The sun is blue, yellow, green – cross out the answers which do not apply.'

Dick managed the first couple of dozen questions without too much difficulty, but he then came to a dead halt. His vocabulary was limited.

177

Next came technical aptitude. I spent the first half hour trying to assemble a lock and the second a bicycle pump. I failed totally on both. Dick performed all ten puzzles swiftly and without difficulty.

Regardless of our intellectual or mental ability, we all have different talents, and the handiwork done by members of this club and on exhibition here today shows how much pleasure they can give to others – and at the same time, to themselves. They have a right to develop their talents to the full – and I congratulate the committee and organizers of this club for the work they have done to enable the members to enjoy their lives.

This place is full of happiness, isn't it? People have the odd idea that where human beings are not blessed with the same degree of mental aptitude as themselves, they are necessarily less happy. I congratulate you all on the measure of happiness which this organization brings not only to its members but also to those who love and care for them.

Thank you, then, for inviting me to be your guest of honour, you, the organizers and committee and your members. I am at your service and proud to be here among you. The very best of luck to you all.

Note: This speech is essentially aimed at the organizers. You must always decide to whom you are going to speak. If you are addressing a school audience, never mind the parents, talk to the youngsters. Thus:

School celebration

Teachers, Parents, Boys and Girls,

I am here as a Governor of the school. Unlike the Governor of a prison who is top boss, a Governor of this school is only one of a group – all of whom work together with the Head and the staff to help you, the pupils, to make the most of your time here.

Why, then, is this school different from others? Why should I and my fellow Governors be proud to be associated with it?

First . . .

Second . . .

Third . . .

Well, I expect you know the story of Henry VIII – and what a happy time he had, didn't he? I say to you – as he said to each of his wives in turn: 'I shall not keep you long!'

Didn't he say that? Unfortunately many of the best historical tales are not necessarily accurate. Like the one about Oliver Cromwell. Charles II definitely did dig him up, lift off the lid of his coffin, chop off his head and put it on a pike on the roof of Westminster for six years – that is the ancient Hall of the Palace of Westminster, the only part of Parliament which is still standing almost as it was when it was first built.

What cannot be proved is the old story that when the head was on the pike on the roof of the Hall, it dripped blood onto the flagstones for six years. Then one night there was a terrible storm and the head blew down with a horrible thud. A huge cat ran out of the crypt, grabbed the head in its teeth and was rushing off towards the door when the Serjeant at Arms – our sort of Head Prefect – drew his sword, speared the cat and grasped old Cromwell's head.

The next part is true. The head was then taken up to Sidney Sussex College in Cambridge and duly buried. It is there to this day.

I do not recommend that you use that story in your history essays – but I do hope that someone will take you to Westminster Hall one day. If you look carefully enough, you might even find Oliver Cromwell's blood still on the flagstones.

Anyway, before my blood is spilled for taking up too much of your time, I will simply wish you well . . . congratulate you all on a tremendous year of success . . . wish you happiness for the holidays . . . (*or as the case may be*).

Good luck to you all.

Note: An imaginative tale enlivens any speech. Draw from your own experience or from anyone else's – but do not talk down to your audience, whatever its age.

At prize-givings, avoid telling children how badly you did when you were young – even if it was true, they will not believe it. Do by all means remember the children who get no prizes. Skip the tale of how dreadfully Winston Churchill did as a boy – and try something like this:

Prize-giving

Mrs Green, Parents, Boys and Girls,

It's marvellous being top of the class, head of the school, a prefect or a monitor, isn't it? Even being in the top form gives you status. You are a senior character, looked up to by the new pupils.

Unfortunately, no sooner do we reach one pinnacle – no sooner do we get to the top of one mountain – than we slide right down again and, once more, become new boys and new girls – 'freshers' as they call them in college.

All you leavers will be feeling a bit nostalgic today. When you start your new school, university or college – at your work – you will be back down at the bottom again.

Naturally, those of you who have won prizes today – and I congratulate you all – will treasure them as a memento of a happy and successful occasion. Still, you will be no higher on the ladder than those of your friends who will be joining you at your work without prizes. And next time, it may be their turn.

In many ways it is a pity that we have to have prizes at all isn't it? Many people here, I know, will have worked very hard and done extremely well but will not be getting rewarded. Never mind. Your turn may come.

Just think of all the successful politicians and scientists – and teachers – whom everybody congratulated and who won all the rich prizes in civilization. Ten years later, where are they? Where is the businessman . . . the captain of industry . . . the big boss. . . ? They retire and are forgotten about and that is the end of them.

Well, you are not retiring, any of you, are you?

Apart from presenting your prizes, which I shall look forward to doing, my task is simply to wish you all well – wherever you are going, whatever you do. I hope that your ambitions will be fulfilled.

As for those of you who remain – I hope that you will have very happy times ahead. Next year, some of you will reach the top. Enjoy it. Jimmy Durante, the famous American comedian, once remarked:

'Be nice to people you pass on your way up because you will pass them again on your way down!'

To all of you who are going up or down, and even to a few who are staying still, the very best of luck to you – and thank you for inviting me to be with you today.

Note: Never mind the parents. They will enjoy your talking to the children. Adapt your words according to the age of the youngsters. Chat to them as if they were your own. A child can see through pomposity or insincerity far better than an adult. You may be elevated onto a platform – but pretend that you are in and amongst them. Indeed, it is sometimes possible to climb off the stage. On great state occasions, the dignities and proprieties have to be maintained. But when talking to children, I try to perch on the edge of a table, to walk down among them, or even to remove my jacket and hang it on the back of a chair – that almost always breaks the ice.

A beginning that I was taught by a member of the Magic Circle – and which requires a certain sleight of hand that I have enjoyed acquiring – goes like this.

Magic opening

Good Morning,

I am sorry that you are all looking so sad. I promise you that I am not going to bore you. So you can relax. There's a chap sleeping at the back – I can see you.

What's this . . . (*holding up a coin in left hand*).

It's an ordinary coin, isn't it? (*vanish coin*).

Now where is it? (*inevitable gasps and cries of 'It's in your pocket . . . It's up your sleeve . . .'*)

No, it's just gone, but you are not going until I have finished talking to you, so you might just as well relax . . .

Note: At one famous school, there was a long pause before proceedings began. It was a small room, with about 50 restless youngsters in it. I said: 'I am sorry to keep you. We shall be starting soon.' 'I shall say when we begin,' the Headmaster reproved me, publicly and rudely. This sort of treatment of a guest is unusual – but one reproof of that sort is too many. Always consult the organizers, chief citizens or bosses of the place or occasion before opening your honoured mouth.

Equally you must choose your opening – and, for that matter, tailor your speech according to the nature and dignity of the occasion. If in doubt, relax.

There are those who regard too informal an approach as a slur – as not recognizing the importance either of the occasion or (worse) those present. Tread warily on the dignity of others.

A charitable occasion

Ladies and Gentlemen,

Some regard homes as chattels to be bought and sold. Others – including everybody here – consider a home to be part of a person's entitlement. So is it not scandalous that so many people are so shockingly housed?

I am delighted to be with you today because you are working to provide roofs for the homeless – and more, to help those in homes to put down their roots and to cope.

These are the twin challenges. First, there is the physical worry of providing a place for people to live in decent happiness and contentment. Second, there are many in our civilization who cannot cope with life, even when they have a home to live in.

It is this second category that provides so many of our most underprivileged and deprived. They are inarticulate; they have no Members of Parliament, because they are on no register; they drift rootless through a world that prefers to disregard them.

Just as those who know no medicine tell the chronically depressed to 'snap out of it', making matters infinitely worse – so those who are able to cope with life tend not to understand the troubles of those who are inadequate.

This organization . . . (*set out its objectives*).

This organization . . . (*set out its successes*).

This organization . . . (*set out its remaining problems and how people can help to solve them*).

To this organization and all who struggle for it – and to those whom it seeks to help – my warm and affectionate greetings. If my colleagues and I can be of help to you, we shall be pleased – meanwhile, we are delighted to be associated with your work.

Trade association

Dear Friends,

We are all part of the same trade/industry aren't we? Some of us are more fortunate than others – and those of us who are here today are certainly very lucky.

It has not all been smooth sailing, has it? We can all remember difficult days when we might have been toppled into trouble.

I know some people here who have fought their way back to the top, after slithering into great difficulty, usually through no fault of their own.

However, this benevolent association of ours is designed to help those who have not been fortunate enough to make success a permanence – who need broad shoulders to lean on.

The association has many achievements . . . (*outline them*). The association has great plans . . . (*outline them*).

This gathering today is designed to . . . (*set out objectives of meeting*).

My colleagues and myself are honoured to be part of your work. I am delighted to be your guest/Chair – and I can assure you that I will do everything in my power to help. There but for the Grace of God goes any of us, in our great industry.

56   Introductions, greetings and thanks

To the Minister

Secretary of State, Ladies and Gentlemen,

We are all very grateful to the Minister for joining our family (*or the family of our trade, industry or as the case may be*) when he could so easily and comfortably have been with his own. We appreciate not only what he has said, but the fact that he has snatched the time to be with us today.

I once asked a friend who is a safety officer how he defined his job. 'Oh,' he replied, 'I'm in charge of accidents!' By that token, the Minister is in charge of illness, deprivation and disease (*or unemployment, or as the case may be*). He deals with our problems and his own with admirable calm – and for the sake of us all, we wish him success.

For our part, we recognize the acute dangers created for our society by any condition of unrest. When people regard all politicians with equal distaste, democracy is in danger. A statesman was once defined as a dead politician. We are glad that there are live statesmen like our guest, concerned with the affairs of our land.

(*Then refer to one or two points made by the guest.*)

So once again I thank the Minister for giving this event the accolade of his lively presence – and I ask you to join me in expressing to him our warmest appreciation.

Apologies for a small audience

There is nothing in the speaker's world more embarrassing than bringing a prominent guest to speak to your organization, membership or club and then to find that – for whatever reason – the audience is pathetically small. How do you handle the situation?

- Make your apologies as best you can – relying on the foul weather, apparent trade disputes or any other excuse that seems reasonable.
- If possible, transfer to a smaller room: a few people in a small room make a fine audience, while a small crowd is lost in a huge hall.
- Adapt your introduction to the occasion. Thus:

Distinguished Guest, Ladies and Gentlemen,

I know that we will all be sorry that the weather (*industrial action or as the case may be*) has kept so many people away. We are to have the treat. We are the fortunate few. I am reminded of a story: Mr Brezhnev and Mr Kosygin were discussing the problems of the Jewish minority wanting to emigrate. Mr Brezhnev said: 'Why don't we let them go?'

Mr Kosygin replied: 'Once you let them out, you will have to release the Ukrainians, the Armenians, the Baptists, the Uzbeks . . . and after that, I will go . . . You will be the only person left . . .'

Mr Brezhnev replied: 'No. I shall not be alone. The Soviet Union will be empty!'

We are far from empty this evening, we have here among us the most distinguished members/some of our top industrialists/some of the most famous executives in our trade/industry.

We have gathered here because we know of the work of our guest —and on behalf of us all, I welcome him to . . .

(*Then give details of the guest's work.*)

Ladies and Gentlemen, I present Mr . . .

Livery dinner: response on behalf of guests

(*Court Night of Armourers and Brasiers Company, Armourers Hall, January 1987. Seventy members and guests, all men. Guests of Honour: The Lord Mayor of London and the Sheriffs. Response on behalf of guests.*)

On behalf of all of your guests, Master, I thank you for this glittering and convivial evening. We enjoyed dining with you by candlelight in this splendid old hall and we much appreciate your hospitality.

I am expecially grateful because I have special leave to be away from my parliamentary barracks. My Chief Whip decided, on balance, that it would be sensible for a Labour M.P. to know something about insider eating.

Which reminds me of the story told by that most genial of Welshmen, Lord Elwyn Jones. He swears that he was in court in the West Country while the jury was being sworn in. One of the jurymen asked to be excused from jury duty. 'What is your reason, Mr Brown?' the judge enquired.

'Well, My Lord,' he replied, 'my wife . . . is about . . . to conceive!'

'I don't think that's what you mean, Mr Brown,' said the judge, 'I think what you mean is that your wife is about to be confined. But whether I am right or you are right, I do agree that you should be there!'

My Chief Whip thought that I ought to be here and I salute him for his good nature.

When you invited me, Master, you made it quite plain that I was to be short. But you need not have seated me in front of an hourglass, however ceremonial!

It is a special joy for me to be here with your other guests. Gunner Janner of Larkhill found himself seated beside this gentleman in his gold braid. I asked him: 'And what do you do?' He replied: 'I look after the Royal Navy!'

To sit alongside the First Lord of the Admiralty and Chief of Naval Staff is indeed a treat. I wish that I, too, had (in the words of W. S. Gilbert in *H.M.S. Pinafore*) 'polished up the handle of the big front door' – so that I might not be a mere Labour backbencher.

As for Lord Delisle and Dudley, I salute his House – also known as life after death. I wonder if you were at a recent Labour Party Conference, My Lord?

[*'Only in spirit,' the Tory peer answered.*]

Then your spirit would have enjoyed with me the sight of wonderful Lord Manny Shinwell, aged 94, the only person in the room to support your House and win a standing ovation by saying: 'With so much unemployment in the country, why do you want to take away my job? Haven't you got better things to do with your time?'

Manny would have enjoyed this evening. Like me, he would have appreciated the pleasures of your good company.

As for your ceremony of the loving cup, what a marvellous idea that is. Where I work, of course, everyone loves each other. So much, in fact, that some of us are said to be stabbing each other in the front. Just imagine the loving cup being passed down the two front benches, before Prime Minister's Question Time.

So, in thanking you, may I finish on a serious note. Looking around this magnificent hall tonight, I was thinking of my grandparents, all four of whom came to this country to escape from pogrom and from persecution. They did not take for granted that marvellous freedom which enables us to come here to differ in convivial friendship, about the way in which the country is run, or even the best way in which it should be defended. They treasured our freedom. And they taught their children and their grandchildren that when you have the good fortune to live in a great and free land like Britain, you must take pride in putting back into the country some of that which it has given to you.

This evening, you have been kind enough to invite me – a man who differs much from many of you – as your guest, to enjoy a happy evening in your good company. Tonight I thank you on behalf of all your guests for your hospitality. Together we must hope that the arms and armour which are on the walls of this hall will, like their modern equivalents, be on show and not in use. May your ancient company flourish in a land of both freedom and peace.

Retirement

Mr Chairman, Colleagues and Friends,
It will seem strange to attend a meeting of the . . . without Arthur Jones presiding over it. In the past . . . months/years, he has established himself as the epitome of all that is best in our trade/ industry/organization. There is much to thank him for.

First, I thank him for the kindly way in which he has referred to me. He has been warm, generous and extremely accurate . . .

I can therefore say with equal accuracy that his qualities of . . . and . . . have enlightened his period of office and helped him to create a vibrant organization.

Most of us here are forthright individuals – or we would not be doing this job. We may disagree as to the best way to serve our customers/clients/firm's business interest. We argue, we debate and we dispute. But we are united in our admiration for Mr . . .

Let me list some of his achievements during the past . . . (*expand on his achievements*).

And now that his period of office is over, we know that we will receive the same unassuming, kindly and affectionate welcome – and the same help – from him as a fellow member of our . . . as we did when he held the highest office and honour that we could give him.

Thomas Mordaunt wrote:

> Sound, sound the clarion, fill the fife
> Throughout the sensual world proclaim
> One crowded hour of glorious life
> Is worth an age without a name.

Our friend, and mentor, Arthur Jones has enjoyed his very crowded hour – and he has put glorious life into our proceedings/company/organization. We thank him – and we wish him well.

Distinguished guests

In the unavoidable absence of our President, I have been asked on behalf of the guests to thank our hosts for the splendid austerity lunch (*smoked salmon sandwiches*). I would wish this sort of austerity on all business people everywhere.

In particular, I thank our two guests for joining us – and for their enthusiastic words. How they adjust – physically and mentally – to their eternal round of the world is a mystery. Maybe it is due to the sustenance provided by the international smoked salmon sandwich.

One of our guests is a lawyer, the other is a financier. When justice and money come together on the same platform, then indeed we have found common cause.

We have listened with immense care to their speeches – and I can assure them that we are happy to associate ourselves with their work. (*Then a few sentences about that work*).

We are involved – and we are all grateful to our guests for increasing that involvement. We look forward to seeing our guests back with us again very soon – and next time for a much longer stay.

57   Business speeches

State of the industry

I am happy to have this opportunity to review the state of our industry – and to appeal on behalf of all of us for government understanding and help. We have honourably adhered to governmental guidelines and advice. We have – as Ministers have sometimes unhappily put it – cut away the fat. But we are becoming extremely and dangerously lean. First, the dangers. They are many.

We face increased competition from countries where employees are paid miserably low wages. We contend with the dumping of goods by suppliers who – directly or indirectly, lawfully or otherwise – are heavily subsidized by their governments. And no government appears ready to help us to meet this unfair competition.

We are against neither competition nor imports. We recognize the need of others to sell. And we must export to live. We know that if we place undue restriction on our imports, then we must expect the same treatment from others to whom we must export. We are against *unfair* competition . . . *unfair* imports . . . *improper* dumping . . . *wilful* subsidy by others, unmatched by governmental aid to our ailing industry.

Add to these overseas miseries, over which we have no control whatever, the results of our own recession; the state of the currency; the weakness of our economy; the problems of overseas demand matched by the collapse of our market – and the reasons for my anxiety are clear.

So let us plan and plot, organize and lobby, work together for the preservation of our industry. Let us learn from the unions that individually we are weak, but if we fight and use our unity, then these times of trouble will have brought great lessons for us all.

Remedies

The diagnosis for our trade is clear – cure the recessional misery. That cure requires capital and investment – but above all, hope and confidence.

The time for cutting each other's industrial throats has passed. We must now work together for the survival of. . . , recognizing that collapse for one is a signal of tempest for all.

So my colleagues and I are proposing the following specific steps, to draw our plight to the government's attention and to take constructive help for our problems – not least in preserving employment in this key area of our industry.

First . . .

Second . . .

Third . . .

I commend these proposals to you. I ask you to accept them unanimously. We need more confidence and you need leadership, which we have now united together to provide.

58   Unions and colleagues

Never talk down to anyone – least of all to trade unions or to your colleagues or workforce. I have watched speeches collapse into ruin at school prize-givings, company occasions, debates at universities and conferences of trade unions – nearly always because the speaker made it plain that he or she regarded the audience as inferior for some reason. Conversely, nearly all the most successful speeches shine because the listener is treated as a colleague, a partner, an equal.

Trade unions are especially sensitive to apparent condescension, even when it is in fact a mask for shyness or apprehension. You only fool your unions once. They will not trust you again. Nor will they accept your invitation to share with them the miseries of recession if you do not also let them benefit in times of profit. Provided that their accounts will not reach the eyes of their creditors, employers are always glad to show the miseries to their workforce. But in days of gloom, the accounts only emerge after due provision has been made for the pension reserve fund and other receptacles for profits that are better unseen.

So the key to a successful speech to employees – and especially to those with the combined strength provided by a well-run union – is: the sharing of information, anxieties and hopes, with sincerity and frankness. Or to use a useful American phrase: 'Level with them . . .'

Disclosure

Mr Chairman, Ladies and Gentlemen,
Thank you for agreeing to meet me today. I would like to explain to you very briefly the position of the company and our plans and hopes for the future. Then I shall be glad to answer your questions.

Our company secretary, Roger White – who is, of course, here with me – has just provided your board with our latest figures. I have provided a summary for each of you, and when I have concluded this introduction, Roger will be glad to join me in answering your questions on these accounts. They provide management with a guide to liability and prospects. And they will give you an indication of the state of business which, of course, provides a livelihood for us all.

Remembering that the period covered is the year/six months/three months from . . . to . . . , let me summarize for you:

First, the turnover during this period increased/decreased from . . . to . . .

Second, our workforce grew/diminished from . . . to . . .

Third, working days lost through illness rose/fell from . . . to . . . ; and from industrial action rose/fell from . . . to . . .

Fourth – and do please treat this information as entirely confidential – in broad terms, at the start of this period we had enough orders on our books to keep us busy/on full-time working for a period of . . . weeks/months. We can now see confidently ahead only until . . .

Our plans for the future are as follows.

We shall make every effort to retain our present workforce. If unfortunately we do have to reduce numbers, we shall try to do so through natural wastage – that is, not replacing employees who leave us. If redundancies do become inevitable – and I repeat that we hope and believe that this will not occur – we shall consult with all unions concerned; and we shall try to arrange redundancies with the minimum of hardship.

Anyway, I repeat that I hope that this situation will not arise. It is certainly the determination of your board and of all the management team to scour the country/the world for orders and to take any steps within our power to keep our organization – with all its skills, experience and comradeship – together. We know that you know the problems – and how much we appreciate your partnership and help. We believe that together – all of us together – we can survive this miserable recession. Thank you – and now please do ask your questions. We shall try to answer them all, frankly and in the confidence that you recognize that we are all working – together – for the future of this, our works/business/undertaking.

Note: The redundancy sections of this speech sets the tone for misery and, of course, should not be used unless that misery is at least in prospect. If you have any alternative joy to offer, then by all means do so. Alternatively, you could use the redundancy section to form a major part of an even more unhappy speech, if redundancies really do become inevitable.

Similar principles apply to speeches to management, thus:

To management colleagues

I appreciate greatly your coming together today. I know how far some of you have had to travel and the difficulty that some of you have had in leaving your work/departments. But it is essential that we confer together on how to meet the current emergency/make the best of the present opportunity/avoid (*or as the case may be*).

First let me refer to the background paper which has been provided to you all. I must emphasize the following points:

1 . . .
2 . . .
3 . . .

The board consider that the following steps should now be taken – but before making any decision irrevocable, we are seeking your views. Our proposals are:

1 . . .
2 . . .
3 . . .

I look forward to hearing your comments and any counter-proposals. We shall value your constructive criticism and your ideas – as we do your comradeship, your partnership and your assistance –without which this business could not survive in such excellent shape.

Note: Accounts (as in the previous example); a background paper (as in this) or some other document, prepared carefully in advance, will avoid waste of time; provide the basis for discussion; and reduce the length of your speech.

Sales team talk

I have asked you – our sales team – to join me today so that we can together plan for the future of the entire business. In the past customers have come to us. In these troubled times, we must go to them – and arrive well ahead of our competitors.

I shall now ask our colleague, Bill Black, to present to you our new product – which will lie at the centre of our effort for the coming year. Bill . . .
(*Mr Black then introduces and explains the product – with appropriate diagrams, charts and/or visual aids.*)

Now you have seen the product and you know the plans. So how do we beat the competition, sell well, and justify the skill, brilliance and the enterprise of our colleagues in research and development? How do we make the most of this great new opportunity? If we succeed, then the company will flourish. Failure is unthinkable – for the company, and for us all.

Note: Visual aids are vital – as a supplement to speech (see Chapter 23). They are indispensable in (a) explaining complicated ideas or machinery; (b) punctuating a lengthy speech or brightening a shorter one; and (c) feeding other people's talents into your talk. (See also Janner on Presentation.)

BOOK THREE

Classic speeches

59   Winston Churchchill:
'Blood, Toil, Tears and Sweat' – 1940

I beg to move,

> That this House welcomes the formation of a Government representing the united and inflexible resolve of the nation to prosecute the war with Germany to a victorious conclusion.

On Friday evening last I received His Majesty's Commission to form a new Administration. It was the evident wish and will of Parliament and the nation that this should be conceived on the broadest possible basis and that it should include all parties, both those who supported the late Government and also the parties of the Opposition. I have completed the most important part of this task. A War Cabinet has been formed of five Members, representing, with the Opposition Liberals, the unity of the nation. The three party Leaders have agreed to serve, either in the War Cabinet or in high executive office. The three fighting Services have been filled. It was necessary that this should be done in one single day, on account of the extreme urgency and rigour of events. A number of other positions, key positions, were filled yesterday, and I am submitting a further list to His Majesty tonight. I hope to complete the appointment of the principal Ministers during tomorrow. The appointment of the other Ministers usually takes a little longer, but I trust that, when Parliament meets again, this part of my task will be completed, and that the administration will be complete in all respects.

I considered it in the public interest to suggest that the House should be summoned to meet today. Mr Speaker agreed, and took the necessary steps, in accordance with the powers conferred upon him by the Resolution of the House. At the end of the proceedings today, the Adjournment of the House will be proposed until Tuesday, 21st May, with, of course, provision for earlier meeting, if need be. The business to be considered during that week will be notified to Members at the earliest opportunity. I now invite the House, by the Motion which stands in my name, to record its approval of the steps taken and to declare its confidence in the new Government.

To form an Administration of this scale and complexity is a serious undertaking in itself, but it must be remembered that we are in the preliminary stage of one of the greatest battles in history, that we are in action at many other points in Norway and in Holland, that we have to be prepared in the Mediterranean, that the air battle is continuous and that many preparations, such as have been indicated by my Hon. Friend below the Gangway, have to be made here at home. In this crisis I hope I may be pardoned if I do not address the House at any length today. I hope that any of my friends and colleagues, or former colleagues, who are affected by the political reconstruction, will make allowances, all allowance, for any lack of ceremony with which it has been necessary to act. I would say to the House, as I said to those who have joined this Government: 'I have nothing to offer but blood, toil, tears and sweat.'

We have before us an ordeal of the most grievous kind. We have before us many, many long months of struggle and of suffering. You ask, what is our policy? I will say: It is to wage war, by sea, land and air, with all our might and with all the strength that God can give us; to wage war against a monstrous tyranny never surpassed in the dark, lamentable catalogue of human crime. That is our policy. You ask, what is our aim? I can answer in one word: It is victory, victory at all cost, victory in spite of all terror, victory, however long and hard the road may be; for without victory, there is no survival. Let that be realized; no survival for the British Empire, no survival for all that the British Empire has stood for, no survival for the urge and impulse of the ages, that mankind will move forward towards its goal. But I take up my task with buoyancy and hope. I feel sure that our cause will not be suffered to fail among men. At this time I feel entitled to claim the aid of all, and I say, 'Come then, let us go forward together with our united strength.'

(*Reprinted, with kind permission of HMSO, from* Hansard, *Fifth Series, issue No. 1096, volume 360, 13 May 1940, col. 1501 to col. 1502.*)

60   Jawaharlal Nehru: 'A Glory has Departed'

Nehru, first Prime Minister of independent India, addressing the Constituent Assembly at New Delhi on 2 February 1948, three days after the assassination of Mahatma Gandhi.

What then can we say about him except to feel humble on this occasion? To praise him we are not worthy – to praise him whom we could not follow adequately and sufficiently. It is almost doing him an injustice just to pass him by with words when he demanded work and labour and sacrifice from us; in a large measure he made this country, during the last thirty years or more, attain heights of sacrifice which in that particular domain have never been equalled elsewhere. He succeeded in that. Yet ultimately things happened which no doubt made him suffer tremendously though his tender face never lost its smile and he never spoke a harsh word to anyone. Yet he must have suffered – suffered for the failing of this generation whom he had trained, suffered because we went away from the path that he had shown us. And ultimately the hand of a child of his – for he after all is as much a child of his as any other Indian – a hand of a child of his struck him down.

Long ages afterwards history will judge of this period that we have passed through. It will judge of the successes and the failures – we are too near it to be proper judges and to understand what has happened and what has not happened. All we know is that there was a glory and that it is no more; all we know is that for the moment there is darkness, not so dark certainly because when we look into our hearts we still find the living flame which he lighted there. And if those living flames exist, there will not be darkness in this land and we shall be able, with our effort, remembering him and following his path, to illumine this land again, small as we are, but still with the fire that he instilled into us.

He was perhaps the greatest symbol of the India of the past, and may I say, of the India of the future, that we could have had. We stand on this perilous edge of the present between that past and the future to be and we face all manner of perils and the greatest peril is sometimes the lack of faith which comes to us, the sense of frustration that comes to us, the sinking of the heart and of the spirit that comes to us when we see ideals go overboard, when we see the great things that we talked about somehow pass into empty words and life taking a different course. Yet, I do believe that perhaps this period will pass soon enough.

He has gone, and all over India there is a feeling of having been left desolate and forlorn. All of us sense that feeling, and I do not know when we shall be able to get rid of it, and yet together with that feeling there is also a feeling of proud thankfulness that it has been given to us of this generation to be associated with this mighty person. In ages to come, centuries and maybe millenia after us, people will think of this generation when this man of God trod on earth and will think of us who, however small, could also follow his path and tread the holy ground where his feet had been. Let us be worthy of him.

A glory has departed and the sun that warmed and brightened our lives has set and we shiver in the cold and dark. Yet, he would not have us feel this way. After all, that glory that we saw for all these years, that man with the divine fire, changed us also – and such as we are, we have been moulded by him during these years; and out of that divine fire many of us also took a small spark which strengthened and made us work to some extent on the lines that he fashioned. And so if we praise him, our words seem rather small and if we praise him, to some extent we also praise ourselves. Great men and eminent men have monuments in bronze and marble set up for them, but this man of divine fire managed in his life-time to become enshrined in millions and millions of hearts so that all of us became somewhat of the stuff that he was made of, though to an infinitely lesser degree. He spread out in this way all over India not in palaces only, or in select places or in assemblies but in every hamlet and hut of the lowly and those who suffer. He lives in the hearts of millions and he will live for immemorial ages.

(*Reprinted, by kind permission of Dover Publications, New York, from* The World's Greatest Speeches [*second revised edition*], *edited by L. Copeland and L. Larner.*)

61 Harold Macmillan: 'The Winds of Change'

Addressing the South African Parliament in 1960 on the theme of emerging, third-world nationalism, Prime Minister Macmillan opened his speech as follows.

Sir, as I have travelled round the Union I have found everywhere, as I expected, a deep preoccupation with what is happening in the rest of the African continent. I understand and sympathize with your interest in these events, and your anxiety about them. Ever since the break-up of the Roman Empire one of the constant facts of political life in Europe has been the emergence of independent nations. They have come into existence over the centuries in different forms, with different kinds of government, but all have been inspired by a deep, keen feeling of nationalism, which has grown as the nations have grown.

In the twentieth century, and especially since the end of the war, the processes which gave birth to the nation states of Europe have been repeated all over the world. We have seen the awakening of national consciousness in peoples who have for centuries lived in dependence upon some other power. Fifteen years ago this movement spread through Asia. Many countries there of different races and civilizations pressed their claim to an independent national life. Today the same thing is happening in Africa, and the most striking of all the impressions I have formed since I left London a month ago is of the strength of this African national consciousness. In different places it takes different forms, but it is happening everywhere. The wind of change is blowing through this continent, and, whether we like it or not, this growth of national consciousness is a political fact. We must all accept it as a fact, and our national policies must take account of it . . .

(*Reprinted, by kind permission of Macmillan London Ltd, from* Pointing the Way 1959–61, *Volume 5 of Macmillan's Biography.*)

62   Martin Luther King: 'I Have a Dream'

Martin Luther King's evocative black masterpiece of hope – 1963

I have a dream that my four little children will one day live in a nation where they will not be judged by the colour of their skin but by the content of their character.

I have a dream today.

I have a dream that one day the state of Alabama, whose governor's lips are presently dripping with the words of interposition and nullification, will be transformed into a situation where little black boys and black girls will be able to join hands with little white boys and white girls and walk together as sisters and brothers.

I have a dream today.

I have a dream that one day every valley shall be exalted, every hill and mountain shall be made low, the rough places will be made plain, and the crooked places will be made straight, and the glory of the Lord shall be revealed, and all flesh shall see it together.

This is our hope. This is the faith with which I return to the South. With this faith we will be able to hew out of the mountain of despair a stone of hope. With this faith we will be able to transform the jangling discords of our nation into a beautiful symphony of brotherhood. With this faith we will be able to work together, to pray together, to struggle together, to go to jail together, to stand up for freedom together, knowing that we will be free one day.

This will be the day when all of God's children will be able to sing with new meaning 'My country 'tis of thee, sweet land of liberty, of thee I sing. Land where my fathers died, land of the pilgrim's pride, from every mountainside, let freedom ring.'

And if America is to be a great nation this must become true. So let freedom ring from the prodigious hilltops of New Hampshire! Let freedom ring from the mighty mountains of New York! Let freedom ring from the heightening Alleghenies of Pennsylvania!

Let freedom ring from the snowcapped Rockies of Colorado!

Let freedom ring from the curvaceous peaks of California!

But not only that; let freedom ring from the Stone Mountain of Georgia!

Let freedom ring from every hill and mole hill of Mississippi. From every mountainside, let freedom ring.

When we let freedom ring, when we let it ring from every village and every hamlet, from every state and every city, we will be able to speed up that day when all of God's children, black men and white men, Jews and Gentiles, Protestants and Catholics, will be able to join hands and sing in the words of that old Negro spiritual, 'Free at last! Free at last! Thank God almighty, we are free at last!'

(Reprinted, by kind permission of George Allen & Unwin Ltd, from What Manner of Man: a Biography of Martin Luther King *by L. Bennet.)*

63   Hugh Gaitskell:
'Fight and Fight and Fight Again'

Speech delivered at the 57th Annual Conference of the Labour Party, Scarborough, 1960.

. . . There is one other possibility to which I must make reference because I have read so much about it – that the issue here is not really defence at all but the leadership of this Party. Let me repeat what Manny Shinwell said. The place to decide the leadership of this Party is not here but in the Parliamentary Party. I would not wish for one day to remain a Leader who had lost the confidence of his colleagues in Parliament. It is perfectly reasonable to try to get rid of somebody, to try to get rid of a man you do not agree with, who you think perhaps is not a good Leader. But there are ways of doing this. What would be wrong, in my opinion, and would not be forgiven, is if, in order to get rid of a man, you supported a policy in which you did not wholeheartedly believe, a policy which, as far as the resolution is concerned, is not clear.

Before you take the vote on this momentous occasion, allow me a last word. Frank Cousins has said this is not the end of the problem. I agree with him. It is not the end of the problem because Labour Members of Parliament will have to consider what they do in the House of Commons. What do you expect of them? You know how they voted in June overwhelmingly for the policy statement. It is not in dispute that the vast majority of Labour Members of Parliament are utterly opposed to unilateralism and neutralism. So what do you expect them to do? Change their minds overnight? To go back on the pledges they gave to the people who elected them from their constituencies? And supposing they did do that. Supposing all of us, like well-behaved sheep, were to follow the policies of unilateralism and neutralism, what kind of an impression would that make upon the British people? You do not seem to be clear in your minds about it, but I will tell you this. I do not believe that the Labour Members of Parliament are prepared to act as time servers. I do not believe they will do this, and I will tell you why – because they are men of conscience and honour. People of the so-called Right and so-called Centre have every justification for having a conscience, as well as people of the so-called Left. I do not think they will do this because they are honest men, loyal men, steadfast men, experienced men, with a lifetime of service to the Labour Movement.

There are other people too, not in Parliament, in the Party who share our convictions. What sort of people do you think they are? What sort of people do you think we are? Do you think we can simply accept a decision of this kind? Do you think that we can become overnight the pacifists, unilateralists and fellow travellers that other people are? How wrong can you be? As wrong as you are about the attitude of the British people.

In a few minutes the Conference will make its decision. Most of the votes, I know, are predetermined and we have been told what is likely to happen. We know how it comes about. I sometimes think, frankly, that the system we have, by which great unions decide their policy before even their conferences can consider the Executive recommendation, is not really a very wise one or a good one. Perhaps in a calmer moment this situation could be looked at.

I say this to you: we may lose the vote today and the result may deal this Party a grave blow. It may not be possible to prevent it, but I think there are many of us who will not accept that this blow need be mortal, who will not believe that such an end is inevitable. There are some of us, Mr Chairman, who will fight and fight and fight again to save the Party we love. We will fight and fight and fight again to bring back sanity and honesty and dignity, so that our Party with its great past may retain its glory and its greatness.

It is in that spirit that I ask delegates who are still free to decide how they vote, to support what I believe to be a realistic policy on defence, which yet could so easily have united the great Party of ours, and to reject what I regard as the suicidal path of unilateral disarmament which will leave our country defenceless and alone.

(*Reprinted by kind permission from the Labour Party Report of the 57th Annual Conference.*)

64   Aneurin Bevan: 'Socialism Unbeaten'

Extract from Bevan's speech to the Labour Party Conference following Macmillan's General Election victory of 1959.

What are we going to say, comrades? Are we going to accept the defeat? Are we going to say to India, where Socialism has been adopted as the official policy despite all the difficulties facing the Indian community, that the British Labour movement has dropped Socialism here? What are we going to say to the rest of the world? Are we going to send a message from this great Labour movement, which is the father and mother of modern democracy and modern Socialism, that we in Blackpool in 1959 have turned our backs on our principles because of a temporary unpopularity in a temporarily affluent society?

Let me give you a personal confession of faith. I have found in my life that the burdens of public life are too great to be borne for trivial ends. The sacrifices are too much, unless we have something really serious in mind; and therefore, I hope we are going to send from this Conference a message of hope, a message of encouragement, to the youth and to the rest of the world that is listening very carefully to what we are saying.

I was rather depressed by what Denis Healey said. I have a lot of respect for him; but you know, Denis, you are not going to be able to help the Africans if the levers of power are left in the hands of their enemies in Britain. You cannot do it! Nor can you inject the principles of ethical Socialism into an economy based upon private greed. You cannot do it! You cannot mix them, and therefore I beg and pray that we should wind this Conference up this time on a message of hope, and we should say to India and we should say to Africa and Indonesia, and not only to them, but we should say to China and we should say to Russia, that the principles of democratic Socialism have not been extinguished by a temporary defeat at the hands of the Tories a few weeks ago!

You know, comrades, parliamentary institutions have not been destroyed because the Left wing was too vigorous; they have been destroyed because the Left was too inert. You cannot give me a single illustration in the Western world where Fascism conquered because Socialism was too violent. You cannot give me a single illustration where representative government has been undermined because the representatives of the people asked for too much.

But I can give you instance after instance we are faced with today where representative government has been rendered helpless because the representatives of the people did not ask enough. We have never suffered from too much vitality; we have suffered from too little. That is why I say that we are going to go from this Conference a united Party. We are going to go back to the House of Commons, and we are going to fight the Tories. But we are not only going to fight them there; we are going to fight them in the constituencies and inside the trade unions. And we are going to get the youth! Let them start. Do not let them wait for the Executive, for God's sake! Start getting your youth clubs, go in and start now! Go back home and start them, and we will give all the help and encouragement that we can.

65 Brian Sedgemore: 'A Long Streak of Spit'

On 8 March 1988, the Commons debated whether a Guardian journalist should be reported to the Committee of Privileges. He had made derogatory remarks about MPs. During the subsequent debate, Brian Sedgemore, Labour MP for Hackney South and Shoreditch, made a classic contribution.

Mr Brian Sedgemore: I begin by declaring an interest. I drink and I have been known to take a catnap in the Library. Indeed, when I once appeared as a barrister before the Lord Chief Justice of England, he said to me, 'I can see you are doing your incompetent best, Mr Sedgemore.'

Nevertheless, I hope that we will take the motion seriously. It is serious for *The Guardian*, that radical newspaper——

Mr Dennis Skinner (Bolsover): What?

Mr Sedgemore: A radical newspaper, which is not only short of money and a decent layout artist, but if I may paraphrase Swift, is in danger of dying by swallowing its own lies. Having said that, I want to defend *The Guardian* and the right of journalists to abuse hon. Members.

All my life I have had the misfortune to be laughed at. You will understand, Mr Speaker – well, perhaps you will not, because perhaps no one has ever laughed at you – that it hurts. The position became unbearable when I was at the school debating society one year and one of my opponents described me as 'a long streak of spit'. I thought, 'Well, this cannot go on.' I was lying in the bath and I had a brilliant idea. I said to myself, 'I know what I'll do to stop it, I'll become an MP. Then I'll get the protection of the all-powerful, all-party Committee of Privileges. No longer will anyone in this life be able to hold me up to hatred, ridicule and contempt.' Imagine my surprise when only last week, as a result of something that I said during proceedings on the Education Reform Bill in Committee, a journalist who is sitting in the Reporter's Gallery described me as 'Derek Jameson's voice coming out of Kerry Packer's body.'

I do not know how hon. Members can worry about 200 Members of Parliament being called 'incompetent, lazy drunks' when a tender, delicate soul like myself is being likened to Sid Yobbo.

I am not claiming that Andrew Rawnsley is entirely innocent. I am not sure how I am supposed to respond, as a paid-up member of the National Union of Journalists, when he argues in his column, as he argues every day, that politicians are even more odious than journalists.

You will be aware, Mr Speaker, that I am not one of those hon. Members who believe in vulgar, personal abuse – [*Interruption*]. I prefer to leave such abuse to the right hon. Member for Chingford (Mr Tebbit) and I am sorry that he is not in the Chamber. I understand that at this very moment he is seeking to raise the standards of artistic appreciation in our country by trying to persuade *The Sun* to set up a Kelvin MacKenzie room at the Tate Gallery to house a permanent collection of nipples. That is the kind of abuse that we could do without. If the right hon. Member for Chingford had not become a Member of Parliament, I am sure that he would have become a PPE – not a graduate in politics, philosophy and economics, but a purveyor of pornography extraordinaire.

I believe that my hon. Friend the Member for Newham, North-West (Mr Banks) will agree that we should judge political abuse by three standards. First, abuse in politics must be treated as an art. Secondly, abuse is at its best when it is in thoroughly bad taste and finally, and this was the only point that my hon. Friend the Member for Newham, North-West picked up himself, abuse should at some stage hint at reality. That is where poor little Rawnsley up there in the Press Gallery, the fearless scribe from Farringdon Road whose goolies are about to be tweaked today, got it wrong.

Mr Speaker: Order. Will the hon. Gentleman seek to use language that is more parliamentary?

Mr Sedgemore: You are absolutely right, Mr Speaker. I am getting carried away. Obviously Mr Rawnsley came to the House and was hard-pressed, like the rest of us, to earn a crust. He did not have a story, and the classic story to make up in the Reporters' Gallery is the 'empty Chamber' story.

Before I finish, I want to ask my hon. Friend the Member for Newham, North-West two questions. I want my hon. Friend to consider some of the best abuse down the ages and I want to give one example from across the Atlantic and one from this side. When my hon. Friend replies and withdraws his motion I want to know how he would respond to such abuse.

How would my hon. Friend have responded to these comments made by Harry Truman?

'Richard Nixon is a no good, lying bastard. He can lie out of both sides of his mouth at the same time and if he ever caught himself telling the truth, he'd lie just to keep his hand in.'

Also, how would my hon. Friend have responded to the classic 18th century argument between Lord Sandwich and John Wilkes?

''Pon your honour, Wilkes, I don't know whether you'll die on the gallows or of the pox.'

To which Wilkes replied:

'That must depend, my Lord, upon whether I embrace your Lordship's principles or your Lordship's mistress.'

A serious point is involved. It is important to preserve the freedom of the press, and that necessitates the freedom of journalists in the Press Gallery to abuse hon. Members down here on the Floor of the House.

BOOK FOUR

Compendium of retellable tales

Introduction

A lively story is to a good speech as spice to a fine meal. A touch of wit, a flash of humour, a shaft of language, each is appreciated by every audience. Everyone likes a good story – whatever his, her or its age. The best tales are like wine. They mature with the years.

As I have sat through millennial miseries of meetings and dinners, many of them extremely boring, I have jotted down on menus, notepads and scraps of assorted paper the best of the story-teller's crop. To create this section of the book, I have raided piles of files, deciphered scrawl and shorthand, rejected some tales, too blue or too terrible to retell – and brought together the mixture that now follows.

Each tale – whether a joke, an aphorism, an illustration, a wisecrack or an unwise gaffe – has been well-used and much appreciated. I have sorted the accumulation into rough sections – although many stories could fit just as well into several of my groupings. Anyway, if you wish to pick out a story for a special purpose, the index should help. Or maybe you will just enjoy browsing your way through some 600 tales which – told or retold – have brought me much pleasure. Use them in good health, in good voice, with careful timing – and with that good fortune that is the essential prerequisite and precursor of every standing ovation.

A tale is only as good as its teller. Bad workmen blame their tools, poor comedians their scriptwriters. Still, tools and scripts must be selected with care, to suit both user and occasion.

Some of these Retellable Tales will suit you, others will not. Most can be adapted.

Sometimes, I have suggested possible changes, in brackets or footnotes. Do not hesitate yourself to change the material to suit your occasion or your audience.

Naturally, it is unhelpful to misattribute a quotation, though, we may all be prepared to accept the paternity of wise words, fathered on us by affectionate quoters – was it not I, who said. . . ? Misquoted ideas are the source of too many libel actions.

There is no end to the oratorical use of the word 'if' – nor to the stories which may embellish it. If (there we go) you decide to use Kipling's poem, please ladle on your vocal melodrama. 'As Kipling long ago claimed, "If you can keep your head when all about you . . ." '

The best 'if' story is a revered classic: 'How was the dinner?'

'If the chicken had been as fresh as the waitress . . . if the waitress had been as young as the wine . . . if the wine had been as mature as the jokes . . . it would have been a lovely evening!'

Or there is the French story: 'If my aunt had wheels, she would be a bicycle!' ('Si ma tante avait des roues se serait une bicyclette' – in case you use it to an audience which Canadians call 'Francophone' – which is not always the same as Anglophile!)

If any readers would care to submit original 'if' stories which I can use in the next edition of this book, I shall be glad to reward them. Meanwhile, please do not think that because a joke or a story happens to be known to your audience, they will reject it. A comedian suggested that there are only two basic schemes for humour – the banana skin and the mother-in-law. All the rest are variations.

The speed at which jokes and stories cross the world is precisely the same as that of transmitted sound. One day you hear a joke in London's Parliament; in Washington the next, a Senator says: 'Did you hear the one about. . . ?' – which is miraculously the same.

In Tokyo and in Torquay and from Sydney to San Francisco, humour is truly universal. You can almost say to your audience: 'Joke no. 81 . . .' They will already know the story about jokes by numbers and the man who laughed uproariously when the comic said: 'No. 96' and when asked why said: 'It wasn't the story, it was the way he told it!'

Which holds the key to the use of humour. Of course the story matters, but not nearly as much as the way it is told.

Leading politicians, lecturers and other perennial public speakers may survive on half a dozen basic speeches. But a repertoire of a few hundred basic stories, old as well as new, with versions authorized and also unauthorized, revised and dated, will suffice for any speechmaker other than those who live off comedy – and they employ unfortunates whose sole job it is to create material which at least appears to be new but which is often a recreation of the old in modern form.

In Chapter 17, you will find some basic rules on the use of humour. These 'retellable tales' are all part of my repertoire and have been used to good and often frequent effect. You will not find that all are suited to your temperament, style or taste – but many should be.

Combined living may destroy love and familiarity may breed hatred. But not necessarily, or marriages would be even more fragile than they are. A tale which is tellable is also retellable.

I hope that you will enjoy reading the collection that follows – and using selections from it, in good health and with fine effect.

66 Presentations, speeches and stories

Opening gambits

As Henry VIII said to each of his wives in turn: 'I shall not keep you long . . .' (*Lord Janner*)

Like the time the toastmaster said: 'Ladies and Gentlemen . . . Pray for the silence of Mr Greville Janner . . .'

The last time our chairman introduced me and was told to be brief, he began: 'The less said about Mr Greville Janner, the better . . .'

Your Chair has just said to me: 'Would you like to speak now – or shall we let them go on enjoying themselves a little longer?'

Why me first?

I have been asked to speak before Mr . . . because I have several dates in (naming two months hence) which I wish to keep. (*Bob Monkhouse*)

Short cut

Guest speaker to Chair: 'How long should I speak?'
    Chair: 'As long as you like. I must be away by five.'

Civic slip

I have to address a lot of conferences. Indeed, last week, somebody said: 'Would you please address a meeting of 150 co-operative women'. (*Mayor of Harrogate addressing conference opening session.*)

Royal introductions

Presenting a stream of notables to the Queen at a reception, I remarked that it must be a strain meeting so many strangers all at one time.
    'It is not as difficult as it might seem,' came Her Majesty's deadpan reply, 'You see, I so seldom have to introduce myself – they all seem to know who I am!'

Compliments   Mark Twain once said: 'I can live for two months on a good compliment.' You have given me enough compliments for several years ... [*Useful response to flattering introduction. GJ*]

AGM   Chair: 'We now come to another annual meeting – after an interval of a year ...'

Audience   I asked your chairman for details of the people I would be speaking to today – numbers, broken down by age and sex – and he replied: 'Yes, they are ...'

Sleep   A new pastor arrived in a country parish. He noticed with dismay that each week during his sermon, the senior churchwarden dropped off to sleep. He put up with this until one week the man snored. After the service he went up to him and said very gently: 'I am sorry to mention this, but it does set a very bad example when my senior churchwarden sleeps during the sermon.'

'Not at all,' replied the Elder. 'It just shows that I trust you!'

Foot in mouth   Conservative MP Andrew Mackay tells of his introduction by the chairperson at a local Tory women's meeting.

'We offer an especially warm welcome to Mr Mackay tonight, since he has refused to accept any payment for his appearance. This means that next time we will be able to afford a proper speaker!'

Off the record?   'How did your speech go?'

'Marvellous. Even the journalists put down their pencils and listened ...'

Quote   'War has devastating results', as Lenin said. And it would be true even had he not said it ... [*Translatable to, from, or for anyone else. GJ*]

Applause   If they clap before you speak, that is faith; if they clap during your speech, that is hope; if they clap at the end, that is charity!

Golden Silence	Business people must first learn when to make speeches. Then they get wise and learn when not to make them.
Pronunciation	An American tourist was crossing Westminster Bridge. He stopped a passer-by and said: 'Sir, could you please tell me. Is this river pronounced "Thems" or "Tems"?' 'Thems,' the man replied. 'Gee, I'm surprised,' said the American. 'I always thought it was pronounced "Tems". Are you quite sure?' 'Yeth,' answered the man. 'I'm thertain!'
Preferred position	Addressing a large meeting, a politician was worried in case his microphone was not working. 'Can you hear me at the back?' he called out. 'I can't hear you,' shouted a man from the front row. 'Would the man at the back like to change places with me?'
To inattentive listener	'Can you hear me? That's good . . . I can hear you too!' (*David Berglas, President of the Magic Circle.*)
Vote of thanks	At least Macbeth knew that when the dreadful banquet was over, he would not be the person required to return thanks.
Jackets off	David Ben Gurion, Israel's first Prime Minister, hated formalities, including jackets and ties. Before Israel's creation, he attended a dinner at the home of the British High Commissioner – in effect the Governor of Palestine. He removed his jacket. The H/C's personal assistant chided him. 'On these important occasions, we wear our jackets, Mr Ben Gurion.' 'I have a special dispensation from Winston Churchill,' he replied. 'How come?' 'Well, I dined with him in London with my jacket off. He said to me: "You mustn't take your jacket off here. That's all right when you're

dining with the High Commissioner, in Palestine!" '

(A useful one, this, if you want to give your guests the option of removing their jackets at dinner party on a formal but hot evening. Or to reassure them, if they do so without prior consent.)

Introduction

Most of you will have heard Greville Janner before; some of you will not have heard Greville Janner before; those who have not heard Greville Janner before will be looking forward to hearing him now.

Food and speech

We should not deliver speeches at table, just as we ought not to eat when we speak.

Short is hard

Winston Churchill always said that for a 10 minute speech he would prepare for 2 hours – but for a 2 hour speech, 10 minutes was enough.

Request time

A famous comedian, Issi Bonn, was most famous for his sobbing rendition of the classic: 'My Yiddisha Momma'. He was once engaged to take part in a West End pantomime: Aladdin.

When Issi saw the script, he said to the producer: 'But when do I sing "My Yiddisha Momma"?'

The producer replied: 'You don't. It's not cabaret, it's a pantomime. It's Aladdin!'

'But my public will demand it,' Issi protested. 'You've got to find a place for it.'

'Impossible.'

After a long argument, the producer finally said: 'Very well, Issi. I'll do a deal with you. You find a place where the song fits into the script and I'll let you sing it.'

For weeks of rehearsal, Issi agonized. Then, one morning, he came to the producer, beaming. 'I've got it,' he said. 'You know the bit when they're all in that cave? They're surrounded by dirty old cups and saucers and lamps? And the genie says? "Well, Aladdin, my boy, what is your wish?" '

The producer nodded.

'Then Aladdin will say: "My wish, genie, is to hear Issi Bonn singing, "My Yiddisha Momma"!'

Lies

I have been economical with the truth. (*Robert Armstrong, Secretary of the Cabinet*)

The classical euphemism? When Winston Churchill was reprimanded in the Commons for saying that a colleague had lied, he apologized. It was a 'terminological inexactitude', he said.

Substitutes

Delayed? Then you may have to send a substitute. The following stories may help.

A visiting American telephoned the parish church in Sandringham, where the Royal Family were on holiday. 'Will their Royal Highnesses be in Church this Sunday?' the voice enquired.

'That we cannot promise,' replied the vicar. 'But we confidently expect God to be there, and we hope that will be incentive enough for a reasonably large attendance!'

Or there was the one about the politician who had to cancel his appointment as after dinner speaker. His host wrote: 'We would be prepared to accept a substitute, but could you please find us someone who is, like you, a wit?'

He replied: 'I'm afraid that I cannot find a substitute who is a wit. But I think I could discover two people who would come in my place and each of them is a half wit . . .'

Oratorical dangers

It's not only an honour to speak to you tonight. It is also bloody dangerous . . .

Distinguished company

I think I am about the only person here whom I haven't heard of . . .

Out of touch

The late Lord Curzon was accustomed to travel by carriage or by cab. One day, neither was available and a fellow peer suggested that he should 'try the bus'. Which he did.

The next day, the friend asked him: 'Well, how did your bus trip go?'

'Terrible,' Lord Curzon replied. 'I told him to take me to 54 Belgrave Square and he refused!' [*Well, our guest of honour is – like Lord Curzon – famous and successful. But he is in touch with our problems . . . GJ*]

Apt stories

If you cannot find a joke to fit the occasion, make the occasion fit the joke.

The renowned Preacher of Dubnow – in eighteenth century Russia – was famous for his vast collection of stories, each one apt to the moment.

A listener asked him: 'How do you manage to have a story for every occasion?'

He replied: 'I'll tell you a story. A traveller stopped off at a country inn. Waiting for his meal, he stepped outside and saw a target, with three arrows in the bulls eye. The innkeeper's son was standing beside it with a bow. "How do you manage to shoot so accurately?" he asked. He replied: "It's quite simple. I shoot the arrows first and then I draw the target around it." '

As with arrows, so with stories . . .

Keeping in touch

To a violinist: 'We cannot expect you to be with us all the time, but perhaps you would be good enough to keep in touch now and again!' (*Sir Thomas Beecham*) [*A super one to direct at a listener whose attention has wandered. 'As Sir Thomas Beecham said to a player, off key . . .'*]

Déjà entendu

I have delivered this speech twice before. Once was to the local Chamber of Commerce and once to patients in Broadmoor. If any of you were there on either occasion, I apologize . . .'

Enough – is not enough

'We've had a belly full, in fact,' said Alleline.

'And like everyone who has had enough,' said Control, as Alleline noisily left the room, 'he wants more.' (*John Le Carré* – '*Tinker, Tailor, Soldier, Spy*')

Introductory thanks

Thank you for that very kind introduction. I am only sorry that neither of my parents are present to hear it. My father would have enjoyed it. And my mother would have believed it.

Fairy tales

'Mummy, why do fairy tales always start: "Once upon a time"?'

'Not always, darling. Father tells ones which usually begin with: "Sorry I'm late love. I got tied up in the office . . ." '

67 Epigrams and definitions, proverbs and laws

Anger

A sage who is angry ceases to be a sage. (*Talmud-Pesahim*)

Argument

My father told me never to argue with an angry man. (*Nahum Goldmann*)

Average man

A defendant in a negligence action pleaded that 'anyone with average intelligence' would not have suffered damage. With shattering accuracy, the judge replied: 'You should perhaps bear in mind that something like one half of the people in this country are below average intelligence!' [*See also Public opinion*]

Balance

Churchill once remarked that there is nothing more difficult than holding up a wall leaning towards you except kissing a girl leaning away from you.

People in our industry are well-balanced – we have a chip on each shoulder! One chip is provided by Revenue, the tax man . . . the other by (the Government, Customs & Excise – or what-have-you).

Change

The UK government was considering switching its vehicles to driving on the right-hand side of the road. Anxious about a transitional change-over period, the Department of Transport suggested effecting the alteration 'by stages . . . starting with the heavy goods vehicles'.

Company

A man is known by the company which he thinks no one knows he is keeping.

Corroboration

Never lie alone. (*Janner's Law*)

Cranks

Crank – a man with a new idea, until it succeeds. (*Mark Twain*)

Danger from fools	Any fool can throw a stone into a lake; but a hundred wise men cannot get it out. (*Greek proverb*.)
Democracy	Democracy – national or corporate – requires the enlightened balance of satisfied self-interest. (*Janner's Law*)
Deterrence	Deterrence requires existence of power; willingness to use it; and knowledge by the adversary that it will, if necessary, be used. (*Abba Eban, Israeli statesman and orator*)
Discretion	If I know something you do not know, then you know that I cannot tell you; and if I do not know anything that you do not know, you will not want to hear me anyway!
Education – and training	The difference between education and training? If your daughter comes home and says she has been having sex education at school, you will doubtless rejoice. But if she says that she has been having sex training, you would have due cause for alarm.
Enemies	Choose your enemies with care. Make sure that they are important. Your importance depends upon theirs. (*Founder of World Jewish Congress, Nahum Goldmann – who maintained that he was unknown until he was publicly attacked by the redoubtable Rabbi Abba Hillel Silver.*)
Friends	The Prime Minister left tonight for a tour of all our friendly European countries. He will be back within a couple of hours.
Friendship	The Greeks say of a true friend: 'I have taken bread and salt with him.'
Genius	A Rabbi visited a kibbutz on the edge of the desert. He said: 'You kibbutzniks are so clever . . . You know how to settle where the trees are!'
Helpful	A driver stopped at a crossroads in a village. 'Excuse me,' he said to a passer-by, 'but does it

matter which of these roads I take to get me to the next town?'

'Not to me it don't,' replied the villager.

Holes
First law on holes – when you're in one, stop digging! (*Denis Healey*)

Ideas
A friend once said to Einstein: 'When I have a good idea, I do not want to forget it. So I keep a notebook by my bed. What do you do?'

Einstein replied: 'I do not understand your question. I have only had two or three good ideas in my life.'

Intolerance
We should not endure intolerance: but we must not endure tolerance. (*Chaim Weizmann, first President of Israel*) [*See also: Tolerance*]

Isolationism
A man once sat in a boat, boring a hole under his seat. 'Don't worry, shipmates,' he said to his fellow travellers. 'It's only under my seat, not yours . . .' (*Talmud*)

Knowledge
Everything I know about this subject would fit into a nutshell and still leave plenty of room for the nut. (*Lord Mancroft*)

Legislation
The effect of a statute is in directly inverse ratio to the amount of noise made during its passage. (*Janner's Law*)

Life?
Confucius says: 'I am asked why I buy rice and flowers? I reply: I buy rice to live and flowers so that I have something to live for.'

Litigation
Litigants fight cases – lawyers win them. (*Janner's Law*)

Men
Men who try too much to be macho do not amount to mucho. (*Zsa Zsa Gabor – quoted by Michael Foot, with reference to Dr Owen, October 1983*)

Opinions
An Iraqui Kurd [*or any other downtrodden citizen: GJ*] was asked whether he didn't have any mind of his own on political affairs. He

replied 'Yes, of course I do. I have my own opinions. But I don't agree with them.'

Optimism   An optimist says that the bottle is half full – a pessimist that it is half empty.

Paranoid?   Just because I'm paranoid don't mean that I ain't got enemies. (*Henry Kissinger*)

Photographs   The road to political oblivion is paved with good photographs.

Plagiarism   Copy from one book and that is 'plagiarism' or breach of copyright. Copy from two or more books and that is 'research'. God gave you eyes? So plagiarize!

Power   Power is wonderful, absolute power is absolutely wonderful.

Public opinion   There was once a Russian doctor who bustled into the ward and said: 'I'm in a terrible hurry. Please give me the average temperature of all the patients . . .' (*Shimon Peres*) [*Useful when asked: 'What is the feeling in the UK about. . . ? GJ*]

Quietude   Chinese proverb: May we live in uninteresting times.

Quotes   UN Resolution 242 is like most sacred texts – more often quoted than read. [*May be applied to most of its kind. GJ*]

Recession, depression and recovery   Recession is when your neighbour is out of work; depression is when you are out of work; recovery is when the government is out of work . . .

Resignation   Never resign – unless a better job awaits. (*Janner's Law*)

Resolutions   The road to political ruin is paved with excellent resolutions. [*See also Photographs*]

Success   Mark Twain bemoaned that he had not seen the Niagara Falls, so they made up a special party to take him there. Afterwards his hosts said: 'What did you think of it?'

Mark Twain paused: 'It's certainly a success,' he said.

Successors Nothing succeeds like a successor.

Survival The porcupine may be less attractive than the rabbit but it has a greater chance of survival and much less chance of being digested.

Systems A system is only as good as those who attempt to deceive it.

Temptation Do not blame the mouse – blame the hole in the wall. (*Talmud*)

Tolerance Tolerance is the ability to put up with opinions which bother us little. [*See also: Intolerance*]

Secrets The vanity of being known to be entrusted with a secret is generally one of the chief motives to disclose it. (*Samuel Johnson*)

If you want to preserve your secret, wrap it up in frankness.

If you want to preserve your secret, keep it to yourself. (*Seneca*)

Tradition It is a long-established tradition . . . as Lord Denning (or anyone else you want to name) would say when he has a new idea . . .

Victory and defeat 'What a glorious thing must be a victory, Sir.' 'The greatest tragedy in the world, Madam, except a defeat.'

Wisdom Just as the bee gathers honey from all flowers, so the wise man gathers knowledge from all men. (*Indian proverb*)

Definitions Politicians – people who will always be there when they need you.

Inflation – a monetary change that allows you to live in a more expensive neighbourhood without moving.

Non-executive director – a person willing to do an honest day's work for a full week's pay.

Executive – a big gun who has managed not to be fired.

Managers – people who take responsibility when things go right.

Small mercies – or don't push your luck

The above is matched by a Talmudic story.

When the Jewish people in Palestine were chafing under Roman rule, they started organizing a revolt. Rabbi Yehoshua called the Elders together and told them this story:

A lion was suffering from a bone, stuck in its throat. Roaring with pain, he called out for help.

A friendly stork said to him: 'Lion, open your mouth wide. I have a long neck and I will reach down into your throat and pull out the bone.'

The lion stopped roaring; opened its mouth; and the stork extracted the bone. The lion sat growling, without a word of appreciation.

The stork exclaimed: 'Lion, I've just saved your life. Don't you even say thank you?'

'Just be grateful,' roared the lion, 'that I did not eat you.'

'And so it is with the Roman oppressors,' said the sage. 'At least we are alive. So stay quiet.'

The Jews did not listen to him. Led by Bar Kochba, the revolt began. In under three years, it was crushed, with monstrous loss of life.

Shouting

Do not shout. When you do, you can hear no voice other than your own. (*Gandhi*)

Experience

You do not have to eat a sheep in order to write about sheep. It is enough to eat a lamb chop. (*Somerset Maugham*)

Pleasing your audience

There are two golden rules for an orchestra: to start together and to finish together. The public doesn't give a damn what goes on in between.

Complication	Let no one say that a subject is too complicated to explain; if he does, that means that he does not understand it. (*Sir Isaiah Berlin*)
Failure – and planning	Politicians and businessmen alike do not plan to fail – they fail to plan.
Mind your words	The frog that opens his mouth reveals his whole body. (*Zen Proverb*)
People	To a scriptwriter, there is no such person as an ordinary one. Stop anyone and listen and you will get a story. (*Lord (Ted) Willis*)
Wit and wisdom	Wit is folly unless a wise man hath the keeping of it. (*Sir Thomas Beecham*)
Marriage	*Hence a man leaves his father and mother and clings to his wife, so that they become one flesh.* (Genesis 2:24)

Does this mean that in reality two individuals are physically fused into one?

No. It means that they *function* as if they were a single entity.

Come and learn: If one leg is temporarily incapacitated, the healthy leg must of necessity assume bearing most of the body's weight until the ill leg can heal itself and reassume its normal share of responsibility. Thus it is written in Scripture: *Two are better off than one. . . . for should they fall, one can raise the other, but woe betide him who is alone and falls with no companion to raise him!* (Ecclesiastes 4:9–10)

However, if one eye is briefly weakened, the healthy, strong eye must of necessity restrain itself and hold back so that the weakened eye can strengthen itself through use, as it is written: *The eyes of the lofty are humbled* (Isaiah 5:15) and *The eyes of the blind shall be opened* (Isaiah 35:5).

Life's wisdom consists in knowing when to be a leg and when to be an eye.

He has delivered my eyes from tears and my

> *feet from stumbling* (Psalm 116:8); All my body *bless his holy name* (Psalm 103:1).

Mud Two Rabbis were arguing. Do you or do you not require your disciples (hassidim) to wear boots in the winter?

First Rabbi: My Hassidim must wear boots.

Second Rabbi: I do not allow my Hassidim to wear boots.

First Rabbi: My Hassidim wear boots because otherwise if they go into the mud, they will get their feet wet.

Second Rabbi: I do not permit my Hassidim to wear boots because if there is mud, then if they are not wearing boots they will be very careful not to go into it. (*Dr Joseph Burg*) [*Lebanon – or Sri Lanka, Afghanistan, Kuwait . . . or anywhere else you feel like invading*]

Tolerance Tolerance is the ability to put up with opinions which bother us little.

Riots A riot is at bottom the language of the unheard. (*Rev. Martin Luther King*)

Contribution v. commitment What is the difference between a contribution to a cause and a total commitment? It's like bacon and egg – the chicken has made a contribution, but the pig is totally committed.

Speculation There are two times in life when a man should not speculate – when he can afford it and when he cannot afford it. (*Mark Twain*)

Weight – and money The difference between weight and money? Money is hard to get and easy to lose. Weight is easy to acquire but hard to lose.

Hope The story of Jonah confirms that you cannot keep a good man down.

Balance A famous West End hotel which caters for Middle Eastern trade served a new dish: chicken and camel stew.

A diner complained to the head waiter: 'I can't taste the chicken.'

'I do assure you that it is camel and chicken stew, sir,' replied the waiter. 'One chicken, one camel . . .'

Now that's balance.

68 Insults

Churchillian

I don't just give offence, I take it. (*Sir Winston Churchill*)

Churchill described Prime Minister Attlee as: 'A sheep in sheep's clothing'; and said of Christian Socialist Chancellor of the Exchequer, Sir Stafford Cripps: 'There but for the grace of God goes God.'

Book reviews

From the moment I picked up your book until I laid it down I was convulsed with laughter. Some day I intend reading it. (*Groucho Marx*)

An author wrote to the perpetrator of a fiercely offensive review: 'I am sitting in the smallest room in the house. Your review is before me. It will soon be behind me.'

Your manuscript is both good and original; the part that is good is not original and the part that is original is not good. (*Samuel Solomon*)

Prejudice

I believe I have no prejudice whatsoever. All I need to know is that a man is a member of the human race and that is bad enough for me.

Lady Astor was the first woman MP. She once said to Churchill: 'If you were my husband, I would flavour your coffee with poison.' He replied: 'Nancy, if I were your husband, I would drink it!'

On another occasion, Nancy said: 'Winston, you are very drunk.'
He retorted: 'Nancy, you are very ugly, but in the morning I shall be sober.'

The late Will Paling, MP, called Churchill 'a dirty dog'. The Tory benches erupted with cries of: 'Withdraw, withdraw . . .'

The old man rose to his feet. 'Not at all,' he said. 'I do not invite the Honourable Member to withdraw. On the contrary, I invite him to repeat what he has said outside this Chamber. And I will then show him what a dirty dog does to a paling!'

Death wish

President Johnson attended the memorial service in Australia for a Prime Minister, recently drowned. He was asked by the press what he would do for peace. 'Anything,' he replied.

'My President,' came a voice from the back. 'Would you take a swim?'

Fence sitting

An American Senator described King Hussein as 'Forever Amber'. [*Could be used for anyone else who cannot make up his mind whether to stop or to go, on a particular issue or generally. GJ*]

Accountants and politicians

Aneurin Bevan coined a marvellous phrase for a heartless human being. Many wrongly believe that he applied it to the austere Sir Stafford Cripps. In fact it was used in rage when he was beaten by Hugh Gaitskell for the Treasurership of the Labour Party. Without naming his target, he said: 'The right kind of leader for the Labour Party is a desiccated calculating machine who must not in any way permit himself to be swayed by indignation ... at suffering, privation or injustice ... for that would be evidence of the lack of proper education and absence of self control.

['*You sir, are – as Bevan once said – a desiccated calculating machine!*' is a splendid insult, especially when aimed at an accountant or a politician.]

Worst enemy

Herbert Morrison was once quoted as saying that he was his own worst enemy. 'Not while I'm alive, he ain't,' Ernest Bevin retorted.

Feminists

I myself have never been able to find out precisely what feminism is. I only know people call me a feminist whenever I express sentiments that differentiate me from a doormat ... (*Rebecca West, 1913*)

Compliment or insult?

Chancellor of the Exchequer David Lloyd George was making an important speech. A Conservative from the Opposition benches kept interrupting him. Eventually, Lloyd George exclaimed: 'I should think that the argument would be plain even to the colossal intellect of the Honourable Member.'

The Tory leapt to his feet. 'Is it in order, Mr Speaker,' he asked, 'for the Right Honourable Gentleman to refer to my colossal intellect?'

'Well,' replied Mr Speaker Lowther very softly. 'I think it is not only in order, but is rather complimentary than otherwise!'

Disaster v. calamity

If Gladstone fell into the Thames, that would be a misfortune; and if anybody pulled him out, that I suppose would be a calamity (*Disraeli*). [*This one is capable of innumerable variations, directed towards your current pet hate. Thus: 'If the Prime Minister/Leader of the Opposition/ managing director of main competitors, were to fall out of an aircraft, that would be a misfortune – if his parachute were to open – that would be a calamity.' GJ*]

Young parents

If you are faced with an inexperienced and youthful opponent, try the insult aimed by US Interior Secretary Harold Ickes at the then young Thomas Dewey, Republican candidate for President: 'Dewey has thrown his diaper into the ring.'

Lying

I do not accuse Mrs Thatcher of lying. She merely has what psychologists call 'selective amnesia'. (*Denis Healey*)

Plagues

I was recently at a charity dinner, with my wife on my right, and a very persistent lobbyist on my left. During the first three courses, he regaled me with horror stories of the way that politicians of all parties had ruined his business and how no country could really survive its treatment by those of us elected to office. Finally, my wife said to him: 'But surely you do make some distinction between the policies of the two parties?'

'There's no difference between you,' he retorted. 'I say: A plague on all your houses.'

My wife smiled across to him. 'When the plague comes to our house,' she said, 'you must come and visit us!'

Memories
I always smile at Mr Smith's jokes. First at their elegant wit, and then again with nostalgia.

Mindless?
Mr Smith didn't say a word till he was ten. His mother didn't know whether he was dumb or just speaking his mind.

Repetition
. . . we were all glad to hear his speech again.

Speechmaking
Mrs . . . has proved the theory that the brain is a wonderful organ that never stops functioning from the moment of birth until you rise to speak in public.

Sleeptalking
Mr . . .'s speeches always do the audience some good; they either go away stimulated or wake up refreshed.

Non-contribution
He makes the same contribution to commerce (or to the subject under discussion) as Cyril Smith* does to hang-gliding . . . [*Or any other well-known man of huge build. GJ]

Libraries
Mr Brown's library was burned down. Both books were destroyed. And one of them he had not even finished colouring.

Progression
I am independent of mind; he is eccentric; you are round the twist.

Proof
A man warmly greets a second hand car dealer. 'I've heard so much about you,' he said. The dealer (or *accountant, estate agent, lawyer* . . .) replied: 'You can't prove a thing!'

Spendthrift   Husband: 'You are a spendthrift.' Wife 'All right. So I like spending money. But name one other extravagance!'

Weddings   Best man: I have been intimate with the bride for many years and a finer woman never walked the streets.

Flattery   When I sit beside Mr Gladstone, I think that he is the cleverest man in the world. When I sit beside Mr Disraeli, I think that I am the cleverest woman in the world. (*Queen Victoria*)

Failure   I cannot make a 'come-back', because I have never been anywhere!

The boss   An executive said to his assistant: 'You are the biggest idiot that I have ever met.' His colleague retorted: 'Well, I have always thought that you were one of the best people to work for. But perhaps we were both wrong!'

Brain power   He has the brain of a flea – and no one has a higher opinion of him than I have!

Fame   His name is a household word – in his own household!

Friends   Abba Eban said of Cabinet Minister: 'It's not that he has enemies. It's just that his friends cannot stand him!' [*This marvellous insult can, of course, be translated against any worthy opponent! GJ*]

Reliability   You always know where you are with him. He will always let you down . . .

Clubs   That famous advocate, F. E. Smith (later Lord Birkenhead), was accustomed to call in to use the toilet facilities of the National Liberal Club, while on his way to the Lords. He was not a member.

　　Eventually, the Committee decided that something must be said. The chairman tackled him.

　　'Good gracious!' F.E. exploded. 'I'm so sorry.

I had no idea it was a club. I thought it was a public lavatory!'

Time-saving

People take an instant dislike to him — which saves them a lot of time.

Memorable?

He is very difficult to forget — but it is well worth the effort.

Anti-antisemitism

My most famous predecessor as President of the Board of Deputies of British Jews was Sir Moses Montefiore. Wherever Jews were in trouble, he would try to help them.

One day, he was at a dinner party, seated beside an obviously anti-semitic peer.

'I am just back from Japan,' said his lordship. 'It is a most delightful country. It has neither pigs nor Jews.'

'Remarkable,' said Montefiore. 'I suggest that you and I should travel there together and it will then have a sample of each.'

Brain transplants

Elderly patient to Harley Street surgeon: 'I want a brain transplant.'

'Certainly. But it's expensive.'

Patient: 'What would it cost me?'

Surgeon: 'Well, an ordinary brain would cost £20,000. But a politician's brain would run to at least £50,000.'

Patient: 'Why?'

Surgeon: 'Because a politician's brain is unused.'

Chattering tongues

My mother-in-law talks so much that when she went on holiday to Majorca, she returned home with a sunburned tongue. [*My mother-in-law is Australian; has never been to Majorca; and uses words with gentle economy. But you can adapt this one for (e.g.) a local politician who has returned from making speeches in any sunny clime. GJ*]

237

Vegetables

It is said that Prime Minister Margaret Thatcher decided to cheer up the Cabinet by taking them out to dinner in a restaurant. The waiter came over with the menu and said: 'Good evening. What will you have, Prime Minister?'
'I'll have a steak, please.'
'And the vegetables?'
She looked at her colleagues. 'They'll have steak, too,' she said.

Dullness

It is the sort of document that is so dull that when you put it down it is difficult to pick it up again. (*Malcolm Rifkind*)

Buried treasure

Why should Saddam Hussein [*or whoever is your current hate*] be buried 20 feet under the ground?
Because deep down, he's not such a bad guy!

Miracle worker

My secretary [*or receptionist or driver or whoever*] is a miracle worker. It's a miracle if he/she works!

Political enemies

It is an accursed doctrine that makes a difference of opinion a matter for personal hatred. (*Lord Acton*)

Someone said of a well known but unlovely politician: 'He has the perfect face . . . for radio!'

Mummified

Not long ago, they dug up a mummy. He opened his eyes and revived. Looking up, he said: 'Is Janner still MP for Leicester West?' [*This should be adapted to the particular purposes and personality in your area – to tease some long standing human institution.*]

Breeding

Buyer, examining a horse: 'He looks a decent animal, but is he well bred?'
'Well bred? Do you know, that animal is so well bred that if he could talk he wouldn't speak to either of us!'

69   Finance, sales and insolvency

Follow-up

Fred won a million pounds in a lottery. His wife said to him: 'What shall we do about all the begging letters?'

'Just keep sending them!' Fred replied.

How to become a millionaire

A bedraggled beggar wheedled a dollar out of Rockefeller, outside his Manhattan apartment block. After handing over the money, the millionaire enquired: 'Why don't you invest in some clean clothing, young man?'

'I appreciate the suggestion,' the beggar replied. 'But if you don't mind my asking, do I try to teach you your business?'

Fellow feeling

A burglar was caught in the garden of a millionaire's mansion, a transis.or radio in his pocket.

'What do you want us to do with him?' asked the police.

'Let him go,' answered the millionaire. 'We all started small.'

The gift of language

Sign on shop: '30 languages spoken here'. Customer comes in and tries to make herself understood in French, but nobody can manage. Another customer says to the shopkeeper: 'I thought you spoke 30 languages here?'

Shopkeeper replies: 'That's the customers . . . not us . . .'

Honour

'Next time a man says that his word is as good as his bond, take his bond! (*Lord Home of the Hirsel – formerly Prime Minister Alec Douglas Home*)

Energy

Britain is a lump of coal in a sea of oil on a bubble of gas. (*Clive Jenkins*)

239

Oil wealth	It's not clever just to have oil, you know. Sardines have oil and they are really stupid. They even get inside the tin and leave the key on the outside. (*Bob Monkhouse*)
Prophecies	It is very difficult to make a prophecy as to the future . . . and in Israel, it is very difficult to be a prophet at all, because of the competition . . .
Cash management	We have just created a new cash flow management programme. This means that we pay when we wish to . . .
Debtors	If you owe £50, you are a beggar. If you owe £5000, you are in business. If you owe £500 billion, then you are Chancellor of the Exchequer (or *Minister of Finance*).
Hyper-inflation	The Chancellor of the Exchequer went into a shop and said: 'I don't think inflation is that bad. Look at those handkerchiefs – £1 each. And shirts for £10. And trousers for £15.' His aide whispered quietly in his ear. 'I'm sorry, Minister. We're not in a man's shop. This is a laundry . . .'
Rise – or raise?	The head of a vast company whose parsimony to his employees was matched by his generosity to the currently governing political party was awarded a knighthood. At Buckingham Palace he knelt before Her Majesty, who tapped him on his right shoulder: 'Rise, Sir Frederick,' she said. Fred remained on his knees. The Queen tapped him on his left shoulder. 'Rise, Sir Frederick,' she pronounced. Still no movement. The sovereign lifted her sword and patted the tycoon gently on his head. 'Rise, Sir Frederick,' she said. Still nothing. A knowledgeable equerry whispered into the royal ear: 'I'd give up, Your Majesty,' he said. 'Sir Fred does not know the meaning of the word "rise".'

A capital story

'Where is the capital of Saudi Arabia?

'A third in Switzerland; a third in London; and the rest in Germany and the USA.'

This story is matched by one I was told in Canada: 'What was the first Polish settlement in the Province of Ontario?'

'30 cents in the dollar!'

Bankruptcy

Nothing in your deposit box? Nothing in your wife's name? Nothing dug into the ground? – You're not bankrupt, brother, you're skint!

Ultimate insolvency

Jack went bankrupt so often that he even put his tombstone into his wife's name.

Liquidation

Noah was the bravest man in history. He floated his company when the rest of the world was in liquidation.

Recession

A deep-sea diver feels tug on rope. Voice on intercom says: 'Come up quickly, the ship's sinking!' [*Suitable for comment on invitation to join political party currently in eclipse. GJ*]

Fair exchange

An accountant opened a new office and a client ordered flowers to be sent to him. The next day a splendid arrangement arrived with a card containing the message, 'Rest in Peace'.

The accountant spoke to his friend and told him what had happened. The friend apologized. 'But,' he said, 'just think of the pleasure that will have been given at the funeral by the card reading "Good luck in your new location!" '

Taxes

We should all pay our taxes with a smile. I tried. But they wanted cash!

Taxing sports

Income tax has made more liars out of British people than golf or fishing.

70 Works, trade and management

Perks
Our staff reckon that they can only take the company's property off our premises at certain times . . .

Welcome
When the Pope landed on a ceremonial visit to the UK, he knelt and kissed the soil.
'I wonder why he did that?' an astonished onlooker exclaimed.
The man beside him retorted: 'You would too, if you'd flown Alitalia and landed safely!'

Fringe benefits
On 'cabbage' (the rag trade term for material offcuts): 'We usually sell cabbage to our staff – if they don't pinch it first . . .'

Working hours
Alistair Cooke passed a country station and found the stationmaster tending his roses. 'How many hours a day do you work?' he enquired.
'Eight hours, sir. Five days a week.'
'Always eight hours? Always five days a week?' said Mr Cooke.
'Yes, always the same?'
'Why always the same?'
'Because if I worked less than eight hours, I wouldn't have enough money to buy roses. And if I worked more than eight hours, I would not have time to tend the roses . . .'

Short-time?
Employer: 'Did you work a full week last week?'
Employee: 'Yes – but I don't want any publicity . . .'

Occupational illnesses
Three well known diseases: Plumbi pendulosis –swinging the lead; Haemophraemia – bloody mindedness; and Non-digitus extractus – failure to pull out the finger . . .

Tell-tale twitch
A man applied for a job as a television announcer. Unfortunately, he suffered from a

242

severe twitch of his right eye. His interviewer said: 'Wouldn't you be better off applying for a job with the radio?'

'No,' the man replied. 'I take one of my special pills and I'll all right for a couple of hours.'

'In that case,' said the interviewer, 'you'd better take one now and let me see how it works.'

The man fished in his pockets and pulled out a packet of condoms . . . then another . . . then a third . . . then a whole pile of them, before finally producing a bottle of aspirin.

'I understand the aspirin,' said the interviewer. 'But why the contraceptives?'

The interviewee looked at him sceptically. 'Have you ever tried going into a chemist's shop and saying: "I'd like a (wink) bottle of (wink) aspirin, please"?'

Job description Fred answered an advertisement offering £1,500 for a man prepared to sleep with a gorilla. He asked whether he could have time to pay.

Unemployment A miner applied for a job at a Rhondda pit. The manager told him to 'come back in the spring'.

'What do you think I am,' asked the man, 'a ruddy cuckoo?' (*Speaker George Thomas, now Viscount Tonypandy*)

Warning The managing director of a great engineering company invited school classes to see round the works. One of the teachers was overheard at the end of the morning saying to his class: 'There you are, lads and girls. You have now seen where you may end up, if you don't do well in your O-levels!'

Passing the buck An Ordinary Seaman was applying for promotion. He was asked to correct the following statement: 'It was me what done it.' He wrote: 'It was not me what done it.' [*Legend has it that he was immediately promoted to Rear Admiral! GJ*]

Trade unions

A trade union is an island of anarchy in a sea of chaos. (*Aneurin Bevan*)

'Differentials' and 'anomalies'

If I earn more than you do, that is a 'differential'. If you earn more than I do, that is an 'anomaly'.

Management – and industrial disputes

The latest argument at a works renowned for its management problems got senior executives so upset that they began to stab each other in the front. [*Also useful to describe feelings in the Cabinet, Shadow Cabinet, boardroom – or where-you-will. GJ*]

Pay day?

A son asked his father for a loan until pay day. His father asked: 'When is pay day?'

The son replied: 'I don't know. You tell me. You're the one who's working . . .'

Leadership

There are two types of leadership. One is where you go in front and lead from there. The other is where you wait to see where people are going and then run around to the front and take over.

Explanations

A personnel director was having great trouble in inducing an employee to sign up under a non-contributory pension scheme – which was in fact far better for him than the current contributory pension scheme. He refused to sign.

Eventually, the personnel manager sent the man to the managing director. 'Alex,' said the MD, 'You must sign. I know that you have been with us for 30 years without causing trouble, but that is no reason for not signing . . .'

Alex 'I refuse.'

Managing Director: 'Alex, you must sign – or I will give you the sack!'

Alex signed.

The next time that personnel manager saw Alex, he said: 'Why did you sign when the managing director asked you to – but you always refused me?'

Alex: 'Well, no one explained it to me properly before . . .'

Supervisors

Two foremen were arguing over whether sex was a pleasure or a chore. The first, a married man with eight children, regarded it as a chore. The second, a bachelor, thought it was the greatest delight in his life. To settle their argument, they called over young Fred, the apprentice. 'So you tell us, Fred,' they said. 'Is sex a chore or a pleasure?'

'It must be a pleasure,' said the boy.

'Why?'

'Because if it was a chore, you guys would make me do it for you!'

Up yours

A worker removed the guard from a machine and lost two fingers on his right hand. He only noticed his loss when he said good night to the foreman!

Once a failure

A man was sacked for trying to kill his foreman. His shop steward begged the employers to give him a second chance.

Never resign

Frederick the Great intended to dismiss one of his Generals. The General wrote to him: 'After the battle, my head is yours. Meanwhile I intend to use it to best effect on your behalf.'

Dismissal

The chairman of a large company called in his directors, one by one. Eventually, only the newest and most junior director was left outside the chairman's office. When his turn came, he found his colleagues sitting around a table.

Chairman: 'Bill have you been having an affair with my secretary, Miss Jones?'

Bill: 'Certainly not.'

'Are you sure?'

'Absolutely. I've never laid a hand on her.'

'Are you quite certain?'

'Of course I am.'

'Very well, Bill. Then you sack her.'

References

'I am pleased to recommend him, for any other job . . .' or 'I am pleased to provide him with a reference for any other job . . .' or 'He was fired with enthusiasm . . .'

Erratic leadership

The following is a useful analogy, when explaining why the Prime Minister, president, managing director or other adversary is likely to perform some unpredictable and dangerous act:

Mr Brown is like the cross-eyed javelin thrower who does not break any records, but who certainly keeps the audience on its toes!

Delanguage

English is a curious language. Consider the words used to take away people's livelihoods.

Nurses are *de*registered. Barristers are *de*barred. Priests are *de*frocked.

Presumably, clerks are *de*filed. Musicians are *de*composed. Politicians are *de*flated. Heavy drinkers are *de*livered. Electricians are *de*lighted. Psychiatrists are *de*ranged. And prostitutes are *de*laid.

Industrial relations

Industrial relations are like sexual relations. It's better between two consenting parties. *Lord Feather (former Chairman of TUC)*

71   Politicians and philosophers

Objectivity

Those who are prominent in political life are objectively described only in their own memoirs. (*Abba Eban*)

Politicians

A politician is a person who approaches every problem with an open mouth. (*Adlai Stevenson*)

Principles

I am a man of principle – but one of my principles is expediency. (*Lloyd George*)

Compromise

Compromise is when you do today that which you swore yesterday that you would not do – and while all politicians compromise, none of them like to be photographed doing so . . .

Balanced concerns

'If I am not for myself, then who will be for me? But if I am only for myself, what am I? And if not now, then when?' (*Rabbi Hillel*)

Middle of the road

The only part of the road worth driving on is the middle – each of the extremes is in the gutter. (*President Eisenhower*)

Experience

Experience tells us that politicians do not always mean the opposite of what they say.

Eggs and baskets

British aircraft manufacturers once suggested to Winston Churchill that he, the Cabinet and 40 other MPs should go up in the newly invented Comet jet aircraft, so as to give confidence to the public. One of his ministers complained that if anything happened to the aircraft, it would be disastrous. The country would be plunged into over 60 by-elections at the same time.

Reluctantly, the old man agreed. 'It all goes to show,' he said, 'that it is potentially disastrous to put all your baskets into one egg . . .'

Opposition

To be in Opposition is no disgrace. In fact, it is

247

an honour. It is the only honour which politicians do not actively seek!

Governmental philosophy

If you do not know where you are going, you will probably end up somewhere else . . .

Media attraction

A microphone has the same effect on him as a lamp post has on a dog.

Sleep

Members of Parliament and Congressmen are people who talk in other people's sleep.

The oldest profession?

Some say gardening is the oldest profession – because Adam was the first man on earth. But the Bible tells us that before the world was created, all was chaos and confusion. And you all know who created that . . . politicians!

Incipient modesty

Your first two weeks in Parliament, you wonder how you got there. Thereafter, you wonder how the others got there.

Substitute?

An MP died. Within a day, a young hopeful telephoned the national agent. 'I hope it's not too soon,' he said, 'but I'm wondering whether I might not take the place of the deceased . . .'

The national agent replied: 'If the undertaker has no objection, I certainly have none!'

Divisions

Two tourists were standing in the central lobby in the House of Commons when the division bell rang. 'What's that?' one of them asked the other. 'I don't know,' she replied. 'I suppose one of them must have escaped . . .'

Person unknown

A Tory Whip telephoned one of his Members in the middle of the night, to tell him to come in to vote. A woman's voice answered the phone – but he heard a male voice in the background saying: 'Tell him I'm not here . . .'

'I'm afraid Mr . . . is not here,' said the voice.

Quick as a flash, the Whip replied: 'In that case, please tell the man who is in bed with you, whoever he may be, that he is required at the House of Commons to vote . . . at once!'

New councillor   Dai Jones is elected a Councillor for the first time. Delighted, he goes to the pub to celebrate.

'Your usual, Dai?' asks the barman.

'Councillor Dai, if you please,' Dai retorted.

When he went to collect his coat in the cloakroom, the attendant said: 'Good evening, Dai.'

'Councillor Dai, if you please,' he replied.

And so it went on with everyone he met. And when he got home, he heard his wife's voice from upstairs: 'Is that you, Dai?'

'Councillor Dai, if you please,' he replied.

'Then you'd better hurry up,' his wife called out. 'Dai will be home at any moment!'

Surprise   St Peter provided a distinguished pope with a bare cell, while giving a Congressman a fine, carpeted and thoroughly heavenly apartment. When challenged by the Pope, St Peter replied: 'We've had plenty of popes up here – but this is our first Congressman!'

Alas   There is nothing so 'ex' as an ex-MP.

Spot the wise man   Bush, Mitterrand and Major met at a conference. 'I need your help,' said Bush. 'I have a problem. I have 18 guards. One of them is a KGB agent. And I cannot find out which one it is!'

'I have a problem that, in its own way, is even worse,' said Mitterrand. 'I have 18 mistresses. One of them is unfaithful to me. And my problem is that I cannot tell which one.'

'My problem is worst of all,' said Mr Major, 'I have 20 people in my Cabinet. One of them is very clever ... [*This happy and – I hasten to add – apocryphal tale, may, of course, be adapted to whichever Cabinet, committee or other national or organized leadership you may desire to defame. GJ*]

Economy   A politician who claimed that it would be possible to get much the same results with half the expenditure illustrated his case with the tale of a Scottish riding school. They supplied each rider with only one spur on the principle that if you can get half the horse to go, there is a good chance that the other half will follow.

Clichés

'My Cabinet Members can do all sorts of things,' commented the King. 'The Duke here can make mountains out of molehills. The Minister splits hairs. The Count makes hay while the sun shines. The Earl leaves no stone unturned. And the Under Secretary,' he finished off ominously, 'hangs by a thread.' (*From 'The Phantom Tollbooth' by Norton Juster.*) [*Like 'Alice in Wonderland', this brilliant children's fantasy is full of fascination for adults – and lessons for speechmakers.*]

Political prophecy

When Prime Minister, Harold Wilson said: 'A week is a long time in politics'. The Japanese say 'In politics, one inch ahead is darkness'.

Underdogs

In the terms of public support, nothing fails like success. (*Ian Mikardo*)

Politics

Politics is the art of looking for trouble; of finding it, even if there is none; of making the wrong diagnosis; and of prescribing the wrong cure. (*Sir Ernest Benn*)

Riposte

The great British Jewish leader, Sir Moses Montefiore, visited Germany. A man walking in the street deliberately bumped into him, snarling: 'Schweinhund!'

Sir Moses courteously stepped back and bowed: 'Montefiore!' he replied.

Deserters

When colleagues started leaving the party in substantial numbers saying that they did not intend to stand at the next election, thereby leaving their embattled leader in very bad times, that was described as 'the ship leaving the sinking rat . . .'

Harnessing hate

This next story is infinitely variable. I have heard it successively used about Carter and the

Iranians, Reagan and the Afghans, Kinnock and
the Militants . . . Use it for whomever you wish.

Michael Heseltine was having his hair cut.
'How are you, Mr Heseltine?' asked the barber —
snip, snip.

'Fine, thank you.'

'And Mr Major?'

'Oh, he's fine, too, thanks.'

A few minutes later: 'Is it true that you and the
PM are getting on much better now?'

'We've always got on well. But why do you
keep asking me about Mr Major?'

'Because whenever I mention his name, your
hair stands on end and becomes much easier to
cut!'

Political satire

Political satire died the moment Henry Kissinger
received the Nobel Peace Prize. (*Tom Lehrer*)

Verbatim

Reporter to President Reagan: 'Did the director
of the CIA carry on covert operations without
your knowing, Mr President?'

Reagan: 'Not to my knowledge.'

**Unseen
brilliance**

Full many a gem of purest ray serene
The dark unfathomed caves of ocean bear:
Full many a flower is born to blush unseen
And waste its sweetness on the desert air.
(*Thomas Gray*)
[*Note: this I quote to MPs who (as, alas, so often
happens) prepare brilliant speeches, questions or
jests, which go either unheard because Mr.
Speaker's eye rests elsewhere – or unrecognized,
because they are unquoted by the media.*]

**Politics,
ambition and
anger**

Churchill was asked: Why did you go into
politics? 'Ambition,' he replied. 'Pure, unadulterated ambition.'

'Then why did you stay in politics?'

'Anger. Pure, unadulterated anger.'

Warning

This animal is dangerous. It defends itself.

72 Parliament, government, democracy and elections

Differences of opinion
We specialize in harmonizing contrariness. (*Sir Shridath (Sonny) Ramphal, former Secretary General of the Commonwealth*)

Family tradition
Franklin D. Roosevelt was asked why he was a Democrat. He replied: 'Because my great-grandfather and my grandfather and my father were Democrats before me.'

'What would happen if your great-grandfather, your grandfather and your father had been horse thieves?' retorted the questioner.

'In that case,' President Roosevelt replied, 'I would have been a Republican.'

News – and advertising
'News is what somebody somewhere wants to suppress; all the rest is advertising'. (*Lord Northcliffe*)

Mania
Soviet dissident Leonid Plyush told a group of MPs the sad story of his incarceration in Soviet mental institutions. When asked what diagnosis he had received from the Soviet psychiatric experts he replied: 'Reformist mania with messianic tendencies.' His listeners agreed that he would have made an excellent MP.

Princely politics
It is very difficult to avoid making party political statements when you talk about almost anything. Sometimes, I fall into great elephant traps and no one notices. Other times, I trip into a very small trap – and all hell breaks loose . . . (*Prince Charles*)

Open government
Sunlight is the most effective of all disinfectants . . . (*US Supreme Court Justice Brandeis*)

Parliament
Our parliamentary system is not good – but it's the best we got. (*Winston Churchill*)

Parliament, government, democracy and elections

Parliamentary democracy is the worst form of government – until you look at all the others. (*Winston Churchill*)

Committees

If Moses had been a committee, the Israelites would still be in Egypt.

A parliamentary committee is a cul-de-sac into which ideas are lured, there to be quietly strangled . . .

Committee inventions

A camel is a horse invented by a committee.

Committee of one

Every committee must be made up of an odd number of people. Three members is too many.

Whipping

An MP complained that the 'whipping' had been so heavy that he could not even get out of the Commons to attend the christening of his son. His friend replied: 'You're lucky. You weren't there when your son was christened. I wasn't there when mine was conceived!'

Elections

A Scottish jury was informed by the judge: 'This is a simple case and no doubt it will not take you long to reach your verdict.'

After the jury had been out for three hours, the judge called them in. 'What's happened?' he enquired.

'We had no difficulty reaching our verdict,' he was told. 'But the trouble is that we're still trying to elect a foreman . . .'

The right of citizens in a democracy exercises the rotatory principle and electors vote the wrong party into power. (*Abba Eban*)

Iraqi elections

In Iraq they have what are called 'Adam elections' – you have the same choice as he had.

Withdraw, withdraw!

MP Willie Hamilton was criticizing Harold Wilson for wanting to go into the Common Market . . . then out of the market . . . then into the market again . . . He described such

253

haviour as: 'The politics of coitus interruptus.' The MP in front of him yelled 'Withdraw . . . withdraw . . .'

The truth

An opponent said: 'How do you know when ex-President Nixon is lying? When he spreads his hands out, he's telling the truth . . . When he wags his finger, he's telling the truth . . . When he shakes his fist, he's telling the truth . . . But when he opens his mouth . . .'

Emigration

A professor decided to emigrate. The dean called him to his office: 'Why do you want to go?' he enquired. 'You have a very good job . . . an excellent home . . . splendid prospects . . .'

'There are two reasons,' the professor replied. 'The first is when I come home in the evenings, I usually find my neighbour outside the door, dead drunk. He keeps swearing at me: "Just wait till we get rid of this Tory government and then we'll slit the throats of all you useless academics!" '

'But the Tory government is in for a while yet,' replied the dean.

'Precisely,' said the professor. 'That's my second reason.'

Tory advance

Conservative statesman: 'I see the status quo as the way forward.'

The choice before us

Vicar, blessing all parties before British election: 'We shall have three hymns today. In honour of the Conservatives: Now Thank We All Our God . . . In honour of the Labour Party: Oh God Our Help In Ages Past . . . And in honour of the Social Democrats: God Moves In a Mysterious Way . . .'

Why we lost

If you are travelling in a rocky ship and feel seasick, it is quite understandable that you would wish to throw the navigator overboard. (*Denis Healey*)

Advice to successor

When Harold Wilson handed over the premiership to James Callaghan, he is said to have left three envelopes in a drawer. They were to be opened in turn, in times of disaster.

Opening the first envelope, after the first disaster, Callaghan read: 'Blame your predecessor.'

After the second, he read: 'Sack your assistant.'

After the third 'Prepare three envelopes . . .'

Successors

After Mrs Thatcher took over from Mr Callaghan, she is reported to have said to him privately: 'You certainly left us a lot of problems.' Jim replied: 'I didn't ask you to take them on, did I?'

Deterrent

Lord Birkett liked to tell the classic tale of the woman in the train who watched the man opposite her tearing up a newspaper and every now and again throwing tiny pieces out of the window.

'Why are you doing that, sir?' she enquired.

'To keep the elephants away,' he replied.

'But there are no elephants,' she protested.

'Yes,' he answered. 'It is indeed wonderfully effective.'

Hardly ever

The Captain of Gilbert and Sullivan's HMS Pinafore was asked whether he was ever sick at sea. He replied: 'Never.'

'What, never?' chorused the sailors.

'No, never.'

'What, never?' the sailor insisted.

'Well . . . hardly ever . . .' the Captain admitted. [*Similarly: The Government – or the Opposition, or the company, or you – may hardly ever be mistaken, out of step, cheating . . . GJ*]

Political punishment

W. S. Gilbert suggested that a judge should 'let the punishment fit the crime'. The following story may be adapted to suit whichever politicians you feel most inclined to insult at the time.

When Winston Churchill died and went to heaven, he was greeted by St Peter who directed him to his room: 'Straight down the corridor, eighth door on the left.' As he walked by, he saw Neville Chamberlain in a cubicle embracing the great cabaret artist, Mae West.

When Winston arrived at his cubicle, he discovered his old sparring partner, Lady Astor – the first woman MP – lying on the bed. He stormed back to St Peter: 'It's disgraceful,' he thundered. 'After all that I've done for the world. It's bad enough putting me in a room with old Nancy Astor. But how can you do that while putting that dreadful Neville Chamberlain with the delicious Mae West?'

'Now, you mind your own business, Sir Winston,' Peter replied. 'How I punish Mae West is my affair!'

Screw loose

Why is (*current central figure in publicized sex scandal*) like an item of (*name your favourite put-it-together yourself*) furniture?

Because lose a screw and the whole arrangement falls apart!

Security – and values

A state which has security but lacks moral values is like a ship without a rudder. But a state with moral values and no security is like a rudder without a ship. (*Henry Kissinger*)

Banana skins

'We specialize in defusing banana skins . . .' (*Sir Robert Armstrong, secretary to the Cabinet, on the roles of his colleagues and himself*)

Foreigners

Stan Cohen, MP for a Leeds seat, is not Jewish. He aquired his name because when his grandfather came to Leeds, someone asked him for his name and he replied: 'My name is Quoin' – which, of course, was written as it sounded, and then his Irish family acquired a priestly Jewish surname.

Returning to the House after an election, Stan told me this enchanting tale. He had knocked on the door of a house and a woman emerged. 'My name is Stan Cohen and I am the Labour candidate,' he said, 'and I hope that I can count on your support.'

'Certainly not,' said the woman. 'I don't vote for Jews!'

'In that case,' said Stan, 'I think you should know that I do not want your vote. But just for the record, perhaps I should tell you that I am Irish.'

'Are you, then?' the woman exploded. 'Goodbye. I don't vote for foreigners!' and she slammed the door.

Diplomatic dance

George Brown, then Labour Foreign Minister, is said to have been at a diplomatic function when the orchestra struck up. As the senior Minister present, he decided to start the dancing. Spotting a likely prey, he said to her: 'Madam, will you do me the honour of this waltz?'

'Certainly not,' said the reply. 'For three reasons. First, you're drunk. Second, this is not a waltz, but the Venezuelan National Anthem. Third, I am the Papal Nuncio.'

Free speech

As Mrs Thatcher used to say to her Cabinet: 'When I want your opinion, I'll give it to you . . .'

The enemy's behind

Jeremy Hanley, MP recalled his first day in the Commons, in 1983. He was startled to find the Rev. Ian Paisley, MP, sitting behind him. 'I didn't realize you were on our side,' Mr Hanley stuttered.

'Young man,' boomed Mr Paisley. 'Never confuse "sitting on your side" with "being on your side"!'

Hard times

Dan Quayle's three hardest years – 2nd grade.

Wooden

When Labour activist Fred Peart was elected as a Member of Parliament in 1935, he arrived at his celebration party in full captain's battledress. He was greeted with rapturous applause. The chairman said: 'Not only is Fred a great Socialist . . . not only is he a great member of the working classes . . . not only is he a great patriot and fighter for his country . . . but he is made of the stuff that Cabinets are made of!'

Pause   If you weren't such a great man, you'd be a terrible bore! (*Prime Minister's wife, Mrs William Gladstone, to her spouse*)

Public bores   He speaks to me as if I were a public meeting. (*Queen Victoria – re: Gladstone*)

Political pessimist   In politics, a pessimist is a former Opposition Leader elected to office and who then receives full information.

Time watches   Vicar to parishioner: 'I don't mind you looking at your watch during my sermon. But when you lift it up to your ear and shake it. . . !'

Sleep – in the Lords   The late Lord Salisbury dreamed that he was speaking in the House of Lords. He woke up and found that he was.

Racial prejudice   Racial prejudice is like a hair across your cheek. You can't see it; you can't find it with your fingers; but you keep brushing at it, because the feel of it is irritating. (*Marian Anderson*)

The dream   I have a dream that my four little children will one day live in a nation where they will not be judged by the colour of their skin, but by the content of their character. (*Martin Luther King*)

Journalism   Winston Churchill was asked why he spent time on lecturing and journalism, instead of devoting himself entirely to his political work. He explained that he needed the money. 'I live from mouth to hand,' he said.

The Whip   'On the day that the press proclaimed that Conservative MP Harvey Proctor was being investigated in respect of allegations of "spanking" and other similar practices, he was absent from the Commons when his name was called out at Prime Minister's Question Time. 'Where is he? Where is he? Where is he?' Labour MPs shouted.

'In the Whip's office!' his colleague, Robert Atkins yelled. The place exploded with laughter.

Secrets

Three MPs were on a trip abroad. After a liquid dinner, they shared indiscretions. The first admitted that he was a secret womanizer; the second that he had severe problems with alcohol; the third maintained that his vice was worse than either of theirs. 'I am a gossip,' he said, 'and I cannot wait to get back to the smoking room in the House to pass on the news that you have just given to me!'

Advice to politicians

When I was first elected, a marvellous old Conservative put his arm around my shoulder and said: 'Your father was a very good friend of mine. We did not agree all the time, but that did not prevent us from being very fond of each other.'

GJ: 'I know. So could you give me some advice on how to behave in this place?'

'Yes. Never do good by stealth!'

The limit

Daughter, to adoring Mum: 'I'm getting engaged.'

Mum: 'Well, that's marvellous. Who is he?'

Daughter: 'Oh, he's very nice. I hope you won't mind, though – he's a Catholic.'

Mum: 'Of course I don't mind. Religion is not important.'

Daughter: 'I hope you also won't mind that he's black.'

Mother: 'Of course I don't.'

Daughter: 'I'm afraid he's also disabled. He's got one eye, a hunchback and no hair.'

Mother: 'That's all right, darling, whatever makes you happy is fine by me.'

Daughter: 'One final thing I should tell you. His father's a Labour MP.'

Mother throws herself out of the window.

Victory

In war, there is no substitute for victory. (*General MacArthur*) [*Also business, politics, sport or other competitive ventures.*]

Feminist

Why did the feminist cross the road? Why shouldn't she cross the road?

Custom and practice?

Ronald and Nancy Reagan had a private audience with the Pope. When they emerged from his Chamber, Nancy said: 'Ronald, did you fart, while you were with the Pope?'

Reagan replied: 'Nope. Should I have done?'

Diaries

My late father, Lord (Barnett) Janner, packed his diary with intricate scrawl. Watching him at a meeting, a colleague said: 'What are you doing, Barny? Looking to see where you are going next?' 'Certainly not,' he replied. 'I'm looking to see where I am now!'

The devil

John Wilkes: 'I ask you to vote for me.'

Heckler: 'Vote for you? I'd rather vote for the devil.'

Wilkes: 'And if your friend is not standing?'

73   Foreigners and diplomats

Foreign Office   A tourist recently asked a policeman in White-hall: 'Which side is the Foreign Office on?' He replied: 'It's supposed to be on our side – but I sometimes wonder . . .'

Ex   When you are a distinguished ambassador, everyone wants you to make speeches and to be guest of honour. When you are an extinguished ambassador, you have to look both for a plat-form and a livelihood . . .

Ambassadors and journalists   An ambassador is a man of virtue sent to lie abroad for his country. A newswriter is a man without virtue who lies at home for himself. (*Sir Henry Wootton*) [*The first quote, written in 1604, is well known. He added the second part later when a journalist teased him about the lack of diplomacy inherent in his first definition.*]

Peaceful solution   Our government is prepared to solve any in-dustrial relations problem peacefully if no other solution is available. [*Adapt to suit your circum-stances – government, committee, organization or as the case may be. GJ*]

Silent diplomacy   Scientist Mark Azbel told of the need for silence by Jews and others oppressed by their rulers: 'A little bird freezes on a cold day and falls to the ground. A passing cow drops a cow pat on it. The bird, revived by the warmth, begins to chirp. A fox appears, hears the chirping, cleans the bird and eats it.'

Moral: 'Not everyone who covers you with manure is your enemy and not everyone who cleans you off is your friend.'

'More important: If you are deep in the shit, don't make a sound!'

Democracy?

Ivor (now Lord) Richard, former British Ambassador to the UN, was asked by an American friend why the United Nations is so undemocratic.

'Undemocratic?' he replied. 'Why do you say that?'

'Because we keep getting outvoted!'

Christmas gifts – and diplomatic problems

A newly appointed British Ambassador to the USA arrived in Washington DC in mid-December. A newspaper man was chatting with him and asked: 'Ambassador, what would you like for Christmas?'

He replied: 'Well, a small box of American chocolates would do nicely.'

On Christmas Eve, the Embassy was shocked to hear the following broadcast: 'We asked various Ambassadors what they would like best for Christmas. The German Ambassador replied: 'A generation of peace for all the world.' The French Ambassador replied: 'Love and Fraternity between nations.' The United Kingdom envoy replied: 'A small box of American chocolates would do nicely.'

English – and American

Never has one language done more to divide two nations. (*George Bernard Shaw*)

Idealism

Yes, India is a country with great ideals – but it is peopled entirely by human beings. (*Prime Minister Mrs Indira Gandhi*) [*or the UK – or anywhere else GJ*]

United Nations?

Former Secretary of State, Dean Acheson: When the United Nations is divided by 50/50, then the decision does not represent 'world conscience'. [Add Yemen, Haiti or Portugal and it becomes world conscience.]

Equality?

Re Israel and her Arab foes: 'They are many and we are one, but we represent 50 per cent of the conflict.' (*Yigal Allon*)

Mind your language

Many years ago, a Canadian MP replied to a suggestion that their proceedings ought to be held from time to time in French saying: 'If the English language was good enough for Matthew, Mark, Luke and John, it is good enough for us!'

Lost opportunities

The Jordanians never miss a chance to lose an opportunity. (*Abba Eban*) [*Adapt to suit circumstances/nation/government/situation. GJ*]

Promotion refuses

The Arab general who conquered Egypt some 1,300 years ago expected the Caliph of Arabia to appoint him governor of the country. In fact, the Caliph only offered him the command of the troops in Egypt, while another man became governor.

The General refused this command, with the memorable phrase: 'Why should I hold the cow's horns, whilst someone else milks her?' (*Anwar Sadat*)

Pure bred?

A polar bear has little boy in tow. Son pulls at his tail. 'Dad,' he says, 'do we have any brown bear blood in us?'

'Certainly not, son,' replies the father. 'We're pure polar bear.'

A little later, tail tugged again: 'Dad. Have we any grizzly bear blood in our veins?'

'How many times do I have to tell you, son – we are absolutely pure polar bear'.

A little later. 'Dad, are you sure that we haven't any koala bear blood in our family?'

'Son, I've told you often enough, we are absolutely pure polar bear – with no other sort of blood in us at all. Only polar bear. But why do you ask?'

'Cos, I'm flipping freezing!'

EEC virtues

What we need are all the attributes of our colleagues in the Common Market. We should have the sovereignty of Luxembourg, the even temper of the Italians, the flexibility of the

Dutch, the initiative of the Belgians, the good nature of the Germans, the reasonableness of the French . . . But we do have in any event the sheer hard work and culinary art of the British . . .

Precedence When the late Aga Khan was due to be guest at a luncheon in the House of Lords, the host wrote to the Garter King of Arms on the question of precedence. After a long wait, he received the following reply: 'The Aga Khan is believed to be a direct descendent of God. English Dukes take precedence . . .'

Brainwashing Chief Rabbi Rosen of Romania tells of his first visit to America. On landing, he was surrounded by press men who asked him some very abrupt and even rude questions. For instance: 'Rabbi, are you not brainwashed in your country?'

He replied: 'Yes, I suppose we are. But then so are you, in a different way. The difference between us and you, though, is that we do not believe what we read in the newspapers and you do.'

Peace A peace treaty is more impressive when it has two signatures on it. (*Abba Eben*)

Ignorance About the policies and motives of the Soviet Union, there is no knowledge – only varying degrees of ignorance. (*President Truman*)

Siberian parrot A Russian dissident trained his parrot to say: 'Down with Brezhnev . . . Down with Marx . . . Down with Lenin . . .'

One day, the KGB called on the dissident. In panic, he shoved the parrot into his refrigerator.

The KGB men searched the house and eventually opened the refrigerator. The parrot emerged shivering.

After an expectant pause, the parrot talked: 'I love Brezhnev . . . I love Marx . . . I love Lenin . . .'

'Little bastard,' snarled his master. 'After five minutes in Siberia, you join the Party . . .'

State secret

Some years ago, a Moscow man was arrested for rushing naked through the streets, yelling: 'Khrushchev is a fool!'

The Judge sentenced him to 25 months' imprisonment. 'You get six months for indecent behaviour,' he said, 'and 19 months for betraying State secrets.'

Moscow morale

A man phoned his friend in Moscow: 'How are you, Ivan?' he asked.

'Fantastic . . . marvellous . . . unbelievable . . . fabulous . . .'

'OK,' said his friend. 'I see you've got someone with you. I'll phone you back later . . .' [*Transpose this one to any current autocracy of your choice. GJ*]

Détente

A Soviet dignitary boasted to an American acquaintance that they had found a new way to make a lion share a cage with a lamb. 'If you don't believe me,' he said, 'then when you come to the USSR we will show you . . .'

True enough, on his next visit the American was taken to Moscow Zoo and there in a cage was a lion lying in one corner and a lamb in another.

'That's wonderful' said the American. 'You must have a very remarkable lion and very wonderful lamb . . .'

'The lion is a good one,' replied the Russian. 'But we have a new lamb every morning.'

One all

For years, I had written to Ambassador Smirnowski, Head of the Russian mission to the UK. My complaints about their treatment of Jews, dissidents, Baptists and other minority groups were all ignored. Then, one day, he came to the Commons for tea, as guest of the Anglo-Soviet Parliament Group – of which I was and remain a member in good standing. The Chair introduced us. I said: 'Your Excellency, I am very pleased to meet you. I did not believe you really existed.'

265

'Why not?' he asked.

'How could I accept the existence of a person who fails to answer so many letters?'

Ambassador: 'Well, I am very pleased to meet you too. I did not believe that a man who wrote so many contentious leters could be so pleasant . . .'

Match drawn . . .

Diplomats v. politicians

What is the difference between a diplomat and a politician?

In civilized diplomacy, diplomats speak well of each other in public and are rude in private. In civilized politics, politicians are rude to each other in public, but friends in private.

Political skill

Political skill is when the Austrians convince you that Mozart was an Austrian and that Hitler was a German. As for Waldheim . . .

Improvements

In New York, I once bought a volume of Shakespeare's collected works in Yiddish. The fly-leaf bore the following modest caption: 'Shakespeare – ubergezetst und verbessert' – 'Shakespeare – translated and improved'!

No solution

God called Gorbachev, Bush and Shamir before him. He slammed them for their part in making the world unacceptable. Then he delivered his own verdict: 'In two weeks' time, I shall destroy the earth. Go back to your people and tell them.'

Gorbachev returned to the Soviet Union, called together his Cabinet and said to them: 'I have two pieces of bad news for you. First, there is a God. Second, God will in two weeks destroy the earth.'

Bush returned to Washington, called his Cabinet and told them: 'I have good news and bad news for you. The good news is: God exists. The bad news is that He will in two weeks destroy the earth.'

Shamir returned to Israel and called his Cabinet together. 'I have two bits of good news for you.' he said. 'The first – that there is a God; the second – that in two weeks he will solve the Palestinian problem!'

[Note: This story is easily transferrable to any other current world leaders – and to the solution of any other insoluble problem. You could (for instance) try the current UK Prime Minister and the Northern Ireland problem; the Indian PM and the problem of Kashmir; the South African President with the problem of the blacks in his country . . .GJ]

74   Business, companies and professions

Auditors

An auditor is an accountant who comes onto the field after the battle is over and bayonets the wounded. (*Don Hanson, Arthur Andersen*)

Auditors – and actuaries

An auditor is like an actuary who has had his personality removed.

Accountancy

If someone asks me: 'What is two and two? I answer: 'Are you buying or selling?' (*Lord Grade*)

Accountants

Three men apply for a job as an accountant. They are asked one question: 'What is two times two?' The first two fellows get it right. The third one replies: 'What figure did you have in mind, sir?' He got the job.

Accountants

An accountant arrived at the gates of Heaven.
'And how old are you, my boy?' asked St Peter.
'Forty-two,' said the man. 'And much too young to have died, don't you think?'
Peter shook his head. 'How odd,' he said, 'I've been looking through your time sheets and according to them, you should be 89!'

Capitalism and Bankruptcy

Capitalism without bankruptcy is like Christianity without hell. (*Eastern Airlines' Chief Executive*)

Risks

A 'calculated risk' was defined by an airline pilot as 'when the engineers on the ground make the calculations and the pilots take the risk'. [*Adapt for any situation where others make the calculation but the risk is yours. GJ*]

Flotation

An accountant and a client were swimming in the sea when the client was swept away. The accountant swam after him, dragged him towards the shore and when he was nearly in, said: 'Are you OK now? Can you float on your own?'

The client replied: 'Even when I'm dying, he wants to talk business!'

Good company Lawyer to judge, well known for his puritanical views and as a pillar of the Church: 'I appear for the plaintiffs – a God-fearing, limited liability company.'

Companies Lord Thurloe once said: 'A corporation has no body to be burned and no soul to be damned . . .'

Unanimity Two directors were doing a crossword. One asked: 'How do you spell "unanimously"?'

The other: 'I am not surprised that you can't spell it. It's only a miracle that you can pronounce the word . . .'

Partners? The owner of an hotel quietly watched as his barman put 50p in his own pocket out of every £1 he took from a customer. When he saw the barman putting an entire £1 into his wallet, he pounced. 'What are you doing?' he asked. 'I thought we were partners!'

Civil servants A civil servant – one who has a valid objection to any possible solution.

Success and failure The then head of the Civil Service, Sir Douglas Wass, pointed out to a distinguished and private dinner of top business executives and lawyers that they could measure their success by winning or losing cases and by their balance sheets (respectively). 'We have no such base to judge ours,' he said. 'The success of a civil servant can only be judged by the absence of obvious failure!'

Police A teacher in a local school required his class to write an essay on the police. Martin wrote: 'Them police are bastards.'

The teacher told the police of the comment.

They invited Martin to the station and gave him the most marvellous day of his life. The next day the teacher set the boys another essay on the police. Martin wrote: 'Them police are cunning bastards!'

Spies

A Russian spy went to Wales and was told to see their contact in Abergavenny, who lived at 25 Cwmbran Terrace. The password: 'The space ship is in orbit.'

By mistake, he called at number 5 Cwmbran Terrace. A woman opened the door. 'Yes?' she enquired.

'The space ship is in orbit,' said the Russian.

'Oh,' said the lady, 'you've come to the wrong address. You will be wanting Dai the Spy. He's at number 25.'

Public relations

Fact: In places, the fabled River Jordan is nothing more than a trickle.

Comment: 'That is what public relations can do for a river!' (*Henry Kissinger*)

Brains

Two army captains were grousing about the stupidity of their respective batmen. They decided to have a bet on which one was more stupid. Captain X called for his batman and said: 'Take this £5 note and buy me a colour TV set down in the village.' 'Yes, sir. Certainly, sir.' The batman saluted and went out into the mess room.

Captain Y then rang for his batman and said: 'Go to the orderly room immediately and see whether I am there.' 'Yes, sir. Certainly, sir.' The batman saluted and left.

The two batmen met in the corridor outside and compared notes.

'Fancy asking me to buy a colour TV set on an early closing day,' said the first. The second replied: 'Imagine making me walk half a mile when he could have used the telephone to see if he's in the orderly room!'

Class distinction When I was serving in the British Army of the Rhine, I found a notice on our HQ board at Christmas. It read: 'Christmas parties will be held as follows: Officers and their ladies, 24 December; non-commissioned officers, and their wives 25 December; and other ranks and their womenfolk, 26 December.'

The 'fearless' press Newspapers are fiercely independent of pressure from their advertisers. Or are they?

Some years ago, I campaigned for legislation to ban the fraudulent 'guarantee' or 'warranty' which in reality removed more rights than it gave – especially when provided with a motor vehicle. I was commissioned to write a full-length feature for a London Sunday paper which carried the front page banner: 'THE fearless newspaper!'

My piece was pungent, accurate, documented and devastating. It was not published. Instead, I simply received my fee. I telephoned the Features Editor. He said: 'I'm sorry, but to publish your piece would have cost us a fortune. You effectively attacked every car manufacturer in the business.'

'So what?' I retorted. 'I thought you were "The fearless newspaper"!'

'That's all very well,' he retorted, 'but you have to have a newspaper to be fearless in!'

Insurers Insurance people present plans to keep you poor while you are alive so that you may die rich.

Insurance The favourite uncle at a wedding dinner announced that he was going to give the bridegroom a life insurance policy. The bride burst into tears. When she was finally calmed, she blurted out: 'I don't like it . . . I don't like it . . . I don't want father to set light to Harry like he did to the warehouse. . . !'

Recession? A man owed $100,000. The night before the sum fell due for payment, he could not sleep. He tossed and turned and he strode up and down.

271

Eventually, he walked around to his creditor's house and knocked on the window. 'What is it?' asked the man.

'I'm very sorry,' replied the debtor, 'but I shan't be able to pay what I owe you tomorrow morning. I've been so worried about it that I couldn't get to sleep. Anyway, I've decided to wake you so that you can now stay awake worrying while I get some sleep!'

Whose trade? Morgan and Dai went on safari. Suddenly, a woolly creature dropped from a tree onto Morgan's back. 'What is it? What is it?' he cried out.

'How should I know?' Dai replied. 'Am I a furrier?'

Enterprise Cohen owned a small tailor's shop and made a modest living. Then two firms of multiple-tailors opened on either side of him. 'What are you going to do now?' asked a friend.

'Don't worry,' said Cohen, 'Everything will be all right. I'll just change the name of my shop.'

'What good will that do?'

'Plenty.'

'What will you call your shop?'

'I shall call it . . . Main Entrance!'

Jewish business Three Jewish men met for dinner.

The first one said: 'Oi!'

The second one said: 'Oi yevay!'

The third said: 'If you boys are going to talk business, I'm off . . .'

Antiques An American and his wife were in Portobello Road. 'It's not bad, Bessie,' he said. 'But they don't make antiques like they used to, do they?'

Wedding present A father-in-law gave his son-in-law 5,000 shares in his business. 'There you are, lad,' he said. 'Anything else I can do for you?'

The son-in-law replied: 'Yes, Dad. Please would you buy me out?'

Business, companies and professions

Commercial progression

A businessman gets on . . . then he gets honest . . . then he gets honoured . . .

Business talk

Movie Mogul Lou Wasserman once invited Sam Goldwyn to meet Clark Gable. 'But you mustn't talk business with him,' he said. 'Promise me – nothing about business and nothing about money.' Goldwyn agreed.

He duly arrived for the lunch with a briefcase which he promptly opened, emptying onto the table $100,000 in dollar notes. 'There you are,' he announced. 'This is what I am not allowed to talk to you about!'

Golfer – a top surprise

'I know you're not meant to take bets when you play against members,' said John Jones to the club professional, 'but I want to ask you a very special favour. As it's my silver wedding, I'd like to play one round with you for £100.'

'You know I can't do that,' said the professional. 'Anyway, I'd have to give you a very large handicap.'

'No,' said John, 'all I want by way of a handicap is three gotchas.'

The professional, who did not want to let on that he did not know what 'gotcha' meant, said: 'OK. But keep it quiet.'

As they were about to tee off at the first hole, the professional felt a hand coming between his legs and grabbing him. 'Gotcha!' John shouted.

Discomforted, the professional prepared to tee off the second time.

'Gotcha!' yelled John, as he grabbed his opponent.

'That's very nasty,' said the professional. 'But we've 18 holes to go and you've only got one gotcha left!'

'That's right.' said John. 'But how will you enjoy playing 18 holes, never knowing when the next gotcha's coming?' (*Bob Monkhouse*) [*Monkhouse used this joke to massive effect at an entertainment industry dinner – his speech*

273

won a standing ovation from his colleagues. Used with sensitivity, it may be told to illustrate any other situation in which you are proposing to keep your opponents, competitors, rivals or enemies in Damocletian suspense! GJ]

Sitting

'Sitting is an eloquent business, any actor will tell you that. We sit according to our natures. We sprawl and straddle, we rest like boxers between rounds, we fidget, perch, cross and uncross our legs, lose patience, lose endurance . . .' (*Le Carré, Tinker, Tailor, Soldier, Spy*)

Conducting

At Covent Garden, Sir Thomas was rehearsing with a new Leader of the Violins and complained: 'We are not together.'

'Well, Sir Thomas,' said the new Leader, 'we can't see your beat.'

'What did you say?'

The Leader repeated it.

'Beat!' exclaimed Beecham, 'What do you think I am, a bloody metronome!'

Doctors and architects

A doctor can bury his mistakes. An architect can only advise his clients to plant vines. (*Frank Lloyd Wright*)

Developers

The government has now developed a neutron mortgage: It wipes out the developer but leaves the buildings intact.

Name dropping

When I met President Reagan – you'll pardon my mentioning it – I have to drop a name or two or you would not think that I am important . . .

Friend to Sir Robin Day: 'Robin, you're the world's worst name dropper.'

Robin: 'I'm afraid you're right. That's exactly what the Queen Mother said to me, only last week!'

Rent rise

Landlord: 'I'm afraid I've got to raise your rent.'

Tenant: 'That's good. I can't raise it myself.'

Workers
I once visited a mill in Nashville, Tennessee. I was taken round by the owner. 'How many people work here?' I asked.
'I'd say about half,' he drawled.

Negotiation
I knew a President of MGM who regarded a contract as a basis for negotiation. (*Edgar Bronfman, President, Seagrams*)

Free speech
Executive to celebrity: 'Do you believe in free speech?'
Celebrity: 'Of course.'
Executive: 'Then how about making one at our annual staff dinner?'

Executive competition
Two executives went on safari. Suddenly, they saw a lion in the distance, heading straight for them, obviously intent on making a kill.
They got up, ready to run. But one of them calmly took off his boots, opened his rucksack and pulled on a pair of trainers.
'You're mad!' cried his colleague. 'You'll never outrun the lion!'
'I don't have to outrun the lion,' he retorted. 'I only have to outrun you!'

Up to standard?
Samuel Goldwyn once employed a ghost-writer to produce a series of articles, to be published under his name. When the job was half done, the ghost-writer fell ill. A substitute took over.
When Goldwyn read one of his pieces, he cried out in anguish: 'That's not up to my usual standard!'

Advertisements
A good advertisement is like a good sermon — comforting the afflicted and afflicting the comfortable.

Supply and demand
Two fine looking women were walking along the street when a frog hopped up to them. 'Please pick me up,' it said. 'Kiss me, and I'll turn into a tall, handsome young accountant.' One of the women bent down, picked up the frog and popped it into her handbag.

'Why don't you give it a kiss?' asked her friend.

'Because,' she replied, 'there are plenty of tall, handsome young accountants. But who's got a talking frog?'

Doctorates

When a wealthy philanthropist was awarded Honorary Doctorates at Glasgow, Oxford, London and Jerusalem someone asked: 'So many doctorates? What does he write? Books?'

The reply: 'No – cheques.'

New job?

'What would you say to a surveyor [*or lawyer or executive or whoever*] who has found a new job?'

'One Big Mac and French fries, please.'

Optimist

An optimist is a manager [*or anyone else in a hard hit profession or business*] who irons five shirts on a Sunday evening.

75   Faith, religion and ethics

Faith

An Italian priest was walking along a cliff top when he slipped and fell – but was caught by a slender sapling growing out of the cliff. He looked down 300 feet at the sea and up at heaven and cried out: 'Is there anyone up there – help!' And a mighty voice cried out: 'I am here. Fear not. Let go of the tree and I will keep you safe.'

The priest looked down 300 feet at the raging sea and rocks. Then he cried out: 'Is there anyone else up there – help, help!'

Greater faith

A nun was driving her little Fiat along the road when it ran out of petrol. She left the car and walked ten miles to the nearest filling station. Regretfully, they said that they had no jerrycan and no other container of any sort. 'Surely you have something which I could put the petrol into?' she pleaded. Thoughtfully the attendant said: 'Well, I can only offer you an old chamber-pot. . . .'

Gratefully, the nun accepted. The pot was filled with petrol; she walked back to the car. And as she was pouring it into the petrol tank, a passing motorist leaned out of the window, saying: 'Well, sister, I wish I had your faith!'

Fowl language

A man was standing on the steps of the cathedral, shooing away the pigeons. 'Bugger off . . . bugger off . . .' he said.

A priest emerged and listened to this performance. 'My man,' he said, 'you really shouldn't talk to pigeons like that. Not on the steps of this House of God. You should say: "Shoo . . . shoo . . . shoo . . ." '

'Look,' he said. 'I'll demonstrate. Shoo . . . shoo . . . shoo . . .' he said to the pigeons. They all flew away.

'There,' said the priest to the visitor. 'I told you all you had to say was: "Shoo . . . shoo . . . shoo . . ." and they'd all bugger off, just the same!'

End of the world

Prominent physicists predicted that a flood would signal the end of the world in three days.

A television station called on leading religious personalities to advise people on how people should react.

The Pope urged his flock to repent their sins; the Buddhist monk instructed his people to seek inner peace by searching for their inner selves; the Rabbi told his followers: 'OK. We've got three days to learn how to swim.'

Optimism

An optimist thinks that all is for the best in the best of all possible worlds. But they say in the Vatican that a pessimist is one who thinks that he is right.

Outside support

I am afraid that I cannot be called a pillar of your church. But I would like to be described as a buttress – supporting you from the outside! [*Ideal for speeches in other people's churches. GJ*]

Civilization

Mahatma Gandhi was asked: 'What do you think of Western civilization?'

He replied: 'I think it would be a very good idea.'

Double crossing

'I once travelled from Amman in Jordan to Damascus in Syria and back again in a day. I was somewhat surprised to find a large sign at the frontier. "Double crossing only permitted for diplomats and for certain priests." ' (*Robert Runcie, former Archbishop of Canterbury*)

True

A man writes to God: 'I am desperately in need of £100. Please, God, help me! He addresses the letter to heaven – and posts it.

In a special, kindly, post office department, the letter is opened. The clerks decide to have a whip-round. They collect £80 and post it back, 'with love from God.'

The following day a letter arrived at the post office: 'Thank You, dear God, for answering my letter. But I think I ought to tell you that those wretched people in the post office stole £20!'

Whose religion? Father Brown (Roman Catholic) and the Reverend Green (Anglican) were arguing furiously over a theological matter.

The priest held up his hand: 'Come, let us not quarrel,' he said. 'You and I are both doing God's work – you in your way and I in His!'

Us We are proud of the inhabitants of our island. There are the Scots who take themselves seriously – as well as anything else they can lay their hands on; the Welsh, who pray on their knees and on each other; the Irish, who will die for what they believe in, even if they do not know what that is; and the English, who proclaim that they are self-made men, thereby absolving the Lord from a heavy burden.

Jewish jokes A Jewish joke is a joke which Jewish people have heard and non-Jewish people would not understand.

Apartheid During the Second World War, the United States fleet paid a courtesy call in Durban. A society lady who was running a big dance one night asked the American authorities to send half a dozen boys along, but to ensure that they included no Jews.

Six black men duly arrived.

'I'm terribly sorry,' said the hostess, 'but I'm afraid that there must be some mistake.'

'No, ma'am,' replied the leader of the party. 'Major Rabinowitz never makes mistakes!'

Jewish wedding The Jewish bridegroom traditionally treads on glass, breaking it into thousands of pieces. Why? 'To celebrate the last occasion when he will be able to put his foot down . . .'

Persistence

A woman was lying on a beach in Miami. She turned to a man lying alongside her and asked:
'Excuse me, are you Jewish?'
He replied: 'No, I'm not.'
A few minutes later, the woman turned again to the man, and said: 'Are you absolutely certain that you're not Jewish?
He replied, angrily: 'All right. So I'm Jewish.'
The woman paused: 'Now isn't that funny,' she said. 'You don't look Jewish!'

Anti-Semitic

A Jewish man was sitting in the corner of a compartment, while two other travellers sat chatting. One said to the other 'Where are you going?'
'To Brighton.'
'Oh that used to be a nice place. But it isn't anymore. It's full of Jews.'
'Where are you going then?' asked his friend.
'To Bournemouth.'
'Bournemouth! You talk of Brighton but you should see what's happening to Bournemouth, with all those Jewish boardinghouses . . .'
The Jew lowered his newspaper and looked at them over the top. 'You know where you two boys should go,' he said. 'You should go to hell. There are no Jews there!'

Many of my best friends

When King Khaled of Saudi Arabia first greeted US Secretary of State, Henry Kissinger, he launched into his renowned attack on the Jews and Israel . . . and how they had taken over the world's banks and financial institutions, its communications and its newspapers, its television and its radio. 'They have even infiltrated into positions of high power in the Foreign Ministries of the world,' declaimed His Majesty.
Then, realizing what he had said, the King added: 'But you, sir, we welcome warmly – not as a Jew, but as a great human being . . .'

Secretary Kissinger replied quietly: 'I thank Your Majesty. Many of my best friends are human beings . . .'

Repeat business

A tailor made a suit for an Anglican parson. He refused to accept any charge. The parson sent him a lovely Bible.

Two weeks later, the same tailor made a suit for a Roman Catholic priest. Again, he refused to charge. The priest sent him a magnificent prayer book.

The tailor was later visited by a Rabbi and made a suit for him. He made no charge. The Rabbi sent him another Rabbi.

The curse of the Plotnik diamond

Dealer shows woman a magnificent diamond. 'This, madam, is the Plotnik diamond. Is it not beautiful? It is one of the largest in the world and is very valuable. But there is a curse which goes with the Plotnik diamond . . .'

Customer: 'What curse is that?'

Dealer: 'Mr Plotnik!'

Oedipus

A Jewish couple sent their son to a psychiatrist. He returned and his mother enquired what had happened.

'He says, I've got an Oedipus complex.'

'Oedipus shmoedipus,' his mother retorted. 'You just go on loving your mommy!'

Blessing

'God bless the Tsar – and keep him far away from us!' (*Fiddler on the Roof*)

Perspective

Ezra Kolet, leader of India's tiny Jewish community – about 7,000 souls out of a population of some 880 million: 'You may take it from me, Ladies and Gentlemen. Numbers are not important!'

Permanent job

Teddy Kollek, Mayor of Jerusalem, kept seeing a man sitting on the roof of his house, looking up at the sky with binoculars. One day, he called out to him: 'What are you doing up there?'

'Looking out for the Messiah,' came the reply.

'Why are you doing that?'
'I am being paid for it.'
'How much?'
'Not much. Just a few pence a day . . .'
'That's pretty poor pay . . .'
'I know. But at least the job is permanent!'

Enemies

Pat Murphy was dying. The Priest arrived to administer the last rites.

'Pat, my son,' he said, 'do you renounce the devil, now and for ever more?'

'Oh, come, Father,' the dying man replied. 'This is no time for making enemies – anywhere!'

[*This is a marvellous story to tell if you are asked to comment on (e.g.) the politics of other countries. GJ*]

No change

David Cohen converted to Catholicism, in the days when good Catholics did not eat meat on Fridays. The following Friday evening, the local priest wandered into his home to find him eating chicken.

'David, my son,' said the Priest. 'You are a Catholic now. You should not be eating meat on Fridays.'

'It's not meat,' said David, 'It's fish.'

'It doesn't look like fish to me,' said the Priest. 'How do you explain that?'

'Well,' said David, 'you poured some water over me and you said: "David, you're not a Jew any more. You're a Catholic". So I poured some water over the chicken and said: "Bird, you're not a chicken any more. You're fish!" '

How tall?

An Antarctic explorer returned to the igloo, late at night. 'How tall is a penguin?' he asked.

'About 3 foot, perhaps 3 foot 6 inches,' his friend replied.

'No, I mean the Emperor penguins. The really large ones.'

'Oh, only about 3 foot 6. Perhaps 3 foot 9 . . .'

'Oh God,' said the explorer. 'I've shot a nun!'

No charge

A Jewish man who had survived the holocaust went to see his Rabbi. 'I have a confession to make,' he said. 'During the war, I saved two Greeks in my cellar.'

'So why did you use your cellar to save Greeks,' the Rabbi enquired, 'when they would probably have survived anyway and there were so many Jews dying? Anyway, I am glad that you did so – even Greeks are entitled to be saved. . . !'

'It gets worse, Rabbi. I'm afraid that I charged them rent!'

'Ah – well, that is not good. But even you had to get enough money to pay for food and to live.'

'That's right, Rabbi. But it gets even worse. They are still there. I have not told them that the war is over!'

A bargain?

A vicar advertised his car for sale at an incredibly low price. He explained to a prospective buyer: 'Well, it has no engine.'

'So how do you make it go?'

'To get it moving,' the vicar explained, 'you say: Thank God! And to stop it you say: Amen! Why don't you try it?'

After looking under the bonnet to check that there was no motor, the buyer clambered into the driver's seat and said: 'Thank God!' True enough, the car darted forward. The buyer steered it through town and onto a dual carriageway.

Suddenly, a lorry pulled out in front of the car. Panicking, the buyer forgot the word to stop. Closer and closer he sped to the lorry. Then he remembered: 'Amen!' he shouted. The car stopped dead, just in time.

'Thank God!' the buyer exclaimed . . .

[*The motor trade version uses: 'Bollocks' and 'F – me!' – and the car stops at the edge of a precipice. GJ*]

Thank God

At Jewish gatherings, grace before or after meals

is generally said by a Rabbi. At one recent gathering, the Chairman pronounced as follows: 'Ladies and gentleman, there being no Rabbi here, let us thank God for his blessings.'

Getting the best deal – Jewish style

The Warsaw butcher's shop was due to open at 7.00 a.m. Meat was in almost invisible supply. A long queue had formed by 5.30.

On the nail of 7.00, the proprietor emerged from the shop. 'Sorry,' he said. 'Not serving Jews today. All Jews go home please.'

Four ill-clad old Jews silently left the queue and drifted into the dawn.

A few minutes later, the proprietor came out again. 'Sorry,' he said. 'We can only serve Party members today. The rest of you should go home.'

Half the queue evaporated.

Five minutes later he was back. 'Sorry,' he said. 'We can only serve officials and functionaries of the Party today. The rest of you must leave.' Only a handful remained outside the shop. The proprietor looked at them: 'Sorry,' he said. 'Today is Tuesday, no meat until Thursday.'

One of the last survivors looked at his neighbour. 'There you are,' he said. 'Those bloody Jews always get the best deal!' (*Told by Rabbi Hugo Gryn, after a visit to Warsaw in 1981.*)

Marrying out

A Rabbi whose son married out of the faith prayed to God: 'What shall I do? Oh, what shall I do?'

A voice came from above: 'Well, you know what I did in similar circumstances. I made a New Testament!'

The difference

What is the difference between God and the Pope?

God is everywhere – the Pope has been everywhere.

Half Jewish

Dorothy Parker was half Jewish, and half-hearted about it. At a party, author Alexander Woolcott made an anti-semitic remark and George S. Kaufman walked out in indignation, saying: 'And I trust that Mrs Parker will walk out with me – half way!'

Communal illness

Psycho-semitic illness is a disease suffered by Jewish leaders and caused by overexposure to their own community.

Health and life

Non-Jewish people, in almost every language, toast each other's 'good health'. Jewish people, in their language, always say 'l'hayim' – to life.

Why? Because non-Jewish people treat the continuation of life as a certainty. So they need health. Jewish history proclaims the uncertainty of life itself.

Light bulbs

There are certain types of joke for which you require a mildly warped sense of humour. These include the never ending light bulb series. As with all humour, you must be very careful not to offend. Adjust the butt of the joke to suit yourself and your audience – which, in general, means to tell it against yourself, your own political persuasion or religion or nationality, and not against anyone else's. That said, here are some of my favourites:

How many missionaries does it take to replace a light bulb?
Three. One to twist it in and two to convince everyone else to do the same.

How many biblical scholars does it take to replace a light bulb?
Biblical scholars never replace light bulbs. They know that they will never find one half as good as the old one.

How many spoiled daughters does it take to replace a light bulb?

Two. One pours Diet Coke. The other calls Daddy to do it.

Jewish mothers What is the difference between a Jewish mother and a terrorist?

With a terrorist, you can negotiate.

Revenge! The traveller at the Hong Kong check out desk was screaming abuse at the woman behind the counter. She remained cool and courteous. When he had gone, the next man in line said to the official: 'How did you manage to keep your temper, when that man was being so thoroughly offensive?'

'No problem,' she replied. 'He is on his way to Chicago. His luggage is heading for Sydney, Australia!'

76   Sex, love and marriage

Sex – with pleasure

George Bernard Shaw was once asked to give a lecture on sex. He rose to his feet and began: 'It gives me great pleasure . . .' And he sat down.

Love and money

'If I lost all my money, darling, would you still love me?'

'Of course, I would, darling. But I'd miss you . . .'

Uncertain future?

A sex questionnaire to college students included: 'Are you a virgin?'

One girl replied: 'Not yet.'

A shepherd's tale

Dai and Morgan went for a dirty weekend in Snowdonia. They found a beautiful shepherdess in a hut and had a lovely time with her.

Three months later, they each received a letter. The shepherdess was in a certain condition.

Dai: 'What shall we do, Morgan?'

Morgan: 'We'd better go and see her, hadn't we?'

Dai: 'I can't get away from work. Tell you what, you go and see her and I'll meet you when you get back and we'll split my day's earnings.'

So off Morgan went, returning that evening. Dai met him at the station.

Morgan: 'I've got some very bad news to tell you. There's been two disasters.'

Dai: 'So what are they, then?'

Morgan: 'The first is – that it's twins.'

Dai: 'Oh God, that's terrible. So what's the second?'

Morgan: 'I regret to inform you that mine has passed away.'

Premarital

Two businessmen talking: 'I never slept with my wife before I was married. Did you?

'I don't know, John. What was her maiden name?'

Welsh virgins

The day after his wedding, Dai returns home.
'What's happened?' asked his mother.
'I found out that Bridget is a virgin,' he said. 'So I left her.'
'Quite right,' said his mother. 'If she's not good enough for the rest of the boys in the village, why should she be good enough for you?'

In love

A well-known peer married at an advanced age. His wife is an attractive Mediterranean lady. When the noble lord fell ill, his wife replied to a telephone enquiry as follows: 'He is still under heavy seduction.'

A wife in the business

I went into the beer business. My wife said: 'I'll drive the people to drink and you can sell it to them.'

Always right

Wife: 'I have my faults. But being wrong isn't one of them.'

Stupidity

Smith came home and found his wife in bed with another man. 'What the hell do you two think you are doing?' he asked.
The wife turned to the other man. 'There you are,' she replied. 'I told you he was stupid!'

Naked truth

Man comes home and finds his wife lying naked on the bed. 'Why aren't you wearing anything?' he asks.
'I keep telling you,' she replies, 'I haven't anything to wear . . .'
He marches over to the cupboard, throws open the door and then says: 'Hello Persian lamb . . . Hello Ocelot . . . Hello Mink . . . Oh, hello Sam! Hello Persian Lamb . . . Hello Coney . . .'

Wrongdoing

Mabel, aged 18, arrived home at four in the morning wearing a mink coat.
'Did I do wrong?' she asked her mother.

Sex, love and marriage

Mother replied: 'I don't know whether you did right or wrong, dear – but you certainly did well!'

Three speech

A woman sued for divorce, claiming that her husband had only spoken to her three times in the course of their marriage. She applied for custody of the three children.

The fodderless child

Our daily diet grows odder and odder. It's a wise child who know his fodder. (*Ogden Nash*)

Fertility

A turtle lives 'twixt plated decks. Which carefully conceal its sex. I think it clever of the turtle, In such a fix to be so fertile! (*Ogden Nash*)

Garlic

The Italians invented birth control – they call it 'garlic'.

Necessity

Gwyneth was on night shift. She arrived home to find her husband, Morgan, in bed with her best friend. She looked down at her sadly and said: 'Bridget – I have to – but you!'

Birth control

When people talk to me about the need to keep down the number of children, I remind them that I was the fifth! (*Clarence Darrow*)

Mothers

A parent's place is in the wrong . . .

Pen pals

For many years, Charlie in London and Bill in New York, were pen pals. They had never met.

One day, Charlie received a letter from Bill, saying that he intended to come to London. 'Please cable back if it's convenient,' Bill wrote.

The following exchange of cables ensued:

Charlie: 'Delighted to welcome you. Will meet you at station.'

Bill: 'Thanks – am black.'

Charlie: 'Don't care if black. Come. Will meet you at station.'

Bill: 'Am Catholic.'

Charlie: 'Don't care if black Catholic. Come. Will meet you at station.'

Bill: 'Am hunchback.'

289

Charlie: 'Don't care if black, Catholic hunchback. Come. Will meet you at station.'

Bill: 'Have only one eye in centre of forehead.'

Charlie: 'Don't care if black Catholic, hunchback with only one eye in middle of forehead. Will meet you at station. How do I recognize you?'

Don't wait

Two men were due to fight a duel. One telephoned the other: 'Charlie, don't wait for me . . . If I'm not there within 5 minutes, please start without me!'

Romance

Fall in love with yourself and you are in for a lifetime of romance. (*Oscar Wilde*)

Self love

He is a self-made man, and he worships his creator. (*Disraeli on John Bright*)

Identification

A man was lying naked on a beach, sunbathing, when he saw three beautiful girls coming towards him. He grabbed at the only clothing within reach – his hat – and put it over his face.

The three girls stopped and looked down at him. The first said: 'Well, it's not my husband.' The second said: 'You're quite right. It is not your husband.' The third one said: 'He's a stranger – he doesn't live in the village . . .'

The bird

A farmer came to town and bought a live chicken. Waiting for his train home, he decided to go to the movies. The woman at the cash desk said: 'I'm sorry, young man, but we don't allow animals in here.'

The farmer went round the corner and stuffed the chicken into his trousers. He returned to the cinema, paid his ticket, and sat down in the stalls. Eventually, two women came and sat beside him.

It was very hot and the chicken became itchy. So he opened up the front of his trousers and the chicken extended its neck.

One woman said to the other: 'Mary, do you see what I see?'

'Certainly I see what you see. If you've seen one, you've seen them all!'

'I'm not sure,' said Mary. 'This is the first one I've seen that eats crisps!'

Evolution

In life, each of us must look after our 'neighbours' – or, as it is sometimes put, we are our brother's keeper. Which reminds me of the monkey in the zoo discussing the principles of evolution and asking: 'Am I my keeper's brother?' [*There is also the tale of the herring, who was separated from his best friend, the whale. He responded to enquiries about his friend's whereabouts with the world's worst pun: 'How should I know. Am I my blubber's kipper?' GJ*]

Misinformation

Businessman to girlfriend: Do I need to wear a contraceptive or are you on the pill?

Friend: You have nothing to worry about. My husband has had a vasectomy.

Free love

He: Do you believe in free love?

She: Have I ever sent you an invoice?

Silent partner

Roger comes home from a rehearsal of his amateur dramatics group and tells his wife: 'I have a marvellous part in the play. I am the husband.'

Wife: 'Couldn't you get a speaking part?'

Blameless

Nobody introduced me to my wife. We just happened to meet. I am not blaming anybody!

Veteran

An 82-year old peer received a letter from an angry MP. It read: 'I understand that you are having an affair with my wife. I require you to call on me at the Dorchester Hotel, at 12 noon tomorrow.'

His Lordship replied: 'I thank you for your circular letter . . .'

Prostitution

A peer decided to bring in a Bill to license prostitutes. He was promised 'government time'. But the Queen's speech made no mention of his proposal; nor did any of the parliamentary speeches that followed it.

So the peer wrote to the Lord Chancellor. 'What would you suggest that I do about my Prostitution Bill?'

The Chancellor replied: 'If I were you, I'd pay it!'

Confession

Eighty-two year old David Cohen goes to confession. On his knees, he tells the priest: 'I had it off seven times last week – and with seven different women.'

Priest: 'Excuse me for asking, but are you a Catholic!'

Cohen: 'No, I'm Jewish.'

Priest: 'So why are you telling me about it?'

Cohen: 'Telling you? I'm telling – everybody!'

Appointment

Blodwen got herself into a certain condition. She did not feel that she could take medical advice in her Welsh home town, so she visited the Harley Street area, looking for a good Welsh name on the plates. Eventually she found one: Dr Ralph Vaughan-Williams.

Blodwen knocked at the door and a woman opened it. 'I've come to see Dr Vaughan-Williams,' she said.

'Have you an appointment?'

'No. But I've come all the way from South Wales and I would be grateful if he could spare me a few moments.'

'You'll have to wait a few minutes, I'm afraid. He's busy reorchestrating the Men of Harlech.'

'Is he, indeed,' Blodwen exclaimed. 'And about ruddy time too!'

Modesty

I conceived at least one great love in my life, of which I was always the object ... (*Albert Camus.*)

I fell in love with myself, at first sight – and time

has proved that my judgment was correct. My lover has never let me down . . .

Anniversary waltz

Humorist A. P. Herbert on his 25th wedding anniversary: Anyone who has been married to someone else for 25 years without an argument obviously has the spirit of a sheep.

Advice

General Mark Clark was asked: What was the best advice you were ever given? He replied: 'To marry my wife.'
'Who gave it?'
'She did.'

Remarriage

Dr Samuel Johnson, describing the remarriage of a divorced friend: 'The triumph of hope over experience!'

Children

During the presidency of Gerald Ford, the Queen and Prince Philip visited the White House. Jack Ford, Gerald's son, lost the studs for his dress shirt. He rushed to the President's room to borrow some. He stepped into the lift, shirt unfastened, hair in disarray. Alas – his parents and their Royal guests were already in it!

Mrs Ford was clearly embarrassed as she introduced her son. The Queen looked at Jack and then turned to his parents, sympathetically: 'I have one just like that,' she said.

Pride

Three grandmothers discussing achievements of their grandsons.

First: 'My grandson's only twenty-five. He's one of Britain's top surgeons. Brilliant – only twenty-five.'

Second: 'My grandson's only twenty-two. He graduated with top Honours at Oxford and is already Vice President of a financial institution. He's only twenty-two.'

Third: 'My grandson is only sixteen. He's already carved out a career for himself. He's been helping the police with their enquiries. And he's only sixteen!'

Reports   Father to son, on reading school report: 'I do not really mind your consistently coming bottom of the class. But I do get upset when they say that you are doing your best . . .'

Infidelity   I have just heard that my wife is having an affair. Really, so who's catering?

Free?   'Do you believe in free speech?
'Have I ever charged you for your focals?'
'Do you believe in free love?'
'Have I ever sent you an invoice?'

Recession   Times were tough in the Brown family. 'You know what,' said Joe to his wife, 'If you would learn to make meals, we could do without the cook.'

'Fair enough, Joe,' replied Mary. 'If you'd learn to make love, we could sack the chauffeur!'

77 Law and lawyers, crimes and courts

The rule of law

This country is planted thick with laws from coast to coast. If you cut them down – and you're just the man to do it – do you really think you could stand upright in the wind that would blow then? (*Robert Bolt – from A Man for All Seasons*)

Justice

Former Lord Chancellor, the genial Lord Elwyn Jones, often said: 'Welsh juries believe in justice. But they are not too dogmatic about it.'

Which is matched by a story of the Glasgow Baillie who sentenced a criminal to 30 days without the option of a fine. 'And count yourself lucky,' he said. 'If there had been a shred of evidence against you, it would have been 60!'

International law

Famous professor Hersch Lauterpacht used to say: 'International law is not much good. It creates laws which the wicked do not obey and the righteous do not need.'

Single-handed

A man asked to be recommended to a one-armed lawyer. When asked why, he replied, 'I'm sick of being told: "On the one hand this – and on the other hand that".'

Lawyers

It is untrue that lawyers do nothing. They just get together and decide that nothing can be done.

Respected professionals

A foreigner was being shown around Westminster Abbey. His guide pointed to a splendid monument: 'There lies a great and honest man and a most distinguished lawyer,' he said.

'That's interesting,' the foreigner replied. 'I never knew that in England you buried two men in the same grave!'

Oh, hell!

A businessman arrived at the pearly gates and

was cross-examined by St Peter. He demanded his basic civil right – to be represented by a lawyer.

'Sorry,' said St Peter. 'We haven't any up here.'

Socialist lawyers

The expression 'socialist lawyer' is a contradiction in terms – like 'military intelligence'. (*Michael Foot*)

Bright boy

A car dealer's son was trying to sell his own vehicle – but failing. His father told him to turn back the clock to 6,000 miles. The following week, the father asked the son whether he had sold the car. 'Certainly not.'

'Why not then?'

'Well, it's only got 6,000 miles on the clock so I decided to keep it . . .'

Costs

Two partners fell out and sued each other. Their lawyers tried to settle the disputes, but failed. Eventually, the case reached court.

Outside the courtroom, Morgan said to his counsel: 'Look, Dai and I used to be very good friends. We were in happy partnership for years. Perhaps we can have a chat and see if we can settle our differences on our own?'

The lawyer replied: 'Why not? But I must warn you. The amount in dispute between you is now less than the legal costs. So even if you settle your dispute, you've got to decide who is going to pay the costs.'

Morgan went to Dai and the two of them disappeared. Half an hour later they returned beaming.

'Have you settled the case?'

'We have,' replied the partners in unison.

'Well, who's going to pay the costs then?'

'Oh, that was easy,' said Dai. 'We've solved the problem. He'll not pay his and I'll not pay mine!'

Wrongdoing

When visiting Egypt, one of our guides

explained his modus operandi. 'If you have to do wrong,' he said, 'you must know the right way to do it.' He called his system: Hinkie Pinky!

Ears

The famous American lawyer, Clarence Darrow, told the story about how easy it is for a lawyer to ask one question too many.

A man was accused of biting off another man's ear. His lawyer cross-examined the witness: 'Did you see my client biting off the victim's ear?

'No sir.'

Instead of stopping there, he went on in triumph: 'So how can you testify that my client bit off the victim's ear?'

'Because I saw him spit it out!'

Banks – and logic

A bank robber came up for sentence. It was his fifth conviction for the same offence and he had been in and out of prison for years.

'Why do you keep robbing banks?' the judge asked him.

'Because that is where the money is,' he replied.

Conducting a case

If the facts are on your side, hammer on the facts . . . if the law is on your side, hammer on the law . . . if neither is on your side, hammer on the table . . .

Modesty

So I asked myself the question . . . We lawyers frequently ask ourselves questions because in that way we know that we will get prompt and intelligent answers . . . (*Lord Denning*)

Lawyers – and rats

Why do they use lawyers instead of rats as laboratory animals in the USA?

There are three main reasons:

First: There are more of them.

Second: Laboratory assistants get less attached to them, so if one dies, no one cares.

And third: There are some things that even rats won't do! Even for money . . . [*Use against your own profession, only! GJ QC*]

297

Chancery
The court of a well-known Chancery judge, now retired (and nameless) became known at the Bar as the 'din of inequity'.

Justice
When I was a puisne judge – sitting on my own, in my own court – I could be sure that justice would be done in that court. But now I sit in the Court of Appeal with two brother judges, the odds against justice being done in my court are two to one! (*Lord Denning*)

Interviewed on his 81st Birthday, Lord Denning was asked whether it was not correct that he bent the law in order to do justice. He replied: 'Certainly not. I just develop it . . .'

Whisky and water
Former Lord Chief Justice, Lord Goddard, was asked what was the difference between whisky and water. He replied: 'If you make the former in private, that is a felony; if you make the latter in public, that is a misdemeanour.' [*The distinction between felonies and misdemeanours has gone, but both acts remain criminal. GJ*]

Dissenting voices
Lord Donaldson, tells of an occasion when he sat in the Court of Appeal with his predecessor, Lord Denning. At the end of a case, Denning turned to him and said: 'Well John, I think we must allow this appeal, don't you?'
Donaldson replied: 'No. It must be dismissed.'
Denning turned to the third judge: 'What do you say?' he asked.
'I'm sorry, Tom,' he replied, 'but I agree with John. The appeal must be dismissed.'
'In that case,' said Lord Denning, 'the two of you will just have to deliver dissenting judgments!'

Equality of opportunity
Courts of this country are like the Waldorf Hotel – open to all! [*High Court judge, explaining the inaccessibility of justice. GJ*]

Perjury
Counsel, cross-examining a man who alleges his

arm and shoulder were hurt in an accident: 'Show me how high you can raise your arm, please . . .' The witness raises his arm a few inches, clearly with great effort and difficulty.

'Now show me how high you could raise it, before the accident . . .'

The arm goes high into the air. [*This tale is of course, best told with the appropriate demonstration. GJ*]

Chinese praise

Chinese man in the witness box in a stamp theft case was praised by the judge. He replied: 'Philately will get you everywhere . . .'

The truth

There are three stories in any law suit: the plaintiff's, the defendant's and the truth.

Ducking the question

Lawyer to witness: 'Did you get the letter?'

Witness (contemplating whether he should answer yes or no – and after a long pause): 'Not necessarily.'

Evidence

Lawyer defending client on charge of causing grievous bodily harm: 'It is our case, my Lord, that there is no evidence that any such affray took place. If it did, we shall prove that my client was not there. If he was there, there is no evidence that he took part in the affray. And in any case, the other man hit him first.'

Unwise counsel

Counsel: 'I hope that you are following me . . .'

Judge: 'Yes – but where are you going?'

Trials

At the 1981 Sheep Dog Trials, how many were found guilty?

Appeal

A businessman had to leave court before the end of the long, hard-fought trial. He left word for a telegram to be sent to him, to inform him of the result.

At the end of the case, the lawyer sent a telegram as arranged: 'Justice has been done,' he read.

The client immediately sent a reply: 'Appeal at once.'

Forgiving

An old Cockney usher used to take visitors to the Lord Chief Justice's Court when Lord Goddard presided: 'Lord Goddard,' he would say, 'is famous as a forgiving judge. Very forgiving. For giving five years . . . ten years . . . life . . .'

Language

Policeman giving evidence of arrest: 'So I cautioned the man and asked him if he could explain his presence, in the early hours of the morning, carrying what appeared to be a house-breaking implement. He made a lengthy reply in a language which I subsequently discovered to be Greek. I told him that I was not satisfied with his explanation and I duly arrested him.'

Cross-examination

The policeman gives evidence of having observed disgusting behaviour by a courting couple in a car. They deny it, maintaining that had he been in a position to observe, they would have heard him coming.

Counsel: 'Was it not a gravel path? What size shoes do you take? Was it not in the silence of the night? I put it to you that had you been near to that car, they would have heard the tramp of your feet . . .'

Constable: 'No sir.'

Counsel: 'You say that they would not have heard the tramp of your feet? Why do you say that?'

Constable: 'I was riding a bicycle.' [*This sort of horror explains why young lawyers are enjoined: 'Never ask a question in cross-examination unless you know the answer.' Theoretically, splendid advice . . . GJ*]

No charge

PC: 'You are under arrest, sir. I am taking you to the police station where you will have to stay the night.'

'And what's the charge, officer?'

'No charge sir. All part of the service.'

Balls

A prisoner went round the cells, selling tickets to the Warder's Ball. One of his mates complained:

'I don't want to buy no ticket for no screw's dance!' The seller replied: 'It's not a dance. It's a raffle!'

Bribery

Lord Goddard once remarked: 'Bribery is like a sausage – difficult to describe but easy enough to smell!' [*My father used to say the same about anti-semitism GJ*]

Commission

A well-known company found difficulty in putting its 'commission' (slush, payola, or what-have-you) through its books. But as it had a hunting lodge in Scotland, it listed the items as 'hunting expenses'.

A visiting customer from overseas* was provided with a suite at Claridges and a girl in it. Unfortunately, he contracted a certain illness for which he had to be treated at the London Clinic. The cost of treatment went into the books as: 'Repairs to gun . . .' [*Choose your favourite country. GJ*]

Corruption

Be specially careful not to bribe tax or factory inspectors or other public officials. 'Do not feed the hand that bites you . . .'

Written evidence

A man appeared in a lawyer's office: 'I have come to you because God has told me you are the best lawyer in the country.'

The lawyer replied: 'If that happens again, please get it in writing.'

Rubbish

To get rid of rubbish nowadays, all you have to do is to wrap it in silver paper, put it on the back seat of your car, and some silly sod will steal it. (*Bob Monkhouse*)

Tact

A company official was in the witness box, giving his opinion. 'Do you consider yourself an expert?' asked the cross-examining lawyer.

'Well, no,' said the man modestly. 'But I am something of a judge.'

'What's the difference between an expert and a judge?' asked the lawyer.

'An expert sometimes makes mistakes,' replied the official. 'A judge – never!'

Judge's functions

Lord Asquith was discussing the functions of the various branches of the judiciary. He said: 'It is the function of the judge in the Queen's Bench Division to be quick, courteous and wrong. But it must not be supposed that it is the function of the Court of Appeal to be slow, crapulous and wrong – for that would be to usurp the function of the House of Lords.'

Conviction

A famous hanging judge, Mr Justice Avory, was discussing with Mr Justice Humphreys the unhappy way in which the courts were being conducted by their junior colleagues.

Avory: 'Any of these young members of the Queen's Bench Division can secure the conviction of a guilty man. But it takes an old hand like you or me to make sure that the innocent do not escape!'

Leading counsel

Litigant arrives at court to find that whilst he is represented by junior counsel only, his opponent has both a junior and a leader. He tugs the gown of his advocate: 'How are you going to manage?' he says. 'The other side have a QC and a junior . . .'

'I'm as good as any two of them,' replies the junior.

A few minutes later, the client again tugs the barrister's gown. 'I'm worried,' he says. 'I've noticed that when the QC is talking, the barrister behind him is thinking. But when you are talking, no one is thinking!'

Speed

An American criminal complained that in New York you are liable to get mugged between the time that you rob the bank and the time that you reach the getaway car.

Terrorism

The Mafia Godfather arrived at the Pearly Gates.

St Peter: 'I'm not sure that we will have you in here. I'll have to ask The Boss.'

'I haven't come to be invited in,' said the Godfather. 'I have come to give you three minutes to get out.' [*This story was also told of Prime Minister Thatcher. GJ*]

Hold up?

A masked man ran into a bank and held up his forefinger at the counter clerk. 'Hand over the money,' he said. 'This is a fuck up!'

Calmly, the assistant said: 'I suppose you mean a hold up?'

'No. I mean a fuck up. I left the gun in the car!'

Those who know not the Lord

Magistrate to prisoner in dock: 'Would you like a lawyer to defend you?'

Prisoner: 'There's no need. The Lord is my defender.'

Magistrates: 'I think that you would be better off to have someone to defend you who is better known in this part of the world . . .'

Rabbit and snake

A blind rabbit became friends with a blind snake. They were complaining that they did not know what they were. 'Let's help each other,' the rabbit suggested. 'You feel around me and tell me what I am and I'll do the same for you.'

The snake agreed and wrapped himself gently around the rabbit, stroking its fur and noting its pointed ears. 'You're a bunny rabbit,' he said. 'Now, what about me?'

The rabbit rubbed its face and its paws over the snake's skin. 'You are very slithery and slimy and difficult to catch hold of,' he said. 'You must be a lawyer . . .'

Whose firm?

The Lord Chancellor – Lord Mackay of Clash-fearn – likes to pay unheralded visits to courts. One day, he dropped in on Wood Green County Court. The usher said: 'I'm so sorry sir, but you cannot come into court. It's sitting in camera.'

Lord Chancellor: 'Ah, but I can. I'm Lord Mackay of Clashfearn.'

Usher: 'I don't care which firm you're with, sir – you can't come in!'

The unfortunate truth

A famous Judge, Lord Ellenborough was addressed by a young lawyer: 'My unfortunate client,' he began. 'My unfortunate client . . .'

'Yes, yes,' said the Judge. 'Do please proceed. So far as you have proceeded hitherto, the court is entirely with you!'

Occupations

I once asked children in a Leicester school what papers they got at home. The majority read the local *Leicester Mercury*. Many took *The Mirror* or *The Sun*; a few the rest – and when I mentioned *The Times*, only one little girl raised her hand.

'What does your father do?' I asked.

'The crossword,' she replied.

At another school, a lad said that they got all the newspapers.

'Every one of them?' I asked incredulously.

'Yes. All of them.'

'What does your Dad do?'

'He's a newsagent.'

Jobs

As a Cambridge undergraduate, I frequently visited Kneesworth Hall, a school for local delinquents. There, I learned much about human nature – and also the need to choose words with care.

One Sunday evening, a visiting preacher addressed the boys thus: 'The theme for my talk is: "If you're going to do a job, do it properly".'

He was astonished to be greeted by prolonged cheering. Most of the lads had done jobs very well. Their regret was that they had been caught doing it.

Time to insure

Client to insurance agent, trying to sell him a new policy: 'How much would I get if the factory burned down this evening?'

Agent: 'About 3 years!'

Lawyers' fees Client to lawyer: 'What are your fees?'
Lawyer: '£100 for three questions.'
'That's an extortionate fee, isn't it?'
'Yes. Now what's your final question?'

Sentencing Before making a plea in mitigation on behalf of a convicted client, I asked him what he would like me to say for him. 'Just be careful,' he replied. 'If you get a short sentence wrong, I shall get a long one . . .'

Knowledge Clerk of Court to accused: 'Are you guilty or not guilty?'
Accused: 'If you don't know, why should I tell you!'

Lawyers What do you need if you see five lawyers up to their neck in concrete?
More concrete.

Choices Why does London have the most lawyers and Cumbria the most toxic waste?
Because Cumbria had the first choice.

[Note: many of the above stories can be adapted to tease your own profession, trade or business. To avoid offence, always make fun of yourself. G.J.]

78 Food, drink and travel

Food for thought

Political life has many drawbacks, one of which is not malnutrition.

Shortage

What is 200 yards long and eats cabbage? A queue outside a food shop in Warsaw.

Patience – and head waiters

Inscription on head waiter's tombstone: God finally caught his eye. [*Alternative: It's coming. GJ*]

We serve all . . .

A man came into Grubb's with an alligator on a leash. He said: 'Do you serve lawyers here?'

Mr Grubb replied: 'Of course we do.'

'In that case,' said the man, 'I'll have two salt-beef sandwiches for me and a lawyer for my alligator . . . [*For lawyers, use doctors, Methodists, Mongolians – or whatever other audience you are addressing. GJ*]

A fare charge

In some countries, cab fares are charged per head. In one of these, a couple with three children stopped a cab and asked what it would cost to be taken to the next town. 'Five dollars for each of you grown ups,' the driver smiled. 'I'll not charge for the children.'

'In that case,' said the father, 'please take the children. My wife and I will take the bus.'

Never satisfied

The host asked his house-guest: 'Will you have coffee after dinner?'

'No thank you. Just brandy.'

'Will you have cocoa before you retire?'

'No thank you. Just tea.'

'Will you have tea for breakfast?'

'No thank you – coffee.'

'Would you like boiled eggs or scrambled eggs?'

'One of each please.'

306

After breakfast the host asked his guest: 'How were your eggs?'
'Not good.'
'Why?'
'You boiled the wrong one!'

Prescriptions

A down-and-out tries to beg a pound from a passer-by.
'What is it then? Drugs?'
'Don't indulge.'
'So I suppose you smoke yourself silly?'
'As a matter of fact, I never smoke at all.'
'Then there is only one answer. Gambling . . .'
'Certainly not. That's a mug's game . . .'
'Then never mind the quid. You come into the car with me and let me take you home to meet my wife. I would like her to see what happens to a man who doesn't drink, take drugs, smoke or gamble!'

Conferences

Some politicians and many business people suffer from a disease called conference syncopation – making irregular movements from bar to bar . . .

Glass houses

Two guests at a cocktail party. One says to the other: 'Look old man, I shouldn't drive if I were you. Your face is getting all blurry.'

Drink and drive?

A Scottish hotel applied for a drinks licence. This was refused because 'the roads in the vicinity of the hotel were unsuitable for drunken driving.'

Blood thicker than whisky . . .

A Scottish friend of mine always carried a hip flask of whisky. One day he fell and felt damp around his hip. 'My God,' he said, 'I hope it's only blood!'

Ugh!

After a party, Fred was found wandering on the rooftops. The drinks were on the house.

Mirage

'Drink makes you look really beautiful, Brenda.'
'But I haven't been drinking, Charlie.'
'I know. But I have!'

No room at the inn?	Smith is refused a room at a famous hotel. I'm sorry, sir, we are full up,' says the head receptionist.
	'If Prince Philip were to come here,' said Smith, 'you'd find a room for him, wouldn't you?'
	'I suppose we would,' said the receptionist.
	'Well, I've got news for you,' Smith retorted. 'He isn't coming. So I'll have his room.'
Early bird	Cyril decided to beat the latest Underground strike by hitch-hiking to work – he got up at 5.30, so as to beat the traffic.
Drinking	One more drink and I shall be under the host. (*Dorothy Parker*)
A la carte	If you eat à la carte, you will get a better choice. But it is nearly always more expensive. And your guests tend to follow your example.
	[*Michael Heseltine, in his resignation speech – referring to the suggestion that it would be better for Britain not to have its own helicopter industry but to be able to buy these and other defence products from any source which may be available.*]
Bookings	Nazi hunter Simon Wiesenthal maintains that he never has any trouble in getting a table in a Vienna restaurant. All he has to do is to ask the management to page Simon Wiesenthal – and half the diners leave!

79   Time

Procrastination

A visitor to Ireland asked a professor: 'What is the Gaelic for manana?'

The professor replied: 'I regret that we do not have any word in the Irish language that conveys quite the same sense of urgency!'

Brevity

We no longer know how to be brief. For instance: the Lord's Prayer consists of 56 words; the Ten Commandments 297 words; the United States Declaration of Independence 300 words; and the EEC Convention on the Importation of Caramel – 26,911 words.

Time limits

No man can enjoy the sunset for more than 15 minutes. (*Goethe*)

Former Israeli Prime Minister Levi Eshkol once chaired a meeting. A speaker who was likely to be boring asked him: 'How long shall I speak? There's so much to say. I don't know where to begin . . .'

Eshkol replied: 'Then I suggest that you start at the end . . .'

Apologies

Counsel apologizes for the length of his speech.

Judge: 'Don't worry – you have shortened the winter for us . . .'

Apologies for lateness

Better the President late than the late President.

Time and tide

An El Al plane was landing in New York. The pilot announced: 'Ladies and Gentlemen, we hope that you enjoyed this flight on El Al and that we shall have the pleasure of your company on future flights.' Then, forgetting that his loudspeaker was still switched on, he added: 'Now all I need is a nice cup of coffee and a woman.'

A pert air hostess rushed up the gangway towards the cockpit. An old Mama put her hand gently on her passing arm: 'Don't hurry, darling,' she said. 'Give him time to have his coffee!'

Confidence

Cricketer Learie Constantine told how he was once walking down the steps of a pavilion on his way to bat when he heard the following telephone conversation. 'You want to speak to Learie Constantine? Oh I'm sorry, he's just gone to bat. Would you like to hold on?'

In conclusion

'Has he finished?'
'Yes, he finished a long time ago, but he is still going on.'

Loquacity

'Am I not running out of time?'
'You have trespassed on the very boundaries of eternity . . .'

80   Health and hospitals

Communication   The operator at a London hospital received a call asking for the sister in charge of a particular ward. When the sister was put through, the caller enquired: 'How is Mrs Goldberg?'

'Doing very well,' Sister replied.

'Is her stomach condition improving then?'

'Yes. The doctor is very pleased with it.'

'Is her blood pressure better?'

'Yes, much better.'

'And how about Mrs Goldberg's chest. Is the infection clearing well?'

'Very well. But tell me, who is enquiring?'

'This is Mrs Goldberg. Nobody tells me nothing, darling!'

Ambition   The Health Secretary visited a hospital and was introduced to three international rugby players, lying in adjacent beds. He asked the first man: 'What's the matter with you?'

'I have piles, sir,' replied the man.

'And what are they doing for you?'

'They give me a brush and some ointment and I apply it for myself.'

'And what is your ambition now?'

'To get back to the rugger field to play for England, sir, as soon as possible.'

'Well done, my boy. I wish you luck.' And he turned to the second man.

'What's the matter with you then?'

'I'm afraid that I've got venereal disease.'

'Oh dear. And what treatment are they giving you?'

'They give me a brush and some ointment and I apply it to myself.'

'And what's your ambition?'

'To get back to the rugger field to play for England again, as soon as possible,' he said.

'Well done, my boy,' nodded the Minister and turned to the third bed.

'And what's your trouble?'

'I have laryngitis,' the man whispered.

'What are they doing for you?'

'They give me a brush and some ointment and I apply it to myself.'

'And what is your ambition?'

'To get the brush before the other two fellows . . .'

Rare?
Patients in a psychiatric hospital were undergoing group therapy. One asked: 'Why are we all here?' Another immediately replied: 'Because we're not all there . . .'

Mad?
Man visits a psychiatrist's office and says: 'My trouble is that no one listens to me.' The psychiatrist says: 'Next . . .'

Lost voice
A singer who had lost his voice knocked on the door of his doctor's surgery. A nurse appeared. The man whispered: 'Is Dr Jones in?' The nurse whispered in reply: 'No – why don't you come in and wait?'

The doctor arrived after about 15 minutes, wrote out a prescription and recommended 'plenty of ice cream.'

The singer duly lodged the pescription with the chemist and went off to the ice cream parlour. He whispered: 'What flavours of ice cream do you have?'

The ice cream man replied, whispering: 'Strawberry and vanilla.'

Singer: 'Do you have laryngitis too?'

The ice cream man whispered: 'No – just strawberry and vanilla.'

Limits on DIY
John needed a pacemaker but could not get one swiftly under the National Health Service. So he went privately to a distinguished consultant. 'I can do the job for you with pleasure,' said the

surgeon. 'But I'm afraid it will cost you £5,000. These gadgets are very expensive.'

'I have a friend who is brilliant with electronics and gadgets,' said John. 'If I provide my own pacemaker with this help, will you do the implant for me?'

The surgeon agreed. John produced the pacemaker and the surgeon planted it in his chest and wired him up.

Three months later, John returned for a checkup. 'Any problems?' The surgeon asked.

John replied: 'Only one. Whenever I get an erection, the garage door opens!'

Just right

Sign over pharmacy: 'We dispense with accuracy.'

Dentistry

Dentist to patient: 'Now, we're not going to hurt each other, are we?'

Medical prophecy

An American doctor gave his patient six months to live – and sent him a bill for $500. By the end of the six months, the bill was still not paid. The doctor then gave his patient another six months . . .

Nurses

Occupational nurses are a race apart. I once asked one 'What do you do when you have a patient brought in with a bleeding leg?' She replied: 'You bind up the bleeding wound; you elevate the bleeding leg; and you call in the bleeding doctor.'

Accidents at work

There is no such things as an Act of God when you are dealing with accidents in industry. The fact is that God has a down on inefficient managers. (*Bill Simpson, then Chairman of the Health and Safety Commission*)

Emergencies

An employee was lying on the operating table in the factory's sick bay, clenching his teeth, while a doctor sewed up a large wound on his scalp. A pair of pliers, had fallen from a scaffold and split open his head. I asked him: 'Haven't you got a hard hat?'

'Yes', he said.

'Where is it, then?'

He replied: 'It's in my locker.'

'Why do you keep it in your locker?'

'It's there for emergencies,' he answered.

Deafness Doctor to personnel manager at very noisy steel works. 'I don't know why you don't just hire deaf people in the first place and then you wouldn't have to worry . . .'

Too late When I asked a steel worker why he was not wearing his ear muffs, he replied: 'I'm already deaf!'

Compensation Apprentice: 'What is a cubic foot?'

Foreman: 'I don't know – but I will make sure that you get full compensation.' [*Or could be a reply by a shop steward. GJ*]

Fall from grace Fred fell 80 feet from a scaffold. By good fortune, he managed to clutch hold of a rope about 20 ft from the ground. After a few moments, he let go and fell on his head.

His friend picked him up and said: 'Fred why did you let go of that rope?'

He replied: 'I was afraid it was going to break.'

Self-recognition An employee had his ear cut off at work. He was told to go to the local hospital and have it stitched back on. When he arrived, he had left the ear behind.

'Where is the ear?' they asked. 'Why didn't you bring it with you?'

'I couldn't tell whether it was mine,' he replied. 'It had no pencil behind it!'

Useless remedy A man suffering from constipation went to his doctor who provided him with a suppository, telling him to leave it in his back passage overnight and that if it did not do the trick, to come back in a couple of days.

Two days later the patient returned. 'It was useless,' he said.

'Did you do as I recommended?' asked the doctor.

'Well,' said the patient, 'we haven't got a back passage in our house. So I put it on top of the refrigerator. For all the good it did me, I might just as well have shoved it up my rear end!'

Open certificate
Morgan was an overworked businessman. He suffered a severe heart attack and his doctor told him that he had to keep 'very quiet' until further notice – no stress, no excitement, no exertion.

'But what about bed with Gwyneth?' he asked. 'Bed is for sleeping purposes only,' said the doctor.

Some months later, when Morgan was feeling much better, he said to Gwyneth. 'Well, it's Friday night and I am quite recovered now.'

'I'm not taking any chances,' said Gwyneth. 'You'll have to get a doctor's certificate before I am prepared to resume our previous arrangements.'

So Morgan went back to the doctor, who examined him and proclaimed himself fully satisfied. 'You may return to work on a part-time basis,' he said. 'You are doing very well.'

'Then how about bed with Gwyneth?'

'That should be all right. Everything in moderation, of course.'

'Gwyneth won't allow even moderation without a certificate from you.'

'Then I shall provide one,' said the doctor, and sat down at his desk, took out his pen and began to write.

Morgan came quietly up behind him. 'If it would not be a nuisance,' he said, 'would you be kind enough to head your certificate: "To whom it may concern"?'

315

Prayer	If you talk to God, you are praying; if God talks to you, you have schizophrenia. If the dead talk to you, you are a spiritualist; if you talk to the dead, you are a schizophrenic.
Jewish hypochondria	How do you recognize the difference between a Jew and a non-Jew? When a non-Jew is thirsty, he goes and gets a drink. When a Jew is thirsty, he goes to his doctor and says: 'Have I got diabetes?' (*Dr Joseph Burg*)
Eye trouble	Patient to eye specialist: 'Every morning, I get up and look at myself in the mirror and I see bleary eyes, lank hair and a sallow face.' Doctor: 'There's nothing wrong with your eyesight.'
Exercise	When I get the urge to take exercise, I immediately lie down and wait until it passes off! (*Oscar Wilde*)

81 Age, death – and the end

Age

The young look forward, the old look back, and the middle-aged look around.

You are young if it is as easy to go upstairs as it is to go down; you are middle-aged if it is easier to go down than up; and you are old if it is just as difficult to go in either direction.

Two elderly men were visiting a brothel on the top floor of a 20-storey block. The lift broke down and they started to climb. One said to the other: 'Wouldn't it be awful if we got to the top and found that the girls weren't there.'

After ten floors, the other replied: 'Wouldn't it be awful if we got to the top and the girls were there!'

Boss to secretary: 'I don't look 50, do I?'
'No – but you used to.'

Distinction

To appear really distinguished, you need grey hair, a wide girth and piles. The grey hairs give you an appearance of wisdom; the girth an appearance of prosperity; and the piles a look of anxiety that can easily be mistaken for true concern.

Alternatives

A distinguished US Senator was asked how he felt on his 80th birthday. 'Very well, thank you,' he replied, 'considering the alternative . . .'

Very nearly

A friend asked an 80-year-old man who had just married a young girl: 'How are you managing?'
'Marvellous,' he replied. 'We do it nearly every night. Nearly on Monday . . . nearly on Tuesday . . . nearly on. . . !'

Don't delay

A streaker ran across Westminster Bridge and passed three elderly ladies. Two of them

317

immediately had a stroke. The third one did not reach out her hand in time.

Pensioners

Two pensioners married. On their honeymoon night, the husband reached for his wife's hand – and held it tenderly. On the next night, he did the same. On the third night, he reached out for her hand, but it was not there.

'What's the matter, Mary?' he asked.

'I'm sorry, dear,' she replied. 'I am too tired tonight . . .'

What for?

Two old men were sitting on a bench in a boulevard. One said: 'Do you remember how we used to run up and down here when we were chasing girls?'

The other replied: 'I remember running up and down – but I've forgotten what it was for.'

Reason to mourn

A man was sobbing his heart out at a millionaire's funeral. No one knew who he was.

'Are you a relative of the deceased?' someone asked him.

'No.'

'So, why are you crying?'

'That's why!' he replied.

Wrinkles

Two old ladies in an old people's home decide to go streaking. A retired sailor is sitting with his wife watching them. She says: 'Look at those two. What are they wearing?'

'I don't know – but whatever it is, it needs pressing!' [*This may be adapted for a named hotel, club or other institution. GJ*]

Happy Ending

Goldstein, aged 75, married a 30-year old. He boasted to a friend how they had done it six times every night during their honeymoon.

Friend: You can die from this!

Goldstein: So she dies, she dies!

Recipe for good life

A reporter was interviewing some venerable men about their recipes for ripe age.

'I don't smoke,' said one. 'And I'm 75.'

'I don't smoke and I don't drink,' said the next. 'I'm 80.'

'I don't smoke, I don't drink and I don't womanize,' said the third. 'And I never have. And I'm 85.'

The reporter turned to a man, leaning heavily on his stick and wobbling, his venerable beard drooping to the ground.

'And what about you?' he said.

'I smoke, I drink and I womanize. And I always have. And I'm 35!' he replied.

Enjoy

Sound, sound the clarion, fill the fife,
Throughout the sensual world proclaim
One crowded hour of glorious life
Is worth an age without a name.

      (Thomas Mordaunt (1730–1809))
[*This last quotation is especially useful in eulogies – particularly for those who died young. GJ*]

Time – and life – and death

Days are scrolls; write on them that which you want to be remembered. (*Spanish-Jewish Sage, Bachya*)

Tact

Jones the Bread, Morgan the Tailor and Evan the Bookie went to the races. Unfortunately, a horse leapt over the rails and smashed into poor Jones, knocking him down and killing him. Morgan and Evan considered the problem: 'Who should tell Mrs Jones?'

Morgan said: 'I'm only a tailor. I have no tact. Evan, you tell her. You're a bookie, so you know how to explain losses . . .'

So Evan went to the village and knocked on the door of the Jones's terraced home. A lady came to the door.

'Excuse me, madam,' said Evan. 'I'm sorry to disturb you. But are you Widow Jones?'

'There's no Widow Jones here,' she replied.

'Do you want to make a bet?' asked Evan.

Will

An old man was dying. His children and his grand-

319

children were gathered round his bed, waiting patiently. Every few minutes, the old gentlemen pointed down to the floor with two fingers of his right hand. Eventually, the eldest son said: 'He is trying to tell us that's where he's put the money . . .'

So they started pulling up the floorboards all over the house – but they found nothing.

That evening, the father rallied and started to chat. Eventually, the son said to him: 'Tell me, father, what were you pointing two fingers at the floor for?'

'Oh that,' replied the father. 'I was just too weak to point them upwards.'

Wills

A man climbed to the top floor of a block of apartments, to the home of a well known call-girl. As she opened the door, he had a heart attack and dropped down dead. His executors asked their lawyers this question: 'Are we bound to carry out the testator's last wish?'

Eternal distrust

During the Congress of Vienna, Metternich was informed that the Russian ambassador had died. 'I wonder what was his motive!' he exclaimed.

Right dead

Here lies the body of William Jay
Who died defending his right of way
He was right – dead right – as he walked along
But he's just as dead as if he'd been wrong.
(*Epitaph on pedestrian's tombstone*)

The will

'What a lovely man my husband was,' the widow boasted to a friend. 'You know what I found after Fred died? I opened the safe and there was a big package, wrapped in brown paper and addressed to me. I opened it and it contained £100,000 in cash!'

'Really,' said the friend. 'Your husband was a saint.'

'But that wasn't all. There were three more packets, one addressed to each of the children. And each contained £25,000 in cash!'

'What a marvellous man he was.'

'And there was even another packet. A small one. Addressed to me. It contained £18,000, "for a memorial stone" – and what a lovely memorial stone I bought with it!' she said, polishing a new diamond ring on her cashmere sweater.

Dust to dust

The great Greek singer, Maria Callas, left instructions in her will that she was to be cremated and her ashes scattered at sea. After the cremation ceremony, her ashes were gathered in an urn which was taken on board a Greek naval vessel, which sailed out to sea, complete with the entire Cabinet and crews from national and international television.

As the ashes were about to be scattered over the side, the television crews requested that the ship should turn about, because the cameras were directly facing the sun. The Captain obliged.

Unfortunately, this manoeuvre resulted in the wind blowing the ashes back onto the deck and sprinkling the distinguished mourners with a light layer of dust.

It is said that at the Cabinet meeting later on that day, the distinguished politicians were still coughing – and flicking specks of ash from their own and each other's clothing!

Floral tribute

Everyone is condemned to the sadness of attending funerals. I treasure one true anecdote which has added a moment of consolation to many a cremation service.

An elegant lady cousin had to attend both a funeral and a wedding on the same summer's afternoon. So she donned a smart, navy blue suit, but put her attractive new floral hat into a paper bag. As it was covered with gay and realistic artificial flowers, it was hardly suitable headgear for a cremation.

In the entrance of the crematorium, a solemn, black-clad man – obviously a cloakroom attendant – held out his hand for her parcel and she gave it to him. Then she sat quietly at the back.

Moments later, the coffin was wheeled noiselessly into the funeral hall. It was crowned with a magnificent floral tribute – her hat!

My cousin sat transfixed during the service, which reached its silent climax as the doors at the far end of the hall slid apart and the coffin rolled gently away, still bedecked with her hat.

The service over, she joined the mourners around the back where all the wreaths had been laid against the chapel wall, accompanied by a simple sign: 'In memory of the Departed'. She stood silently – wondering whether she dared remove her floral tribute from the rest. Watching the sad faces of the family of the deceased, she decided that her hat must be sacrificed. She went to the wedding hatless. When she returned that evening, her hat was gone.

Brotherly love

During the lingering, final illness of my wife's beloved uncle, Emeritus Chief Rabbi Sir Israel Brodie, I often sat by his bedside while he told me marvellous and generally whimsical tales from the Talmud. My favourite explains the nature of brotherly love: I have used it often and always with impact at functions of and for charities, fraternal organizations and the like . . .

A father died and left his fields in equal parts to his two sons, one of whom was a bachelor; the other was married, with many children.

One moonless night, after the harvest had been brought in and stacked, the bachelor crept into his field and carried half a dozen sheaves from his pile, took them across the boundary line and quietly placed them on his brother's heap. The next morning, he was amazed to find that the two piles were still the same size.

The following night, the brother repeated the process. Still the piles were no different.

The next night, the bachelor tried again. This time, as he was carrying the bundles across his field, he met his married brother, coming in the other direction and himself laden with sheaves. 'What are you doing?' he asked. 'Please let me give you some of my wheat. I do not need it, I am single and have no family to keep. You have a wife and children – many mouths to feed.'

'Not so, brother,' came the response. 'You must save for your old age. You will have no wife or children to look after you. You must keep the corn for yourself.'

So the two brothers stood together and looked up to heaven and called on the Holy-One-Blessed-Be-He. 'Tell us,' they called out, 'which one of us is correct?'

A voice descended from above. 'You are both right,' it said. 'And so great is your love that upon these fields will I build my Temple.' And tradition has it that He did.

Death

Cicero: Life is a great play. The final act is a tragedy.

De Gaulle: Life is a magnificent voyage, ending in a shipwreck.

Hell

Stalin died and went below. Shortly thereafter, St Peter answered a knock on the door. He found the devil outside, seeking political asylum.

Life after ...

'The House of Lords? Life after death, my boy ...' (*Ex-Cabinet Minister – now a Peer*)

Musical death

After a concert in a private home, a lady approached famous pianist Paderewski and asked about one of his selections. 'What a beautiful piece,' she said. 'Who composed it?'

'Beethoven, madam,' he answered.

'I see,' she said. 'And is he composing now?'

'No,' replied Paderewski. 'He is decomposing.' (*Useful for speech by a person who has retired from office or work. 'I am no longer*

> distinguished ... I am extinguished. Which
> reminds me of the story of Paderewski ...')

Certainty

When your mother-in-law dies, how will you dispose of her body?

I'll have her embalmed, cremated and the ashes solemnly buried. I'll not be taking any chances ... [*This can, of course, be adapted to yours (or anyone else's) current pet hate – as known to your audience. GJ*]

Is anyone in?

The redoubtable Cardinal Newman met his friend, Chief Rabbi Hertz. 'I had a remarkable dream, Chief Rabbi,' he said. 'I dreamed that I went to the Jewish heaven.' 'Oh yes,' said Chief Rabbi Hertz. 'And what did you find?'

'Well, I came up to great, golden gates, studded with precious stones. I turned the handle and looked in – and guess what I saw?'

'What did you see?'

'I peeped in and the place was absolutely packed with people – singing psalms, playing cards and discussing business.'

'What an amazing dream,' exclaimed the Chief Rabbi. 'How strange it is that I had one so similar. I dreamed that I came to the Catholic heaven. There were mighty, wrought iron gates, studded with niches, filled with the statues of saints. I pulled open one of the doors – and guess what I saw? Not a soul. . . !' [*This is useful as an illustration of an empty meeting . . . or no one turning up at a party . . . GJ*]

Worries

When I look back on all these worries, I remember the story of the old man who was on his death bed. He had had a lot of trouble in his life, most of which never happened. (*Winston Churchill*)

Alternatives

For seven days after the death of a Jewish person, prayers are held. On each evening of this 'shiva', tradition calls for someone to speak good words about the deceased.

When David died, prayers were held as usual. At their end, the Rabbi said: 'Who will say something about the departed?' Silence.

'Someone must speak.' Silence.

'Won't anyone say anything?' Silence.

Eventually, a man at the back said: 'OK. So I'll speak.'

The Rabbi thanked him and called him forward. He looked up, paused, and then said: 'His brother was worse!'

Political

Mrs Thatcher died and went up to heaven where she was greeted by God: 'Welcome, my dear girl.'

She replied: 'First, I am not your dear girl. Second, you are sitting on my seat!'

Dealing with death

Three mothers talking.

Mary: 'I'm like the Peer who says he wants his body to be fed to the dogs, at the Battersea Dogs' Home. At least let's do something useful after we've gone.'

Sally: 'Not me. I want my body to be run over by a road roller. Really thin. Then I can be put through my daughter-in-law's letter box. That would teach her a lesson.'

Janet: 'I want to be cremated and my ashes scattered in my local supermarket. And then at least I can be sure that my daughter will think of me every now and again.'

Longevity

Interviewer to German Chancellor Adenauer, on his 80th birthday: 'And can I expect to interview you again on your 90th birthday, Chancellor?'

Adenauer: 'I don't see why not. You look perfectly fit to me.'

Reporter to local celebrity, on his 90th birthday: 'To what do you attribute your longevity?'

Reply: 'I suppose, to the fact that I ain't yet died!'

Sympathy

Mary Brown was approaching her 90th birthday. Her family decided that the best present they could give her would be — a portrait of herself. So they arranged for a distinguished painter to visit her, to discuss how she would like the portrait done. 'With sympathy, please,' she said.

On her 90th birthday, the painting duly arrived. It was magnificent. But on her shoulder sat a tiny, elf-like man, with his hand pushed down through the front of her dress.

'Who's that man?' she protested.

'You said that you wanted the painting done with sympathy,' said the painter. 'So I looked up "sympathy" in the dictionary and it said: "A little fellow feeling in the bosom . . ."!'

Lord (Manny Shinwell, on his 100th birthday: 'They say that to have reached the age of 100 is a miracle. You may take it from me that it is nothing of the kind. It is an affliction.'

I then asked him the name of the doctor who had produced this marvellous affliction, he retaining all his faculties and brilliance.

'Never mind doctors,' he said. 'I'll give you the name of my whisky.' (It was Glenfiddich).

Death

The Earl of Sandwich to John Wilkes: 'I do not know, sir, whether you will die on the gallows or of the pox.'

Wilkes: 'That, my Lord, will depend on whether I embrace your principles or your mistress.'

Index

Index

language 239
law 295–305
laws 223–31
lawyers 295–305
leadership 244
legislation 225
lies 220, 234
life 225
liquidation 241
litigation 225
longevity 325
love 287–94
management 244
managers 228
marriage 229–30, 287–94
memories 235
men 225
money 230
millionaires 239
name dropping 274
nurses 313
oil 240
opening gambits 216
opinions 225–6
optimism 226, 276, 278
paranoia 226
parliament 252–60
partners 269
peace 264
people 229
perks 242
photographs 226
plagiarism 226
plagues 234
police 269
politicians 227, 233, 237, 247–67
power 226
precedence 264
prejudice 232–3
press 271
principles 247
procrastination 309–10
professions 268–74
pronunciation 219
prophecies 240, 250
prostitution 291–2
proverbs 223–31
public opinion 226

public relations 270
quotes 226
recession 226, 271–2
references 245
reliability 236
religion 276–86
repetition 235
resignation 226
resolutions 226
riots 230
risks 268
royal introductions 216
secrets 227, 259
security 256
sex 287–94
shouting 228
silence 218
sitting
sleep 217
speechmaking 235
speculation 230
spendthrift 236
spies 269
substitutes 220
success 226, 269
supervisors 245
survival 227
sympathy 326
systems 227
tact 319
taxes 241
temptation 227
time 309–10
tolerance 227
trade unions 244
tradition 227
travel 306–8
unemployment 243
United Nations 262
victory and defeat 227, 260
weddings 236, 272
wills 319–21
wisdom 227
workers 275
working hours 242
worries 324
wrinkles 318

Sedgemore, Brian: 'A Long Streak of Spit' 208–10